TD
196
.P4
B87
1997

Burger, Joanna.

Oil spills.

$29.95

OIL SPILLS

OIL SPILLS

● ● ●

Joanna Burger

RUTGERS UNIVERSITY PRESS
New Brunswick, New Jersey

Library of Congress Cataloging-in-Publication Data

Burger, Joanna.
    Oil spills / Joanna Burger.
       p.   cm.
    Includes bibliographical references and index.
    ISBN 0-8135-2338-9 (alk. paper)
    1. Oil spills—Environmental aspects. I. Title.
TD196.P4B87   1997
363.73'82—dc20   96-8340
                                   CIP

British Cataloging-in-Publication information available

Manufactured in the United States of America

For my husband, Michael Gochfeld,
who is always there for me

Contents

Tables and Figures

Tables

Preface

Technology has far too many advantages to enumerate, but one overwhelming disadvantage is the potential for industrial and chemical accidents. Oil spills are among the most ruinous of these—and are becoming more so as supertankers increase in size and as world transport routes multiply and handle more traffic. To supertanker, transfer, well, and pipeline accidents has been added the horror of intentional bombing of tankers and setting afire of hundreds of oil wells in the wake of military retreat, as happened during the Gulf War.

Oil spills, however, differ dramatically from other types of industrial accidents, such as chemical spills and nuclear mishaps. Except among the crews aboard ships, and they are almost always rescued, there are few human fatalities. We fear oil spill accidents much less than other accidents, but the potential for damage to the environment, and to humans whose lifestyles are closely intertwined with the environment, is very great.

Most books on oil spills either focus on a particular gigantic spill that captured our attention, such as the *Exxon Valdez*, or deal with particular aspects of spill cleanup, tanker safety, or the difficulties of arctic or offshore drilling activities. Others are very technical, providing comprehensive details on supertanker construction, shipping lanes, or oil refineries. In my coverage of oil spills, I begin with the history of oil and its uses, as well as a chronology of major oil spills. I then move on to the immediate events surrounding an oil spill, its biological effects, and finally, its effects on people, including health risks and the social, economic, and aesthetic impacts. In general, I focus on marine and other aquatic spills because these are more numerous and we know more about them. I will take you on a journey through a number of oil spills, often from the perspective of the scientists and others who lived through them.

Until I saw an oil spill slowly seep through an estuarine system I studied and loved, I could not have believed the devastation it would create. In its wake, it leaves not only the oiled birds and struggling seals we see on television, but hundreds and thousands of dead mussels and barnacles, crabs and fish, and a sense of profound loss and frustration on the part of local residents, who stare in disbelief at their fouled beaches.

Acknowledgments

I am grateful to the many people who have discussed the effects of environmental insult with me. I particularly thank Michael Gochfeld, who provided comments on the ms, has traversed many an oil-stained beach with me, worked long hours in libraries, and patiently helped me visit the site of the *Exxon Valdez* despite my broken ankle. I thank Anne and Alex Gochfeld, David Gochfeld, L. J. Evans, and Karen Reeds, who read and provided valuable comments on earlier versions. I also thank Carl Safina, Mike Gallo, Anne and Alex Gochfeld, Bernie Goldstein, John Brzorad, Keith Cooper, L. J. Evans, Fred Grassle, Michelle LeMarchant, Larry Niles, Ian Nisbet, Joel O'Connor, Kathy Parsons, Stan Senner, Robert Tucker, Guy Tudor, and William Vesterman for references, advice, and encouragement.

Tom Benson, David Gochfeld, Debbie Gochfeld, Susan Seyboldt, Robert Ramos, and Kathleen Jeramiassen of Rutgers University, and Michael Cooper of the Media Resources Department of UMDNJ–Robert Wood Johnson Medical School helped with graphics and library research. Several others who worked with animals before and after the oil spill on the Arthur Kill provided invaluable insights, including John Brzorad, Keith Cooper, Gordon Johnson, Lynne Frink, Angela Cristini, Alan Maccarone, Kathy Parsons, Robert Tucker, and Ramona Haebler.

My work on the *Exxon Valdez* oil spill would not have been possible without the help and hospitality of Dave and Andy Sonneborn, Ken Warheit, George Divoky, and several others who attended the *Exxon Valdez* seabird workshop in 1995, and Russellyn Carruth for her legal views on the spill and logistical information. Guy Tudor, Michelle LaMarchant, Bert and Patti Murray, Mary and Charlie Leck, and Lehr Brisbin discussed pollution and the state of the world with me, and I thank them. I particularly benefited from discussions with Stan Senner, science coordinator for the *Exxon*

Valdez Oil Spill Trustee Council. Photographs were provided by the Oil Spill Public Information Center, Michael Gochfeld (California, Alaska), and David Policansky (*Exxon Valdez*). Finally, I thank Karen Reeds (science editor at Rutgers University Press) and Carole Brown (copy editor) for their help and patience with the manuscript.

My research over the years on oil spills and related toxics has been supported by the New Jersey Department of Environmental Protection (Office of Science and Research, Endangered and Nongame Species Program), National Institute of Environmental Health Sciences (Grants ESO 05022 and ESO 05955), U.S. Environmental Protection Agency, Department of Energy (Consortium for Risk Evaluation with Stakeholder Participation), Environmental and Occupational Health Sciences Institute, and the Bureau of Biological Research.

OIL SPILLS

Chapter One
Introduction

● ● ●

The world runs on oil. Because oil is our main source of energy, but is unevenly distributed throughout the world, we spend time and money transporting it over the high seas and in pipelines to distant lands. This inevitably results in accidents: accidents while drilling for oil, accidents while transferring oil to vessels, and accidents while transporting oil over the oceans. Occasionally, these leakages are massive and catastrophic, but often they are smaller and chronic. Although the major transport and transfer activities occur in the oceans, ports, and rivers, accidents are not limited to these areas. Wherever oil is drilled, stored, handled, refined, transported, and transferred, there is the potential for spills. Few other environmental problems are as common or ubiquitous.

Oil is here to stay, at least until we discover some other means to power our world, to move our vehicles, to heat our homes. It is imperative that we understand the risks and hazards, as well as the benefits, of this power source, and learn from past errors.

In this book I concentrate on marine and other aquatic oil spills because they are the most common, the largest, and the best known. These include several of the more recent or dramatic oil spills, such as the *Amoco Cadiz*, the *Exxon Valdez*, the *Sea Empress*, and the massive oil spills during the Gulf War. Although not an aquatic oil spill, the Usinsk pipeline rupture in Russia is also described, as its location presents special problems that are worth noting. I provide an overview of the nature of oil spills, the ecological problems they cause, the types of cleanups and their efficacy, the legal and social consequences of spills, their long-term impacts, ways to prevent them, and alternatives to oil. Few catastrophes caused by humans have such potential for immediate environmental damage and long-range effects, yet with proper precautions, the number and size of oil spills can be reduced substantially.

I have long been aware of the trouble caused by oiled waters. As a child in Niskayuna, New York, I watched gulls on the Mohawk River sink in a wash of sticky oil. Like many, I watched with sadness the otters and birds blackened with oil from the *Exxon Valdez*—"tarred and feathered" took on a new meaning. Little did I dream that within a year I would have my very own spill in the Arthur Kill, near Rutgers University. Then, while the world was glued to the TV, watching the Gulf War, intrigued by the sight of tanks moving over the desert and missiles hitting their targets, my attention was directed at the burning oil wells. I worried about the wildlife drowning in a sea of oil, and feared for the aftereffects of the fallout and smoke on surrounding agriculture and on the global climate.

Before examining the history of oil, oil drilling, and oil spills, come with me on a personal journey to two oil spills, one relatively small, the other very large. The Arthur Kill spill in New Jersey was a small spill that happened in 1990; the *Exxon Valdez* accident in Alaska in 1989 was the largest tanker oil spill in U.S. history. The Arthur Kill spill took place in a narrow and short river surrounded by industrialized and urbanized communities in the shadow of New York City; the Alaska spill occurred in a very wild and remote area of fiords, glaciers, and wide expanses of open water.

Arthur Kill

A great egret slowly moves along the edge of the mud and water, searching for prey (Fig. 1.1). The egret is pure white, a stately bird on long, spindly, black legs. It peers into the calm water, its long, yellow bill pointing downward. Its neck is so far extended that the bird looks like it will topple forward, but it remains motionless, watching. Seconds, then minutes, go by, and still it remains silent. Not a muscle moves. Nearby, two young great egrets feed. They are more awkward than the adult, they walk a bit faster, they move ever so slightly when they stand, and their strike is slower. The adult catches two fish in a row; the young manage to catch only one fish between them, even though they make several strikes. It is early August, and this may well be parent and young. These young birds no doubt were hatched on nearby Prall's Island, one of the largest heronries in the northeastern United States, home to many different herons, egrets, and ibises.

The mudflat is quite wide, enough for scattered flocks of ducks and gulls to sleep quietly, many sitting flat on the mud, others standing with their bills tucked in their back feathers. Now and then a bird opens one eye, peers around, and falls back asleep. Several semipalmated sandpipers and

Figure 1.1. Great egret feeding along the Arthur Kill.

dunlins forage along the water edge. The tight-knit flock actively probes in the mud for small invertebrates. They briefly look up at passersby, and then continue their rhythmic pecking.

A few yards away a great black-backed gull picks at a dead fish left behind by the receding tide. The fish is so large that it may have died of old age. Large fish are an indication of a healthy ecosystem; if oxygen levels are low or pollution heavy, such fish do not survive. This scavenging gull is quite harmless to the other birds now, but on other days, black-backs can be ravaging predators, killing a healthy scaup duck as it bobs in the water.

Nearby, at the edge of a creek, the mud is dotted with tiny holes, and hundreds of fiddler crabs scurry over the mud in search of bits of algae. Females shovel the algae into their mouths with both claws, but the males are able to eat with only one; their other claw is greatly enlarged and is used for defense and courtship. The courtship season is past, and for the most part, everyone feeds serenely.

A black-crowned night heron sails into view, sending the crabs scurrying for their burrows. Within seconds, they have disappeared. The heron lands and stands motionless, peering at the holes, waiting for a fiddler to venture forth. The crabs have only a few hours to feed when the tide is out, and so they emerge quickly, first one, and then another, emerge to walk cautiously across the mud. The night heron strikes swiftly, scooping up three or four before they can return to the safety of their burrows.

Beyond, a sea of salt hay and cordgrass sways gently in the breezes. It is a lush green, although a slight tinge of yellow and brown gives a hint of approaching fall. A marsh hawk, or harrier, skims across the salt marsh, just inches above the grass, searching for voles hidden in tiny grass runways. The stark white underparts with black wingtips indicate that the hawk is a male. Suddenly he dips out of sight into the grass and comes up with a dark, limp vole. Flying to an exposed log, he begins unceremoniously to rip the vole apart.

This pristine scene could be seen anywhere along the eastern coast of North America, wherever lush salt marshes provide nurseries for many species of invertebrates and fish, and support numerous colonies of nesting birds. The presence of young egrets and harriers usually indicates that the ecosystem is healthy and functioning well. Both egrets and harriers are top predators that feed on large fish and small mammals. Top predators are usually the first to disappear with environmental degradation and pollution.

The small boat drifts slowly in the current, and my view encompasses open water, mudflats, and salt marshes. Beyond the salt marshes superhighways extend in all directions, leading past oil tanks; tall, dilapidated warehouses; and eventually, the looming buildings of crowded cities. Cars and trucks race along, oblivious to the natural world not far below them. I am on the Arthur Kill, a small waterway that separates Staten Island, New York, from New Jersey. "Kill" is the Dutch word for creek, and is a small reminder of the role the Dutch played in settling northern New Jersey. Although only fifteen miles long, the Arthur Kill passes through one of the most densely populated and most highly industrialized regions of the world. The salt marshes here are largely a forgotten world, a jewel that has not been discovered by the masses of people that live in the metropolitan New York City area.

The vast import, storage, and transfer of oil that occur here makes oil spills inevitable, and every year there are hundreds of small spills. This chronic oil pollution surely takes its toll, though it receives little media attention. Who can worry about a hundred spilled gallons, or even a thousand spilled gallons; yet the small amounts add up, particularly when they happen year after year in the same bay or waterway. On January 1, 1990, however, a leak from an Exxon pipeline dumped 567,000 gallons of oil into the Kill, awakening first biologists and conservationists, then governmental agencies, and finally the public to the exquisite little ecosystem that flourishes in the midst of the oil tank farms, storage facilities, bulkheads, tenements, and highways that line its shores.

For years before the 1990 oil spill, many biologists worked on the Arthur Kill ecosystem, studying fiddler crabs and other invertebrates, fish, and birds. Thus, when the oil spill happened, baseline information on the ecological resources of the area was available, certainly unusual for most regions and for most oil spills. In other chapters I describe this spill and its immediate effects in detail, but for now, we are moving along the Arthur Kill five years after the spill, assessing its ability to recover.

For me, the presence of a functioning ecosystem is proof that the system is not polluted beyond repair or sustainability (Fig. 1.2). The mere presence of active heronries, breeding marsh hawks, and abundant fiddler crabs indicates that this is a system worth saving. To many people who see the Kill only from the turnpike and warehouses, the habitat appears a deserted area, littered with old tires, abandoned cars, ruined wharves, and other debris. But the animals that live here have defined its value, and any system that can support one of the largest heronries in the Northeast and be home to a thriving population of marsh hawks speaks for itself.

As I drift down the waterway, I am struck by its recovery. In 1990 the shores were covered with oil, the water's surface had an oil slick that gleamed red, green, and blue in the sun, ducks and gulls covered with oil lay dead along the shores, diamond-backed terrapins and fiddler crabs were forced from their winter hibernation, emerging from their burrows to die from exposure to the cold. Even muskrats and raccoons that visited the oiled banks became ill and died.

Now, the ducks and gulls that fly across my bow are clean, and the fiddler

Figure 1.2. Author in a salt marsh along the Arthur Kill five years after the spill.

crab numbers have nearly returned to prespill levels. Yet there are still signs of the spill. Along some shores the mudflats are wider than they once were, for some of the oiled cordgrass that died has not grown back. On some of the smaller creeks that meander within the marsh an oil sheen is still visible at low tide, and clumps of oil cling to the mud and lurk under decaying driftwood.

While most of the creeks have hundreds or thousands of fiddler crabs that emerge during low tides to feed on the algae, the creeks directly across from the pipeline still have lower populations than before, attesting to the severe effects. Some of the crabs in the more heavily oiled creeks are a bit more aggressive than crabs in the unoiled creeks. Oil that seeped down into the marsh peat may still contaminate new generations of crabs. Such subtle behavioral differences that are evident even years later make me wonder whether ecosystems ever recover completely, and whether the forces of nature can obliterate the effects of an oil spill in only a few short years.

The Arthur Kill spill was relatively limited, in a small ecosystem, in a heavily populated region of the world. But oil spills often occur in remote regions, and these spills may be huge by comparison. After my experiences with the Arthur Kill, my desire to walk the shores of a region where a massive oil spill occurred is overpowering, and I head for Prince William Sound in Alaska, where the largest oil spill in U.S. history happened less than a year before the Arthur Kill spill. The trip is daunting, since I recently broke my ankle while in Indonesia, and the cast came off only days before I am due to leave for Alaska.

Exxon Valdez

A few minutes after midnight on Good Friday, March 24, 1989, the tanker vessel *Exxon Valdez* went aground on the well-marked Bligh reef. It spilled almost eleven million gallons of crude oil along the shores of Prince William Sound and the Gulf of Alaska, covering an area that, by comparison, would stretch from Connecticut to North Carolina. Whether the captain was under the influence of alcohol, was too tired from twenty-four hours of loading the tanker, or was just trying to avoid colliding with drifting icebergs mattered not to the thousands of animals that died in the following days and weeks.

Prince William Sound is very, very large. Larger by far than I could have imagined from the pictures that I watched on TV of oil-stained beaches and dead birds. It has taken us over an hour to fly here from Anchorage in a small float plane. An endless expanse of coastline stretches ahead, small bands of rocky shores fringe hilly islands, and spruces and hemlocks plummet to the rocky beaches.

The spruce-covered hills and mountains that border the sound give way to majestic mountains that rise over four thousand feet above the water, peaks that are covered with snow and glaciers all year. Over a thousand glaciers flow toward Prince William Sound; some are small and dainty and wind through narrow valleys, others are massive, stretching for miles in every direction. Most are slowly receding; their forward movement is not keeping pace with melting at the edge, where huge pieces of ice break off and fall into the sound. The ice edge is never silent, for shearing ice tinkles continuously, and huge splashes break the lullaby of the gently moving ice. Near the edge of some glaciers the pack ice is so thick that most marine mammals avoid it. Only the small, dark-gray harbor seals, known locally to some as glacier seals, find this home.

Far above the glaciers, on the steep slopes, the spruce trees give way to tundra meadows where moss and lichens abound, and above these are the barren, rocky mountaintops. A few small, blue flowers remain snuggled among the lichens. A coal black mother bear with her three cubs makes her way slowly across the tundra, searching for berries. Only a few weeks ago she was down at the water's edge, where the cold glacier streams rush to meet the sound. Here she fished for pink salmon that were returning to spawn in the streams of their birth. The young bears were awkward and unable to catch fish at first, but gradually they learned. It is early October, the fish have stopped running, and she has returned to the mountains to search for small berries and to dig up roots.

As we fly south over the sound the field of broken ice slowly gives way to open water, where a few small icebergs drift quietly southward, toward the Gulf of Alaska. From our floatplane view, we can see how far the icebergs extend below the surface, creating eerie blue green shapes that are much larger than the ice that rises above the surface.

A large, starkly white glaucous-winged gull flies slowly above the water, searching for prey. It is a youngster, and has not yet attained the silvery grey back of an adult. It rises higher, sails over a small spruce-covered island, and disappears in the distance. Kittiwakes skim over the water far below, their heads bent low, searching for fish just beneath the surface. Not far away a group of thirty kittiwakes swirls above the water, each one plunging now and then to skim the surface, emerging with a small fish. The white trailing edge of their black-tipped wings stands out against the greenish blue water. Logs longer than two railroad cars seem like matchsticks against the miles of open water. A lone kittiwake perches on one log, peering over the calm waters. As the plane circles Sleepy Bay on LaTouche Island, the kittiwakes scatter, only to land on a small, jagged, rocky island a few yards offshore. They stand motionless, and watch the intrusion.

The pilot circles several times to search for large rocks hidden below the surface that could rip the paper-thin aluminum pontoons of the float plane. Finally we land and glide across the water toward shore. He cuts the engine, and we drift to rest a few feet from the rocky rubble in Sleepy Bay. The horseshoe-shaped cove is exposed to open sound, and the rocks are mostly gray, and rounded by eons of pounding waves and winter storms. Exploring the shore, I notice that up near the high-tide line brown and golden seaweed with large inflated bladders form a wide band, rotting, accompanied by hundreds of tiny insects. The mass of *Fucus* smells oddly fishlike. I move slowly along, bursting the pale yellow bladders, watching as masses of tiny insects gather to feed on the tender inner surfaces that are now exposed.

The beach is fringed by dense spruce and hemlock trees. The spruce look organized and trimmed, but the hemlock have an awkward look, with branches hanging out too far here and there. The dead trunk of a spruce tree glistens silver in the sun; a few broken branches are all that remains of a once-majestic giant. Such trees provide places for hairy woodpeckers to feed and find nesting holes, as well as wonderful perch sites for bald eagles to survey their domain.

The shore is peaceful now; the bustle and confusion that followed the oil spill are gone. This was one of the heavily oiled beaches, and it received massive cleanup. It was easy to land here, the oil was very obvious, and the gentle slopes were hospitable to work crews.

Standing here now, it is hard to imagine the thick layers of black ooze that covered every stone and seeped between the rocks to poison the intertidal organisms living far below. There is no indication of the total devastation, at least from a first glance. A majestic bald eagle sweeps across the water and sails up to a dead spruce far above the bay. A magpie flies from the underbrush and lands close by, concealing its flashing black-and-white wing pattern. The magpie is curious about my activities and stands sentinel duty quietly, waiting and watching.

The air is warm, the sun bright, and the sky very blue. Wispy white clouds drift over the mountains, coalescing as they reach the Gulf of Alaska beyond. The pilot calls this a rare calm day for the sound. He flew for the cleanup crews during the spill, ferrying people back and forth to remote beaches. He is amazed at how different the beaches now look.

I hobble along the rocky shores toward the distant point; it is not easy going under any circumstances, and I worry that my broken ankle, which is not quite healed, might give way. Only by walking, however, do I truly feel the vastness of this Alaskan scene. This is but one small cove along 150 miles of the sound that were oiled. The 150 miles is as a crow flies, however, and does not do justice to the undulating coastline, small islands, and deep channels and fiords that make up the shoreline here.

This tranquil scene does not completely hide the presence of oil. The odor is ever so faint, and might not be noticeable if I did not know about the spill. At the far tip of the cove I find a few rocks where thick, black, marbled asphalt still clings—a visible sign of the spill. This was missed by the cleanup crews, or clung so tenaciously that the high-powered water hoses could not dislodge it. Even the force of six years of winter storms has failed to wash the rocks completely clean. It was fortunate that this oil spill happened in an area of such violent weather, for the relentless harsh winds and high waves scour the rocks, removing most of the oil, and leaving only the most persistent asphalt.

Slowly I make my way back toward the waiting floatplane, walking on the mats of dead *Fucus* at the high-tide line. Although the golden brown and yellow algae are mushy and slippery, the mat cushions my step, and the pain is less.

We careen noisily into the air and head for Block Island, on the south shore of Eleanor Island. This beach was also heavily oiled by the spill. On our way, we pass hundreds of smaller beaches and coves, guarded by boulders that jut from the water, making it impossible to land boats or floatplanes. Many of these beaches received no cleanup, and were left to the forces of nature. Now there seems little difference between the cleaned and uncleaned beaches, except on closer examination one sees that more oil clings between the boulders. Nature was almost as effective as the busy crews that toiled in the cold and freezing rain.

From the air, we watch four white-sided dolphins slide through the water, change course, and head west. We follow overhead, mesmerized by their sleek black-and-white bodies as they glide through the water in an undulating pattern. Unexpectedly, they stop, change course, and begin to circle, breaking the surface more often than before. Suddenly a huge triangular dorsal fin breaks the surface. The dolphins are swimming around three orca whales, mobbing them in the same way that birds attack a hawk in the air. This is quite amazing, as orcas feed on dolphins, and usually the dolphins avoid them. One orca is staying quite low in the water, but the others break the surface, revealing their large dorsal fins.

All four dolphins leap out of the water at the same time, and then dive under, still circling the orcas. The orcas seem to be circling one another as well, and emerge above the surface only once in a while, but they do not sound and go deep. Instead, the swirling party moves slowly away, while the dance continues.

Block Island beach is also horseshoe-shaped, but is much smaller than Sleepy Bay, with more large rocks lurking just below the surface, making it trickier to land safely. This beach has a wilder feel, the rocks and boulders on shore are larger and more jagged, and some are much taller than I. The same small, gray rocks line the shore, and dense spruces plunge to the cove. Kittiwakes guard this waterfront, refusing to move as our plane glides in.

A wrackline of *Fucus* is very high on the beach, a testament to the recent high tides. Nearly a hundred jellyfish the size of dinner plates are strewn about the pebbles, looking like clear plastic Frisbees with striking deep-brown rosettes radiating from the center. The beach here has recovered a bit more than Sleepy Bay, for beds of bluish black mussels line the boulders, and small white barnacles cover some of the rocks. The largest mussels are no bigger than a thumb but still they cling tenaciously to the rocks, and will one day be clean enough for the native Alaskans to harvest.

Figure 1.3. Hanging glacier on Prince William Sound.

The view from this cove is spectacular. Spruces and gigantic boulders frame a wide expanse of open water. In the distance to the northwest, snow-covered mountains rise from the deep green waters. There are too many peaks to count, each one more beautiful than the next. Most rise at forty-five degree angles or more, tumbling one upon the other. Massive sheets of ice plummet from some of the peaks, forging valleys in the solid rock. Some glaciers end abruptly, hanging in the high valleys (Fig. 1.3). Others, however, plunge all the way to the sound. A few icebergs drift close to the far shore.

On the highest reaches, hidden below boulders and small rocks, we find patches of viscous, black oil still remaining from the spill (Fig. 1.4). A few tiny, black beach fleas are caught in the mass, and though I try, I am unable to free them. The smell of oil lingers; the oil has not hardened into asphalt, and probably it never will, given that some of the solvent it contains has not evaporated. Once I learn how to search for the oil, I find more and more bits and pieces here and there. Some that are exposed to the surf have been worn nearly smooth. The oil will remain until it is removed by humans, or by the ravenous storms of winter that will one day reach this high.

Prince William Sound is breathtaking, the land rugged and unspoiled, and the wildlife abundant and charming. It is very, very large, and completely untamed. Sitting here, it is possible to believe that I am alone in the world, that the sedate life of Anchorage is merely a dream, that the hustle

Figure 1.4. Top, *scene looking northwest from Block Island in 1995;* bottom, *bits of oil remained hidden under the rocks.*

and bustle of the Arthur Kill does not exist, and that only the forces of nature can prevail and endure. Surely humans cannot influence such a rugged and wild land.

To the casual visitor to Prince William Sound, the ecosystem has recovered completely from the oil spill. I am struck by the vastness, the majesty, and the hordes of seals, sea lions, and kittiwakes that are everywhere. Thousands of kittiwakes still nest on rocky islands in the sound, and hundreds of seals bask on rocky ledges, the males still court females, and young are still born. However, my pilot reminds me that the waters are not as good for fishing, the populations of harbor seals are not as large, and the killer whales swim in smaller pods. The little crevices and crannies of many beaches still harbor bits of viscous oil, and thick sheets of asphalt still cover some of the rocks. I cannot dislodge them even when I pry with my cane. At very low tide, the blue green orangish sheen of oil coats some rocks, giving off the faint odor of oil. It is hard to find these reminders of the oil spill, but they are there.

Just knowing that bits of oil remain can spoil the image of this pristine wilderness for some people. Knowing that some of the seabirds have not recovered their former numbers, that there are fewer sea ducks in the winter, that there are fewer pink salmon in the summer run, and that there are fewer seals and killer whales diminishes the majesty for many. To those who daily wander the coves and beaches of Prince William Sound, to those who count this as home, to those who feel this is their ancestral homeland, the sound is not yet free from the taint of that awful day in March when a tanker went aground.

Chapter Two
A Brief History of Oil
● ● ●

Crude petroleum, or oil, is a liquid or semiliquid mixture of hydrocarbon compounds. Petroleum can take the form of natural gas, oil, or asphalt, and its chemical composition varies from place to place. In general it contains sulfur, oxygen, nitrogen, metals, and other elements. The hydrocarbons are the decayed remains of small marine animals and plants that flourished in the shallow inland seas that once covered large areas of the continents. Over hundreds of thousands of years, these tiny organisms lived, reproduced, and died, and their remains drifted to the sea bottom. For the past 600 million years, incompletely decayed plant and animal remains were buried under thick layers of rock, which often accumulated one layer at a time. There, aided by the pressure of these rock layers and temperatures of 210–250°F (99–121°C), this organic matter changed into the complicated hydrocarbons we call petroleum. Because petroleum is formed from organisms that lived millions of years ago, it is called a fossil fuel.

Since the Paleozoic era (570–245 million years ago), this organic matter has been slowly moving to more porous and permeable rocks, such as sandstone and siltstones, where it becomes trapped. The oil would not continue to accumulate, however, except for the presence of impermeable rock lying over these reservoirs. These trapped oils are called pools, and a series of pools within a common rock structure is called an oil field. Some oil fields extend laterally in the rock over several miles and may be several hundred yards deep.

A typical oil deposit includes natural gas, oil, and salt water. When a drill cuts into the rock where the petroleum is deposited, natural gas rushes out, followed by oil, and finally by salt water. When only salt water comes from a well, the supply of oil may be exhausted, and the well is usually abandoned.

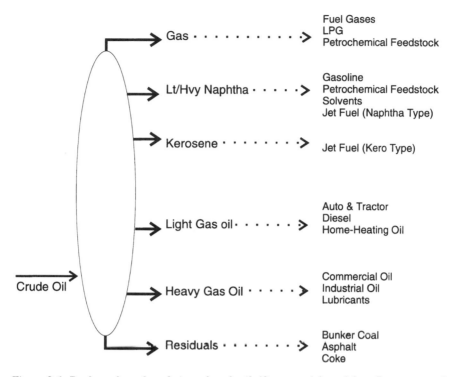

Figure 2.1. Products from the refining of crude oil. (Source: *Adapted from Department of Energy, 1994,* International energy annual report [*U.S. Department of Energy, Washington, D.C.*])

Crude oil is a mixture of many different hydrocarbons with a wide range of boiling points, and hence, a wide range of viscosities at a given temperature. Some of the different hydrocarbon components of petroleum are dissolved natural gas, gasoline, benzine, naphtha, kerosene, diesel fuel, light heating oils, heavy heating oils, and tars of various weights. They are separated from each other by elaborate refining processes (Fig. 2.1). The components are then further refined and combined into other products such as solvents, paints, asphalt, plastics, synthetic rubber, fibers, soaps and cleansing agents, waxes and jellies, medicines, explosives, and fertilizers.

Accustomed as we are to the use of sophisticated drilling equipment to tap oil deposits, we're often unaware that in many places oil flows to the surface of its own accord. Oil seeps from the surface rocks or lies in sticky masses of asphalt all over the world. One of the most famous oil seeps is in West Los Angeles, at the Rancho La Brea tar pits, where coyotes, wolves, great lions, pumas, lynx, saber-toothed cats, and giant ground sloths were trapped in the mass of sticky, black petroleum over 35,000 years ago. Over

90 percent of the animal remains are those of predators, suggesting that this must have been an incredible place for them to lie in wait for unsuspecting prey. The remaining animals are plant eaters such as bison, horses, camels, antelopes, deer, mastodons, and elephants. It is home to one of the most complete assemblages of Pleistocene fauna in the world.

In the early days of Spanish California, Rancho La Brea was a vast cattle ranch, named for the abundant asphalt that was used for roofing material. The buried bones were merely a nuisance for the people extracting oil and asphalt. Not until the early 1900s did scientists recognize the importance of the tar pits. Today, the site is surrounded by high-rise buildings and busy streets. Thousands of people visit the park each year to see the bones of these exotic animals protruding from the tar. This tar is gooey enough to trap pigeons and squirrels even today, and they slowly sink as I imagine mastodons did so many centuries ago.

Early Uses of Oil

The modern world is so dependent on oil that it is easy to forget that people have been using oil since prehistoric times. From the archeological record, we know that for over six thousand years people have used petroleum in the form of asphalt, pitch (bitumen), and liquid oil. Ancient civilizations living in the Mesopotamia river valleys used local asphalt from hand-dug pits as building cement, for ornamental purposes, and for caulking boats. The legend of the Flood described in Genesis of the Bible records only one of many inundations of the low-lying river lands of Mesopotamia, and a well-caulked Ark was a necessity.

The Elamites, Chaldeans, Akkadians, and Sumerians mined shallow deposits of oil-derived pitch or asphalt, which was exported to Egypt to preserve the mummies of great kings and queens and for mosaics to adorn their coffins. During the early centuries of this millennium, the wrappings from these disinterred Egyptian mummies were used for medicines. Nile boats were caulked with asphalt, and the infant Moses was cradled in a raft of bulrushes "daubed with pitch" when he was set adrift. People in the Egyptian and Euphrates valleys also used pitch from cedars of Lebanon to augment the oil pitch. Asphalt pitch was particularly valuable where trees were no longer available or were in great demand for construction or firewood.

Archeological remains in Khuzistan, Iran, show that asphalt was commonly used for bonding and jewel setting during the Sumerian epoch (4000 B.C.). Asphalt was reportedly used as a cement in the Tower of Babel, as well as in the walls and columns of early Babylonian temples. The Babylonians even set clay cones and tiny semiprecious stones in bitumen to form elaborate mosaics as early as 600 B.C.

Plutarch wrote that Alexander the Great, when near Kirkuk in Iraq about 331 B.C., was impressed by the sight of a continuous flame issuing from the earth, probably a natural gas seep set ablaze. The Roman orator Cicero used oil lamps in the first century B.C. The Chinese first used oil as a fuel around A.D. 200. They employed pulleys and hand labor to suction the oil from the ground through hollowed-out bamboo pipes. Natural gas was also produced from these wells and transported through pipes. This method of drilling was not to be emulated in the West until the 1800s.

Liquid oil served as a purgative and wound dressing for the ancient Egyptians, aiding the healing process and keeping wounds clean. Oil was quickly adapted for warfare, however. Oil-filled trenches were set aflame to defend cities in ancient times. In Persia, natural gas was produced from shallow, percussion-drilled wells, and the Arabs developed the first distilling processes to obtain flammable oil products for military purposes. During the siege of Athens in 480 B.C. they used arrows wrapped in oil-soaked clothes. The Byzantines used "Greek fire," porous pots filled with Median oil that was ignited by gunpowder and fuses, against the Muslims in the seventh and eighth centuries A.D. At close range, Greek fire was propelled through tubes onto Arab ships attacking Constantinople in A.D. 673, nearly destroying the fleet. The Saracens used Greek fire against St. Louis during the Crusades, and the Knights of St. John used it against the invading Turks at Malta. The Mongols also burned petroleum products in their siege of central Asia. Bokhara fell in 1220 because Genghis Khan threw pots full of naphtha and fire at the gates of the castle, and it burst into flames. People poured from the city, or died in the flames.

During the Renaissance, shallow veins of crude oil and asphalt were discovered in the Far East, and brought to Europe by travelers. These early importers were richly rewarded for their wares, and trade routes soon developed. Sufficient oil from local sources was already available by the seventeenth century to light the streets of Modena in Italy and of Prague in Czechoslovakia. In 1726, Peter the Great issued ordinances regulating the transport of oil from Baku on the Caspian Sea, by boat, up the Volga. Oil had become a valued commodity to barter, trade, or steal. Up to the 1700s in Europe and the East, oil was extracted principally for fuel, medicines, jewelry, and weapons. By the beginning of the 1800s, however, rock asphalt was in demand for road building. By the end of the Napoleonic Wars, rock asphalt was being used extensively to build roads.

In the New World, the Indians of Venezuela caulked boats and hand-woven baskets with asphalt, and liquid oil served medicinal and illuminating purposes. Native North Americans incorporated oil in magic and medicines. They mixed dried weeds and flowers with oil to create permanent paints. When the early settlers arrived, they bought "Seneca oil" and "Genesee oil" from the Indians. The first barrel of Venezuelan oil to be exported was sent to Spain by Castellanos in 1539 to alleviate the gout of Emperor Charles V.

Columbus discovered a large tar lake on the island of Trinidad, and he and others filled cracks in their ships with tar. Alexander Humboldt in his explorations in the early 1800s also traveled to Trinidad specifically to obtain asphalt to repair his boats. Such repairs were essential for these early boats, and Trinidad was often the last stop on the return voyage to Europe, so boats could be readied for the dangerous journey across the Atlantic. Today, this tar lake is a tourist trap, literally, for unsuspecting visitors may park their cars on seemingly firm tar, only to find them sunken a few hours later, after the tar has softened in the warm sun.

Oil in the Modern World

The modern era of commercial use of oil began in 1820, when a small-bore lead pipe was used to transport natural gas from a seep near Fredonia, New York, to nearby consumers, including the local hotel. In 1852, Polish farmers in Pennsylvania asked a local pharmacist to distill oil they obtained from a local seep, hoping to produce vodka. The pharmacist boiled the oil, and then collected and cooled the vapor. It was not drinkable, but they tried burning it, and kerosene was invented. The invention of the kerosene lamp in 1854 created a large-scale market for the commercial product, and soon small towns everywhere were ablaze with light. Kerosene was such a successful product that Colonel Edwin L. Drake drilled the first percussion oil well to a depth of 69 feet near Titusville, Pennsylvania, in 1859. He obtained a constant flow of liquid oil, and the modern oil industry was born. Kerosene was the chief finished product from Drake's well, and it soon replaced whale oil for lamps.

Little use was made of petroleum until the development of the gasoline engine and its application to automobiles, trucks, tractors, and airplanes in the twentieth century. Even at that, until the end of the 1960s, solid fuels, such as wood, coal, and peat, were the major sources of energy for the world, although the transition to liquid fuels had happened much earlier in the United States. The change occurred partly because of the rapid growth in oil transport, and partly because of technical advances that made use of fossil fuels both easy and less expensive than other energy sources.

Today, the world runs on fossil fuels, notably oil. Although much is used for transportation (in the United States alone, vehicles burn 43 percent of the nation's oil), we depend on oil for a variety of other products, includ-

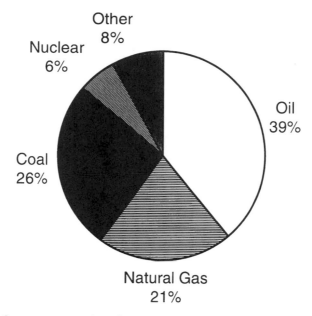

Figure 2.2. Current consumption of energy resources. These relationships are expected to remain over the next twenty years. (Source: *Adapted from Department of Energy, 1994,* International energy annual report [*U.S. Department of Energy, Washington, D.C.*])

ing lubricants, fuels, dyes, drugs, and many synthetic fibers and plastics. Overall, oil accounts for nearly 40 percent of the world's consumption of energy and is expected to hold this level well into the twenty-first century (Fig. 2.2). Oil production and consumption have risen steadily in the twentieth century. Since the early 1980s, consumption has risen from 53,000 barrels a day to 60,000 barrels a day (Fig. 2.3).

Oil not only plays a pivotal role in our economic lives, but spills over into literature and entertainment. Newsmen regularly liken oil spills to other catastrophies such as the fires in Yellowstone and devastating earthquakes. In the novel *True Grit*, set in Oklahoma in the early 1870s, Rooster Cogburn says to the bad guys, "We have got a bucket of coal oil! In one minute we will burn you out from both ends"—not unlike the Arabs lobbing oil-tipped arrows in ancient times. In one of Frederick Forsyth's early books, the hero tries to prevent the bad guys from blowing up a supertanker and fouling the world with millions of gallons of oil. High school english teachers link the *Exxon Valdez* to the morals learned in Coleridge's "Rime of the Ancient Mariner." And movies such as the *Free Willy* sequel depict the exploits of a boy trying to free a killer whale from a coal black oil slick. This is a bit close to home, since whales were affected by the *Exxon Valdez* spill.

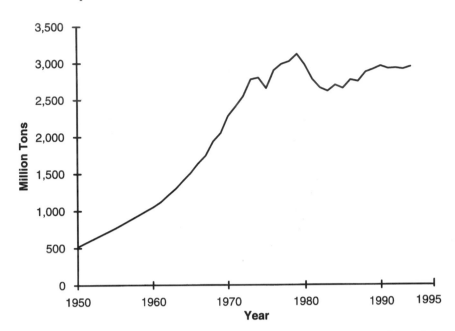

Figure 2.3. World petroleum production from 1950 to 1995. (Sources: *Adapted from Department of Energy, 1980,* International energy annual report [*U.S. Department of Energy, Washington, D.C.*]; *Department of Energy, 1994,* International energy annual report [*U.S. Department of Energy, Washington, D.C.*])

Patterns of Production

In the early part of the twentieth century, dominance in oil production went back and forth between the United States and Russia. Russia produced more oil than the United States between 1898 and 1902, mostly from Baku on the Caspian Sea. But oil drilling in that country declined when the available technology was unable to extract any more oil. The discovery of vast oil fields in the Urals and Siberia after the Second World War and the application of modern drilling techniques renewed production, and by 1974 the USSR was again the world's largest producer of oil. It lost this lead to the Middle East shortly thereafter.

In the 1920s Mexico occupied the position of the world's second-largest producer of oil. It depended on oil from seepages that required only shallow wells. However, Mexico's oil production soon decreased. Subsequently, many oil fields were discovered in Venezuela, which replaced Mexico in second place. Venezuelan oil production reached a peak in the mid-1960s;

thereafter, unfavorable tax and labor legislation discouraged exploration and exportation, and production fell off. In 1996, Venezuela again opened up to foreign oil concerns and it plans to double its production over the next ten years. Over the past two years it exceeded its OPEC quotas, and it plans to continue doing so.

Several countries that were early producers of oil—Romania, Germany, Indonesia, Brunei, Trinidad, Argentina, Brazil, and Colombia—continue to do so today. Although their output has remained steady, their relative contribution to the world's production has declined because of the increased production of oil in the Middle Eastern countries.

Oil was discovered in Iran in 1908, in Iraq in 1927, and in Saudi Arabia in 1938. However, the remarkable expansion of the Middle East oil industry did not begin until 1946. By 1974, the oil fields from Turkey to Oman were producing nearly 50 percent of the world's oil. These oil fields are notable for the size of their reservoir beds. Saudi Arabia is by far the largest oil producer, followed by Iran and Iraq. The small countries of Abu Dhabi, Kuwait, Oman, and Qatar are also important producers.

African countries also emerged as important oil producers after the Second World War. Large accumulations of oil were discovered in Algeria, Libya, Egypt, and Nigeria. Other African countries are just beginning offshore drilling operations, including Ghana, Congo Republic, Cameroon, Ivory Coast, Gabon, and Angola. In 1996, large offshore reserves were discovered in Nigeria. A 14,700-foot well has been drilled, which could significantly increase that country's oil production which already accounts for 90 percent of its foreign exchange.

In Asia, Indonesia has been an exporter of oil since the last century. The Philippines and Malaysia also produce oil commercially. The typical landscape pattern of Southeast Asia, many small islands surrounded by water, encourages offshore exploration and drilling, a trend that increases the importance of these oil-producing regions. Although China was truly the first country to drill for oil over eighteen hundred years ago, because of lack of industrialization, it produced only a small amount of oil in the twentieth century. Modern techniques employed in the last twenty years, however, have made China an important oil-producing country, yet for its own energy needs it still relies mainly on coal. In recent years, the emergence of the North Sea Basin in the northern Atlantic as an oil-producing region has turned Britain into a major producer of the world's oil.

Currently, the majority of the known oil reserves reside in the Middle East, followed by North America (Fig. 2.4). The Organization of Petroleum Exporting Countries (OPEC) have the greatest reserves, with Saudia Arabia leading the pack. OPEC countries include Algeria, Ecuador, Gabon, Indonesia, Iran, Iraq, Kuwait, Libya, Neutral zone, Nigeria, Saudi Arabia, Venezuela and United Arab Emirates. Other major producers include

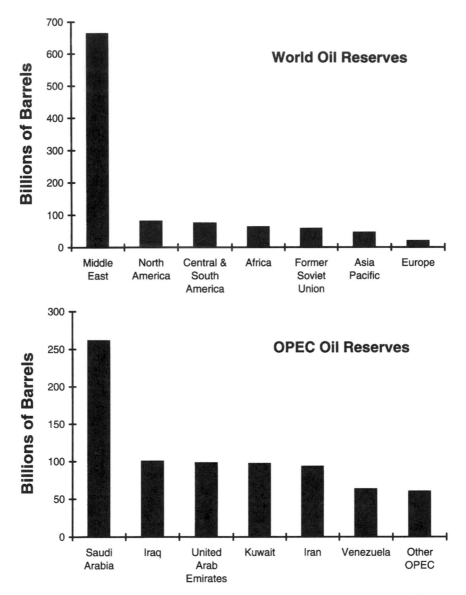

Figure 2.4. World and OPEC oil reserves. (Sources: *Adapted from Department of Energy, 1992,* International energy annual report [*U.S. Department of Energy, Washington, D.C.*]*; Department of Energy, 1994,* International energy annual report [*U.S. Department of Energy, Washington, D.C.*])

Venezuela, Libya, Indonesia, and Romania. The global pattern of oil deposits influences production and transport patterns, and thereby determines the potential distribution of oil spills.

Initially, oil reserves were exploited on land, where it was easy to explore and drill from solid ground. Geological investigations, however, revealed extensive offshore oil supplies, and technologies developed to explore coastal waters using seismic geophysical surveys. Offshore oil drilling, with its elaborate technology to deal with oceanic environments, began about seventy years ago off the coast of California. The first successful offshore oil well began operating in 1947 from a wooden platform built in sixteen feet of water off Louisiana. Most offshore exploration and drilling, however, has taken place only within the last twenty-five years. Today, there are thirty-eight hundred platforms operating in the U.S. Gulf Coast waters alone—in depths of ten to three thousand feet.

Offshore oil operations involve several activities, including exploration, drilling, construction work, production, maintenance and repair, and ultimately transport of oil or gas to refineries. Commercial quantities of offshore oil must be transported either by tankers or pipelines to the mainland for refining. One concern about offshore drilling regards the eventual need to remove offshore structures when they are no longer in operation. The usual method is to cut them into sections with explosives. The use of explosives, however, poses a danger to endangered sea turtles, marine mammals, and fish.

Transportation Methods

Part of the problem with oil is that in very few areas of the world does consumption balance production (Fig. 2.5). The greatest geographical difference between production and consumption occurs in Europe, largely because Europe contains few oil reserves but is highly industrialized. OPEC countries, however, produce far more than they use. China comes close to having its energy needs and resources in balance, but as it develops technologically, the gap between reserves and consumption will also widen.

The pattern of distribution of oil worldwide, however, has varied from time to time. For example, although in the mid-1970s, OPEC's oil production accounted for 55 percent of the world's production, its share declined to only 29 percent in the mid-1980s, but rose again to over 40 percent in the 1990s. Politics, oil prices, wars, energy conservation practices, and other considerations all have influenced oil production in the Middle East.

At present, most oil is transported in an unrefined state as "crude," and

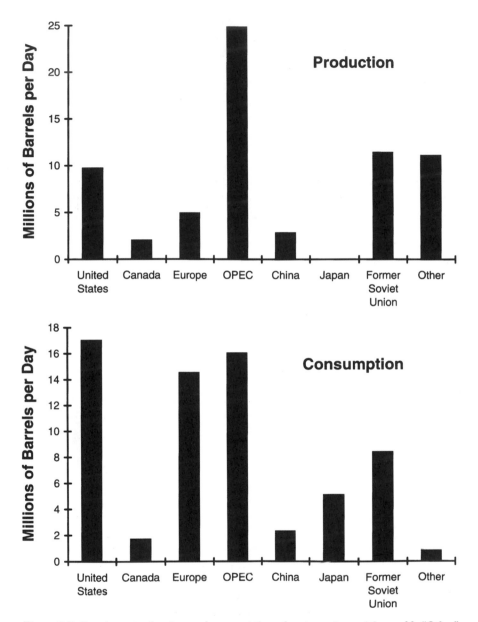

Figure 2.5. Petroleum production and consumption of major regions of the world. "Other" includes Australia and New Zealand. Arctic oil reserves are included with each country that has them. (Source: *Adapted from Department of Energy, 1994,* International energy annual report [*U.S. Department of Energy, Washington, D.C.*])

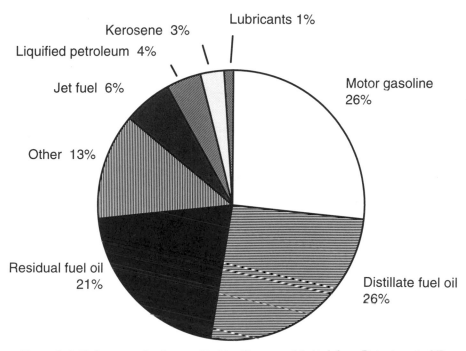

Figure 2.6. Refinery production worldwide. (Source: *Adapted from Department of Energy, 1994,* International energy annual report [*U.S. Department of Energy, Washington, D.C.*])

refineries are located near the ports of entry. Worldwide, fuel oil accounts for most of the refinery production (Fig. 2.6). Surprisingly, jet fuel accounts for only 6 percent of the world's refinery production, even with the immense increase in air transportation in the last twenty-five years.

Very soon after Drake's well went into operation, people discovered how to transport oil globally. The refined oil in the form of kerosene was put on sailing vessels in five-gallon cans, six cans to a wooden case, and sent to Europe. In the late 1800s, a sailing vessel was built in England to carry oil in bulk in barrels. By 1886, the first oil "tanker" was designed to carry oil in compartments rather than in barrels. Oil tankers are now the primary method of transportation, and traditional shipping lanes have developed over the oceans between the oil-producing countries and the importing countries. At present, major oil routes go from the Middle East to Japan, Europe, and the United States (Fig. 2.7).

Increasingly, however, oil is transported through pipes over vast distances to refineries. Today there are more miles of oil pipelines than of railroads. Pipelines have the advantage of being able to operate around the clock, under all kinds of weather. However, the initial investment required for

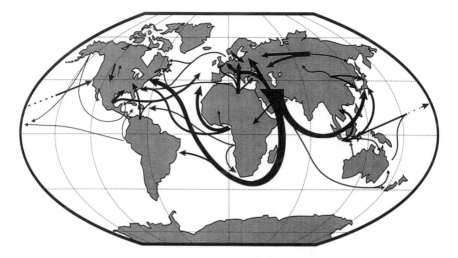

Figure 2.7. Major transportation routes of oil. The size of the arrow indicates the relative relationship. (Source: *Adapted from Department of Energy, 1988,* International energy annual report [*U.S. Department of Energy, Washington, D.C.*])

pipelines is far greater than for tankers, and royalties must be paid to countries transited. Heavy crude oils cannot be transported easily through pipelines because they are too thick to flow freely. Furthermore, it is hard to imagine building pipelines that stretch from the Middle East to Japan or the United States.

Sources of Oil Spills

Given the millions of barrels of oil that are transferred from one vessel to another and being transported around the world, it is inevitable that some of this oil will be spilled. Spills present an acute hazard to humans, other animals, and the environment.

The big spills receive worldwide attention, and vivid images of the spreading spill and the cleanup operations remain before the public. Information about oiled birds, mammals, and vegetation is gathered, both for the hungry public and to prepare a legal case for damage assessment. Dead bodies are collected and counted for the record. Gradually, information on oiled birds and mammals gives way to discussions about legal settlements and how to prevent future spills.

Small spills happen during all the same operations as massive spills, but they are often ignored by both the public and governmental agencies because their effects seem small and inconsequential. By themselves, they do not cause immediate death and destruction or foul the environment. No birds covered with oil sink in a black slick. Evidence of a small spill is fleeting, and it is soon forgotten.

In the past, many small spills came from the dumping of oil-contaminated ballast water and tank washings. It was normal practice to discharge this dirty water directly into the sea while tankers were sailing toward their loading ports. Although each tanker released only a little waste oil, with all the supertankers crisscrossing the oceans, the oil added up. In 1964, growing public sensitivity to this pollution problem provoked major oil companies to agree to stop this process. The best way to dispose of ballast water is still unclear, however.

Today, small spills occur during the transfer of oil from tanker to tanker and from tanker to refinery, around oil refineries and storage facilities, and from damaged underground pipes. Leaks from the vessels themselves sometimes go unnoticed. Day by day however, the small spills add up, until the amount of oil spilled equals a larger spill. The effects also add up, as the plants and animals must adapt to small levels of oil in their daily environment. Chronic, low-level exposure to oil can be just as devastating to plants and animals as a single, huge, short-term spill, and the effects may be longer-lasting because organisms never have time to fully recover from environmental insult.

Whenever a large oil spill occurs, the media focuses attention on the oil industry and related activities. Everyone becomes conscious of the problems of oil spills, and this heightened awareness leads to more care in the handling of oil at all levels. The number of small spills decreases because everyone is being more careful to attend to safety regulations and to follow proper handling procedures. Oil spills were occurring almost daily in the Arthur Kill prior to the large spill there, but in the succeeding years, these little spills decreased sharply. For example, in the two years before the spill there were 275 and 261 spill incidents in the Arthur Kill; but in the year following the Exxon oil spill of 1990, there were only 177 spills.

Although the U.S. Coast Guard monitors large spills, small spills often are ignored. They are reported, but no monitoring scheme assesses the amount of oil that is spilled per year, or the level of hydrocarbons that are present in aquatic environments. Yet the organisms that live there must adapt to the oil pollution that is present every day, as well as to the massive spills that occur infrequently.

Several factors have contributed to the growing number and size of oil spills over the years, including increases in the amount of oil shipped and the size of oil tankers, as well as continued discovery and drilling of offshore oil resources. This increase in the amount of oil moved around the world markedly contributes to the oil pollution problem. Today, oil accounts for over half the annual tonnage of all sea cargoes. Crude oil is

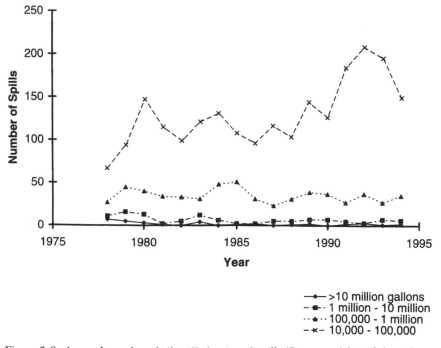

Figure 2.8. Annual number of oil spills by size of spill. (Source: *Adapted from Cutter Information Corp., 1995,* International oil spill statistics: 1994 [*Cutter Information Corp., Arlington, Mass.*])

carried by tankers to overseas refineries, while refined products are carried in smaller vessels.

One of the most important trends in tanker construction has been the tremendous growth in sheer size. In the 1930s, the largest tanker carried only 20,000 tons of oil, but in the 1960s there was a dramatic increase in the size of tankers, and many supertankers could carry 500,000 tons. By the early 1970s, maximum tanker size reached 800,000 tons and over three football fields long, their current size. This size difference adds to the likelihood of accidents because supertankers are harder to maneuver, and it takes longer for them to stop or change course to avoid other ships, icebergs, or other obstacles.

Offshore drilling provides the oil industry with one of the major technological challenges in the industry. The discovery, drilling, and transport of oil from offshore facilities creates unique problems. Large ships, barges, and submersibles are required for laying pipes or transporting oil. Inclement weather accompanied by high winds, waves, and cold severely limits the activities of the crews. The transfer of oil from a supply ship to a barge is

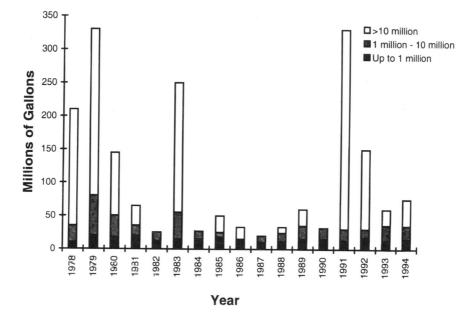

Figure 2.9. Gallons of oil spilled annually from 1978 to 1994. (Source: *Adapted from Cutter Information Corp., 1995,* International oil spill statistics: 1994 [*Cutter Information Corp., Arlington, Mass.*])

more dangerous and difficult under hazardous weather conditions, providing many opportunities for the spilling of oil and injury to the crew.

While most oil transport occurs on the water, and it is here that people worry about spills, it is prudent to remember that oil is also moved over land. Oil is stored at large installations in steel tanks and then must be transferred to pipelines or vessels, resulting in the potential for spills. Specially designed road or rail tank cars, necessary to transport petroleum products, normally are divided into a number of separate compartments. They are loaded through the top or the bottom, either by a hose or a pipe, providing yet another opportunity for spills.

It is disturbing to examine the number of spills that occur worldwide, as well as the total gallons spilled annually (Figs. 2.8 and 2.9). The largest spill in the world dumped 240 million gallons into the Persian Gulf, but most spills are smaller (Table 2.1, Fig. 2.10). Since 1978 only thirty-four spills have involved more than 10 million gallons for one incident. The *Exxon Valdez* spill is number 28 on that list. Even with all the media and regulatory attention devoted to oil spills, one to three spills of over 10 million gallons happens each year. Furthermore, the amount of oil spilled annually has not decreased during this time. The total amount of oil spilled in a given year is directly related to the number of huge accidents (or wars) that year. One or

Table 2.1. The Biggest Oil Spills Worldwide

Name and place	Year	Cause	Millions of gallons
1. Terminals and tankers, Persian Gulf	1991	War	240.0
2. Ixtoc-1 oil well, off Mexico	1979	Blowout	140.0
3. Nowruz Field, Arabia	1980	Operations	80.0
4. Fergana Valley, Uzbekistan	1992	Operations	80.0
5. *Castillo de Bellver,* off South Africa	1983	Fire	78.5
6. *Amoco Cadiz,* off NW France	1978	Grounding	68.7
7. *Atlantic Express* and *Aegean Captain,* off Trinidad and Tobago	1979	Collision	48.8
8. Well, 480 miles SE of Tripoli, Libya	1980	Operations	42.0
9. *Irenes Serenade,* Greece	1980	Grounding	36.6
10. *Torrey Canyon,* off SW UK	1967	Grounding	35.0
11. *Sea Star,* off Oman	1972	Collision	34.0
12. Storage tanks, Shuaybah, Kuwait	1981	Operations	31.2
13. *Urquiola,* off N Spain	1976	Grounding	29.0
14. *Hawaiian Patriot,* N Pacific	1977	Fire	29.0
15. *Braer,* Shetland Islands	1993	Grounding	25.0
16. *Sea Empress,* Wales	1996	Grounding	24.0
17. Pipeline, Usinsk, Russia	1994	Burst pipe	23.0

Source. Adapted from Cutter Information Corp., 1995, *International Oil Spill Statistics: 1994* (Cutter Information Corp., Arlington, Mass.).
Note. Ship names are in italics. For comparison, the *Exxon Valdez* spill resulted from a grounding in Prince William Sound, and only 10.8 million gallons leaked from the ship. Locations of these oil spills are shown in Figure 2.10.

two catastrophic accidents in any given year can increase the amount of oil spilled onto the land and into the oceans substantially. During the same time there has been a steady increase in the number of small spills, while the number of large spills has remained relatively constant. The small spills of less than 100,000 gallons apiece collectively add up to about 10 million gallons a year, worldwide.

In summary, the amount of oil that flows into the ocean, barring large accidents, comes primarily from operations near shore (Fig. 2.11). With the increase of oil tanker size and capacity (Fig. 2.12), the potential for accidents has increased. Natural seepages account for only about 10 percent of the oil that reaches the ocean. Overall, from 20 million to 340 million gallons of oil spill onto the earth and into the oceans each year— variations are due merely to how many large spills occur in the oceans.

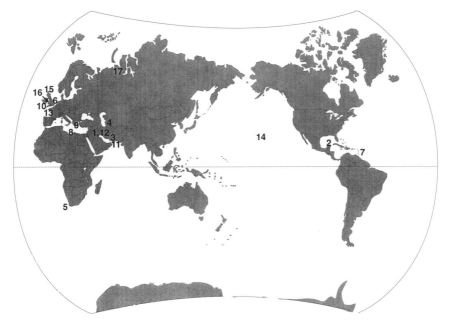

Figure 2.10. The locations of the sixteen worst oil spills in history.

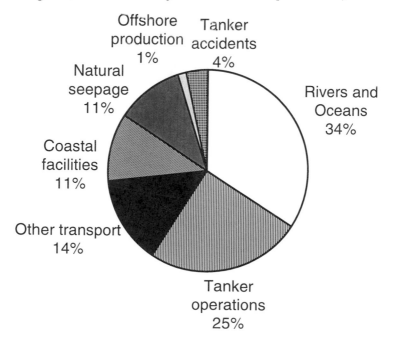

Figure 2.11. Sources of oil entering the oceans each year. About two billion gallons enter the oceans from spills and other accidents. (Source: Adapted from National Research Council, 1991, Tanker spills: Prevention by design [National Academy Press, Washington, D.C.])

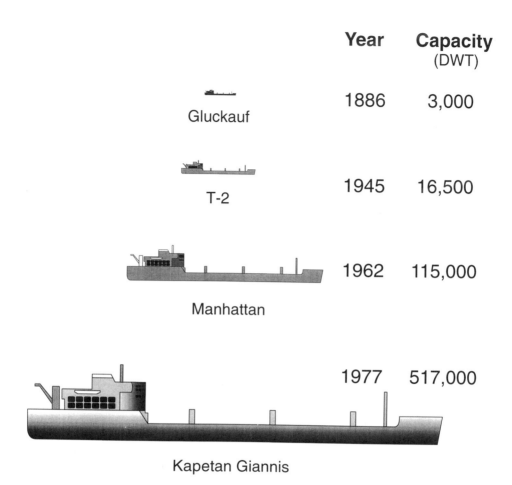

	Year	Capacity (DWT)
Gluckauf	1886	3,000
T-2	1945	16,500
Manhattan	1962	115,000
Kapetan Giannis	1977	517,000

Figure 2.12. Change in oil tanker size over time.

Chapter Three
Early Oil Spills:
From the *Torrey Canyon*
to the Mid-1980s
● ● ●

Since the 1960s, when oil tankers grew from relatively small vessels to supertankers that require several miles in which to stop, there have been major oil spills of over ten million gallons nearly every year. Some of these captured worldwide attention, while others of even greater magnitude passed unnoticed. Oil spills in the coastal waters of western Europe and North America receive intense media attention, largely due to a freedom of the press that is nonexistent in many other parts of the world. When news filtered out about spills in the USSR and some other countries with tight information controls, restricted access made it impossible to find out the severity of the spill or the damage it caused. Although our information is imperfect for many parts of the world, it is clear that accidents occur wherever there are major oil exploration and drilling operations and along the transport routes, whether they be over land or over the ocean.

In this chapter and the next I describe the very early spills we hardly remember, as well as some of the largest and most spectacular, the ones we all read about in the papers (Figs. 3.1 and 3.2). They captured our attention, and we followed every detail of the spreading oil, the dying wildlife, and the thousands of volunteers who tried, often in vain, to save oiled animals and clean soiled beaches. We watched in astonishment and dismay as the Iraqis intentionally set fire to the Kuwait oil wells during the Gulf War and released crude oil into the Gulf in a desperate attempt to clog desalination plants. In contrast, there was much less information in the press about the recent oil spill in Arctic Russia. I also describe the much smaller spill that occurred in the Arthur Kill, because it illustrates the political, social, and scientific problems created by a spill in an urban area sensitized to environmental quality.

For the most part, I discuss the spills chronologically, to examine the

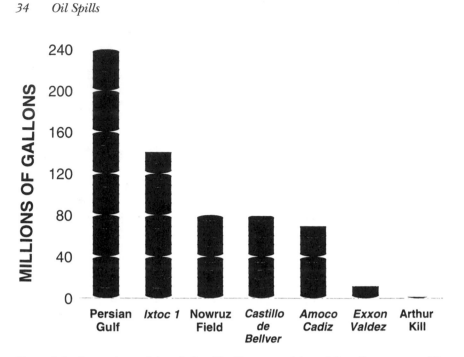

Figure 3.1. Comparison of size of oil spills. (Sources: *Adapted from Department of Energy, 1994,* International energy annual report [*U.S. Department of Energy, Washington, D.C.*]; *Cutter Information Corp., 1995,* International oil spill statistics: 1994 [*Cutter Information Corp., Arlington, Mass.*])

advances in oil spill containment and cleanup technologies. From each spill we learn about the enormous ecological and social costs, as well as how better to avoid, contain, and clean up these accidents.

Oil is measured in metric tons, barrels, and gallons. A ton is a measure of weight, while the other two are volume measures. It is difficult to go between these two measures because the weight of different oils varies. Nonetheless, the following will help:

Measures of Oil

Barrel = 42 gallons
Metric ton = 2,204 pounds
Metric ton = 7–9 barrels
Metric ton = 240–378 gallons

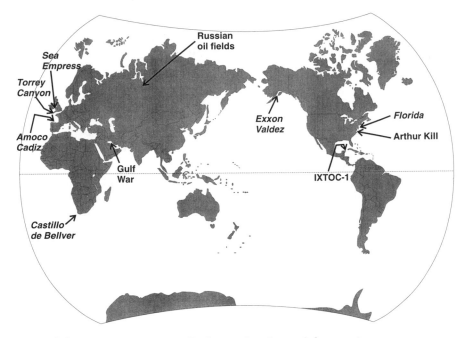

Figure 3.2. Locations of the oil spills discussed in this and the next chapter.

Torrey Canyon, off England, March 1967

In March 1967, the 118,285-ton supertanker *Torrey Canyon* carrying oil from Kuwait stranded on the Seven Stones in the Scilly Isles, causing the world's first massive marine pollution event. Pressure to beat the tide at Milford Haven led the ship's master into a catastrophic impromptu decision to steer between the Seven Stones and the main islands. Confusion and bad judgment put the ship on the rocks, it broke open, thirty-five million gallons of crude oil leaked out, and the beaches of Cornwall and Brittany were fouled. The horror of oil spreading out on the open seas without a method of containment and the impending certainty that the oil would reach the shores remained a vivid image for local residents for years. Although oiling of shores and wildlife was not new, this was the first oil spill catastrophe, and the world would never again have unlimited faith in humans' ability to transport oil safely.

Society was not prepared to contain the oil, clean it up, rehabilitate wildlife, or even assess the effects of the spill. Restoration of oiled beaches and imperiled wildlife was not an option. In fact, the British government waited a full ten days before attempting by aerial bombing to burn oil still left in the tanker. The salvager's desire to save some of the vessel was deemed more important than preventing the spread of more oil. Finally, jet planes bombed the tanker, setting fire to the crude oil in her hull and on the surface of the ocean for a mile around. Flames shot two-hundred to three-hundred feet into the air, smoke rose a mile and drifted southeast for miles, and finally dropped soot into the English Channel.

The oil threatened the beaches of the southern coast of England, Britain's main holiday area. Immediate pressure was exerted to save the beaches. The British responded by using detergents to emulsify and disperse the oil—some 2 million gallons (10,000 tons) were used to treat Cornish beaches, and another half million gallons were sprayed at sea. For wildlife, this treatment proved more damaging than the oil itself. The detergent was toxic to limpets and barnacles, and to planktonic organisms floating in the sea.

The worst victims were diving birds, such as guillemots, razorbills, cormorants, and shags. Gulls, which I have always felt were quite bright, appeared to avoid the moving oil slick, and few were affected. Total casualty counts for the *Torrey Canyon* were 20,000 guillemots and 5,000 razorbills, but these were estimates, not counts, of oiled birds. The British, a nation of bird lovers, rallied to try to save the birds. Unfortunately, of the nearly 8,000 birds brought in for care and rehabilitation, only 450 were still alive a month later, and only about 80 were ever set free.

Remarkably, there seemed to be no permanent effects on the British fisheries and shellfisheries, or on the seals. However, no one did a detailed damage assessment, and no long-term studies were made at seal breeding colonies.

France had an entirely different experience with the *Torrey Canyon* spill. The oil took longer to reach French shores, which gave that country more time to consider alternatives. The French opted for mechanical means to remove oil from the beaches of Brittany rather than use chemical means as in Cornwall.

Unlike earlier, smaller spills, an international team of scientists and engineers was convened to help the French with the decisions about oil spill cleanup technologies. The scientific advice led to the choice of powdered chalk. The chalk binds the oil into particles, which then sink to the bottom. The French estimated that 3,000 tons of chalk would sink 20,000 tons of oil. Chalk had an advantage over the detergents used for other spills, in that its effects were not nearly so disastrous for the flora and fauna.

Several committees in France and Britain that evaluated the effects of the *Torrey Canyon* spill concluded that if such a disaster ever occurred again, a team of scientists should be appointed to help with the coordination of the cleanup. In hindsight, their conclusion seems obvious, yet it marked a real change in the approach to spills. They also urged that the cargo should be removed as fast as possible to prevent further leakage and prolonged effects on the environment. This illustrates how each successive spill has advanced our understanding of how to reduce the effects of oil spill accidents.

The *Florida* Barge Accident, at West Falmouth, Massachusetts, September 1969

On the evening of September 15, 1969, a tugboat pulled out of Tiverton, Rhode Island, and headed for the power plant on the Cape Cod Canal. During the night, the towline broke, the radar failed, and the barge went aground on submerged boulders near the mouth of West Falmouth Harbor. Before oil could be removed from the barge, 175,000 gallons of light refined oil spilled on the shores of Buzzards Bay. Although this was not a large spill by *Torrey Canyon* standards, it is interesting because it is one of the best-studied oil spills in U.S. history.

The coffee-colored oil slick was visible for several miles, and driven by strong north-northeast winds, it headed for Wild Harbor. Cleanup crews used booms to contain the oil and dispersants to break it up. But their efforts had little effect on the movement and impact of the oil. Miles of beach were littered with windrows of dying, dead, and decaying marine organisms. With each succeeding tide, the beach was strewn with more dead scallops, lobsters, marine worms, and fish. Losses to the shellfish industry alone amounted to over $250,000 from the direct mortality of scallops and soft-shelled clams, not counting losses of lobsters, fish, and hard-shelled clams.

There was mass mortality of benthic or bottom-dwelling organisms, and many fish such as scup and tomcod washed up on shore. To examine the effects, researchers trawled the bottom off New Silver Beach in ten feet of water—they discovered that 95 percent of the animals were dead and the rest were dying. This massive dieoff within the benthic community triggered one of the most complete, comprehensive, and long-term studies of an oil spill. The studies continue today, and they find that oil still remains in the sediments of the marshes.

The greater the concentration of oil in the subtidal sediments and marsh muds, the greater the mortality. For several years the number of species in the heavily oiled habitats was reduced, and fluctuations in population numbers was greater than usual as oil moved through the food chain and was recycled. Shortly after the spill, an opportunistic species of worm called *Capitella* underwent a population explosion. This relatively resistant worm took advantage of the initial impact, and its populations exploded in the vacuum left by the demise of other species. In many marsh plots *Capitella* accounted for 99 percent of the individuals, while in nearby control plots none could be found.

The spill was relatively small, and the president of the cleanup company predicted a full recovery within four to six weeks. Indeed, to the casual observer the beaches soon looked clean enough for people to return and swim. In the weeks following the spill, however, the oil continued to spread to beaches and mudflats. Six months after the spill some sites that were normal right after the spill were now contaminated. By the spring, the subtidal (below the low tide line) polluted area was ten times larger than immediately after the spill, covering five thousand acres. Some five hundred acres of marsh and river were also polluted. Oil residues were found in a number of organisms for many months, and in some cases, for many years. Ten years later, spilled oil persisted in subtidal environments.

There were many sublethal effects on a number of organisms that live between and below the low tide line. Fiddler crabs were perhaps the best studied. Mortality was high initially, and even those crabs that survived were severely affected. They had decreased escape responses, decreased burrowing activity, increased molting, inappropriate display of mating colors, high winter mortality, abnormal settlement of juveniles onto the bottom, and skewed age and sex ratios. Their decreased ability to dig burrows resulted in higher winter mortality, as many failed to dig down deep enough and died with the winter frosts. These severe sublethal changes affect population size and stability. Many of these effects persisted for over seven years, when studies on the crabs ended.

The effects from the oil spill lasted for many years and included decreased population levels of many species, decreased species diversity, decreases in growth and reproductive rates, and changes in the population age structure and predator–prey interactions. In short, the communities in the marshes and the adjacent bottom-dwelling organisms were severely disrupted. Study of the West Falmouth marshes continues even today, and persistent oil residues can still be found in the tissues of some organisms and in the marsh peat.

Amoco Cadiz, off Portsall, France, March 1978

The *Amoco Cadiz* tanker was driven ashore by gale force winds on the northern shores of Brittany in March 1978. Unlike the relatively primitive *Torrey Canyon,* this was a state-of-the-art vessel, built for safety. Just off the coast, the ship's steering was lost. A large tug came to help, but heavy swells snapped the towing cables from the tug, and the ship drifted onto rocky shoals some twelve hours later. A total of 68.7 million gallons of Iranian crude oil flowed over the seas, more than double the amount of the *Torrey Canyon* disaster eleven years earlier. Tentacles of black oil moved menacingly toward the shore.

The crew was airlifted to safety, but the captain remained on board with the damaged ship. As day turned to night, the vessel foundered on the rock. With a screech of metal and a shower of sparks the ship broke in two, and water began to pour over the bridge. A helicopter returned to save the captain, just as the sea seized the broken vessel, pulling it down. For months, the bow protruded from the shallow water like a giant, menacing shark on the rocks of Portsall.

The immediate cause of the accident was failure of the steering gear and failure to summon assistance immediately, but the formal examination showed faulty design of the machinery. If the ship had been equipped with two steering gear systems instead of one, the accident might not have happened. The legal reports cited the master captain guilty of "gross dereliction" for waiting until 140 minutes after the grounding to issue a general distress call, ruling that he should have issued a distress call some seven hours earlier, when the first towline broke and certainly should have done so immediately upon grounding.

The *Amoco Cadiz* was a 228,513-ton oil tanker that was truly international. It flew a Liberian flag, but it was built by the Spanish, owned by Americans, and sailed by an Italian crew. The ship did not fly an American flag because U.S. laws require that such ships have an American crew. Because American wages are higher than elsewhere, owners avoid having American crews. This complex issue of nationality of supertankers on the high seas makes overseeing them difficult: Regulations that apply in one country do not apply in another, and crews may not even be aware of regulations.

The oil washed ashore along about four hundred miles of the French coast, which harbored a vigorous fishing industry and attracted tourists from all over Europe. The fishing boats remained in port and along the shores, coated in oil. Edible crabs and shore crabs, species of commercial value, lay dead and dying in the oil along the beach. Oil covered some two thousand acres of oyster beds in rich fishing grounds that provided a third of France's seafood. A multimillion-dollar seaweed industry was threatened. Months after the oil spill the oyster beds were still damaged.

The effects on other creatures were massive as well. In the days and weeks following the spill, millions of dead razor clams and sea urchins washed ashore. Adult finfish were poisoned, and thousands of birds died in the aftermath of the spill. More than 4,500 oiled birds, of thirty-three species, were collected along beaches in northwestern France and the Channel Islands in March alone. Of the casualties, 31 percent were puffins, 22 percent were razorbills, and 16 percent were guillemots. Obviously, the number of birds that actually died was far higher.

Huge cleanup crews arrived to try to remove oil from the beaches, while others force-fed avian victims of the spill. Volunteers tried to remove oil from feathers with towels, but procedures to prevent shock and thermal stress were unavailable. The world had not yet developed extensive technologies to clean beaches and to rehabilitate injured wildlife. The use of microorganisms to hasten the degradation of the oil was still in the early stages of development. Amoco immediately set aside two million dollars for a research program to examine the effects of the spill, and the French government provided money as well. Although commercial fish stocks were well known by local fisherman, information on other fish and invertebrates was virtually nonexistent.

Because of the extensive oiling, recovery was slow, different species returned to the beaches and tidal waters at different rates, and population levels recovered to prespill levels at disparate times. On heavily oiled beaches, snails, periwinkles, crabs, and other invertebrates suffered very high mortalities—100 percent on some beaches. Amphipods, tiny shrimplike creatures that swim on their side and are the prey base for many young fish, had decreased in density from 6,000 to only 15 individuals per square yard.

Sand eels, an important forage fish eaten by large fish and fish-eating birds, suffered high mortality close to the spill. Several other species of small forage fish also died in droves. In the estuaries east of the grounding, the 1978 year class of flatfish (flukes and flounders) that would have been eggs and larvae at the time of the spill was entirely absent. The following year, there were at least some individuals in the first-year age class in the estuaries and offshore areas. Within the bays and estuaries, mullet, pollock, and mackerel were emaciated and listless, and grey mullet were covered with sores. Over 40 percent of them had fin rot, and many eventually died. Not until 1980 did a substantial proportion of eggs and young fry survive.

About 40 percent of the total fish sold in France came from this region. Principal seafoods of the region were, in order of descending value, finfish, crustaceans, cultured oysters, other mollusks, and marine algae. Seaweed production was an important part of the local economy, as some six hundred people gathered the algae. The severe impact on the industry and on consumers' food budgets lead to public pressure to do something about oil spills. Although severely impacted at first, the seaweed *Laminaria* actually grew better a few weeks after the spill than before, because of the release of high concentrations of nitrogen and phosphorous from decaying organisms. Initially, the seaweed was shorter than usual, but this effect soon passed, and the seaweed flourished in the nutrient-rich environment, upsetting the ecological balance even further.

The *Amoco Cadiz* oil spill marked the first time anyone tried to determine exactly what happened to the oil itself. In previous oil spills, little attention was directed at finding out what fraction washed up on shore to foul the beaches. For this spill, a wide variety of techniques were employed to determine the fate of the oil, including determination of distribution and concentration of oil in the water column (a cross section of water from the

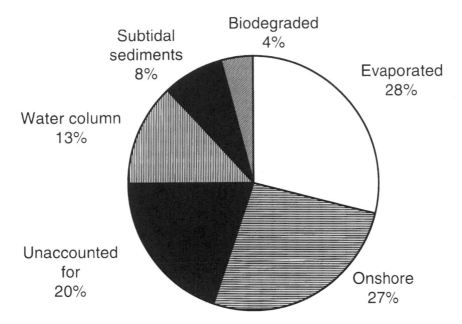

Figure 3.3. Fate of the oil from the Amoco Cadiz *over the first month after the spill.* (Source: *Adapted from E. R. Gundlach, P. D. Boehm, M. Marchand, R. M. Atlas, D. M. Ward, and D. A. Wolfe, 1983, Fate of the* Amoco Cadiz *oil,* Science *221)*

surface to the bottom), measurements of oil quantity at sampling stations, use of aerial photographs, and chemical monitoring of shoreline sites. Of the total oil spilled, 28 percent evaporated, 27 percent was deposited on shore, 13 percent was dispersed in the water column, 8 percent was deposited in subtidal sediments, and only 4 percent was degraded by microbes, leaving 20 percent unaccounted for (Fig. 3.3). Some of the oil remained dissolved in the water column for seven months, while onshore oil was visible for at least two years (Fig. 3.4).

In the wake of the *Amoco Cadiz*, concern mounted regarding the elusive goal of oil tanker safety. As early as the late 1970s, the U.S. Congress began to move on a tanker safety bill that would require double bottoms or double hulls on all new American tankers and segregated ballast systems on all tankers, new and old. When a supertanker is completely unloaded, the crew refills the tanks with water so that the ship floats smoothly in the ocean during its return voyage. Separate compartments add to the stability of the boat. In addition, all tankers that call in U.S. ports would be required to have backup radar and improved emergency systems. This upset the Intergovernmental Maritime Consultative Organization (IMCO), an international body that sets standards for ships, although some critics argued

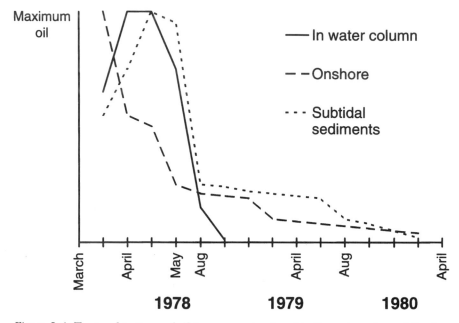

Figure 3.4. Temporal patterns of oil presence on land and in the water column following the Amoco Cadiz *oil spill. (Source: Adapted from E. R. Gundlach, P. D. Boehm, M. Marchand, R. M. Atlas, D. M. Ward, and D. A. Wolfe, 1983, Fate of the* Amoco Cadiz *oil, Science 221)*

that this organization was largely representative of ship owners. In any case, the IMCO failed to adopt the separate ballast tank system in the late 1970s, and the U.S. Congress backed down on its bill. It was to be many years before international shipping recognized the problems of supertanker construction.

Ixtoc 1 Well Blowout, Gulf of Mexico near Carmen, Mexico, June 1979

The Ixtoc 1 well blew and caught on fire on June 3, 1979, near the city of Carmen in the Gulf of Mexico. Because the fires happened close to home and the event was so close in time to the *Amoco Cadiz*, it awakened the American people to the potential for total disaster. This spill was remarkable for two reasons. It was the second-largest release of oil into the environment (140 million gallons), and it happened on an offshore exploratory well site. It became obvious that offshore operations are very vulnerable and that safety issues around these wells are extremely important.

Intensive exploration for oil in the mid-1970s in Mexico turned up oil fields so immense that they threatened to overturn conventional wisdom about the world's oil supplies. These oil supplies were heralded as equal to those in the Persian Gulf, although this turned out to be inaccurate. Even so, oil exploration was at a fever pitch—centered from Tampico south, including most of the Yucatan Peninsula. Much of the exploration was concentrated offshore, creating the potential for accidents.

The well blew early in the morning, and the first estimates put the loss of oil at over 400,000 gallons per day. As the flames rose higher and the oil flowed freely, Petroleum Mexicanos (Pemex) claimed that half the oil was burning, and another 30 percent was being lost by evaporation. As is often the case with optimistic views of the owners, this was wrong. No crude oil was burning off, only natural gas. Nine days later, a slick over one hundred miles long and fifty miles wide was moving west. At the time, it was the largest slick ever reported. Attempts to cap the well failed, and Pemex frantically drilled two wells nearby to release some of the pressure, but this failed to have an effect. To the northeast of the spill, fishing grounds where the shrimp boats from the town of Carmen normally landed shrimp worth over fifty million dollars a year were nearly destroyed. The slick was then blown north toward the Florida and Texas coasts some five hundred miles away. When it reached the coast of Texas, the aged oil was no longer as acutely toxic to invertebrates and fish, but Texans worried about sublethal effects. Later studies indicated that the oil caused a decrease in the number of species and the total population size of intertidal invertebrates. Mollusks, amphipods, and polychaete worms were greatly reduced in numbers near Padre Island, Texas.

The fires burned on and the crude oil continued to flow into the ocean. Skimmers were brought in, but with the wind and waves, they could not recoup much of the oil, and this effort largely failed as well. Finally, in desperation, in the late summer of 1979 Pemex injected over a hundred thousand tennis ball–sized steel and lead balls in a heavy solution into the maverick well, and the flow was reduced by half. Still nearly 300,000 gallons spilled into the water each day. They next tried to stop the flow by lowering a 310-ton steel cone "sombrero" over the well, and this decreased the flow to about 74,000 gallons a day. In mid-October the oil on the sea was still burning, four months after the well started to burn. The Ixtoc 1 fire finally died on March 23, 1980, when the last of three cement plugs went into the crippled well and sealed the gusher. Each plug consisted of one thousand sacks of cement jammed into the well from the two relief wells. Amazingly, through all this, only one worker died in the containment efforts.

Cleanup costs were very large—the U.S. Coast Guard spent over $8.5 million alone. Pemex estimated that their total bill was $219 million: $132 million for capping the well and containing the damage, and $87 million in lost oil revenues.

Although the ecological dangers to the Gulf coast were undoubtedly enormous, little effort was made to conduct detailed, long-term studies. The greatest ecological threat of the Ixtoc 1 oil spill was to the endangered Kemp's ridley turtle, which lays its eggs exclusively on an isolated stretch of beach at Rancho Nuevo in northern Mexico, just south of Brownsville, Texas. The females come ashore in one massive group to dig nests about twenty inches deep in May or early June. The young hatch in late July or early August, and would have to swim through the oil. With money from the U.S. Office of Endangered Species, an American graduate student and a Mexican biologist successfully airlifted ten thousand baby turtles from the beaches to a region of the Gulf of Mexico free from the oil. Many of these would have perished without help.

Castillo de Bellver, off Cape Town, South Africa, August 1983

Just after midnight on August 6, 1983, the Spanish tanker *Castillo de Bellver* caught fire seventy miles west of Cape Town. Seven hours later it broke in two, and shortly thereafter the back section sank in nearly five hundred yards of water. With some difficulty, rescue tugs towed the front half farther out to sea, where it was sunk in three thousand yards of water a week later. Oil continued to leak from the stern until January 1984, five months later. During this time over 78 million gallons of oil washed into the sea. Even now, the stern may still contain up to a million gallons of oil. Rusting and breakdown may one day release this oil into the region, and the stern remains a time bomb.

Because of the great quantities of oil that leaked from the broken tanker and its proximity to vulnerable coastal seabird colonies, there was widespread concern for ecological damage. Over 300,000 seabirds nest in colonies in the Saldanha Bay region, and thousands of migrant shorebirds stop here in both spring and fall.

The world watched with a careful eye after the tanker caught fire. Over the next few days, the winds shifted to southerly, and with the prevailing north- to northwest-moving Benguela current, the oil was carried offshore in a northwesterly direction. Cleanup crews used over 60,000 gallons of dispersants on the landward edge of the slick. About 10 percent of the oil burned off the water, and another 40 percent evaporated, leaving half of the original amount in the slick. The oil mostly remained at sea, and the

Figure 3.5. Gannet colony near Saldanha Bay, site of the Castillo de Bellver *oil spill.*

only visible damage was the oiling of some 1,500 gannets (related to boobies). Most of these oiled birds were picked up from Saldanha Bay, where they were gathering at a breeding colony on a rocky island (Fig. 3.5). Most were only lightly oiled, and about 65 percent were released after cleaning and rehabilitation. No counts were made at sea, however, and heavily oiled gannets may never have drifted to shore.

Local people were concerned about the black rain that fell for the first few days on the farms to the west of the burning tanker. Snowy white sheep were blackened by the rain, and wheatfields were no longer a vibrant green. There were no apparent long-term effects from the rain, however, and the soot washed away with later storms.

Concern ran high among fisherman, because the slick moved across the spawning, nursery, and recruitment grounds for a number of commercially important fish. More than 50 percent of the annual South African commercial rock lobster catch comes from the region between Dassen Island and St. Helena Bay, as does half of the ocean fish catch from purse seines. Nevertheless, the spill had little effect on the fishery, at least from the initial reports. The lack of immediate effects on fish was an accident of the strong winds and the Benguela current, which carried the slick away from the spawning grounds, and not a result of cleanup methods. Subtle effects on the local fishery were difficult to determine, however, both because no long-term studies were conducted and also because the fish they depend on live mainly in the oceanic waters, where it is impossible to follow individuals from the juvenile stage to adulthood. Fish that spawn in streams are easier to catch and follow than those that live entirely in the ocean.

In summary, the early oil spills, those that preceded the *Exxon Valdez*, were remarkable for a number of reasons. By the mid-1980s the world had already experienced the largest *accidental* oil spills in history. No single accidental spill after that time involved as much oil. Also, major accidents happened nearly everywhere in the world; no place was immune. And finally, we were exposed to the full range of accidents: Tankers ran aground, tankers burned, tankers collided, oil wells blew out and burned, and oil spilled on the land. Most of the major technologies we use today were available by the mid-1980s. All we have done since that time is improve the methodology; improve the legal penalties and responsibilities for cleanup; and make more money available for cleanup; damage assessment, and restoration. The next decade would see an increase in scientific studies of the effects of oil spills on natural resources, an increase in the realization that there are a variety of economic losses that can and should be compensated, and an increase in awareness that there are a variety of nonmonetary losses and stresses associated with oil spills.

Chapter Four

Modern Oil Spills: From the *Exxon Valdez* to the Present

● ● ●

Exxon Valdez, Prince William Sound, Alaska, March 1989

When the *Exxon Valdez* went aground in Prince William Sound it profoundly changed the way Americans viewed oil spills. This was the largest spill in U.S. history, and the sheer magnitude alarmed even the most complacent supporters of big industry and the oil companies.

On March 24, 1989, the 211,469-ton American-owned and -operated tanker became stranded on Bligh Reef in Prince William Sound (Fig. 4.1). The supertanker had just been fully loaded with Alaskan crude oil at a transfer terminal just across from the tiny village of Valdez. The oil had surged through a gigantic pipeline that stretches from the north slope of Alaska to Valdez. The town is on one side of the narrow bay, the oil terminals on the other. Mountains rise to over four thousand feet, and snowfields and glaciers plummet to the sea. Winter still remained in the sound, and icebergs of various sizes drifted from the base of several glaciers.

As is the custom in many ports, a pilot boarded the tanker to steer it through the treacherous waters. On leaving Valdez Narrows, an arm of water leading from the port to Prince William Sound, the port pilot left the ship, and the captain took over. After altering the course to avoid ice, the captain left the bridge in charge of the third officer. The vessel was headed straight for shoal water. The captain had instructed the third officer to alter course to starboard to clear the ice, but the execution of the order was delayed, and the vessel headed straight for Bligh Reef, barely covered with icy waters. The crew tried to shift the ship's course, but the ship refused to shift, and steadfastly headed for the reef. Too late, the crew realized that the unresponsive ship was locked in autopilot mode. The 1,400-foot-long

Figure 4.1. Top, *the Valdez facility, where the* Exxon Valdez *took on its cargo of Alaskan crude;* bottom, *Bligh Reef, where the tanker ran aground.* (Bottom photo courtesy of D. Policansky)

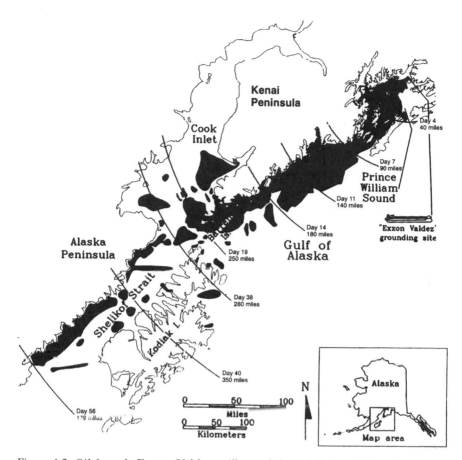

Figure 4.2. Oil from the Exxon Valdez *spill spread through Prince William Sound and on into the Gulf of Alaska.* (Source: Exxon Valdez *Oil Spill Trustee Council, pers. comm.*)

supertanker became impaled on the reef and immediately began to leak oil.

Over the course of the next few hours, over 11 million gallons of crude oil—of the over 50 million gallons on board—spread over the water. The world watched in wonder as day after day the spreading oil moved like a malevolent creature southwest through Prince William Sound, into the Gulf of Alaska, and on to Kodiak Island by forty days after the spill (Fig. 4.2). Winds and currents pushed the oil toward the western shores of the sound, and along the eastern part of the Gulf of Alaska, where it fouled beaches and killed fish and wildlife (Fig. 4.3). Within days the oil reached remote beaches at the end of convoluted fiords. Had the oil spill occurred

Figure 4.3. Oiled bird at the Exxon Valdez *spill site.* (Source: Exxon Valdez *Library*)

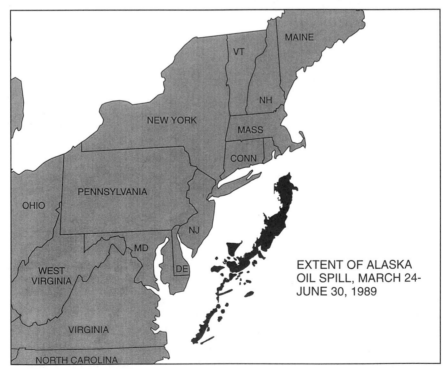

MAINE

VT

NH

NEW YORK

MASS

CONN

PENNSYLVANIA

OHIO

NJ

MD

WEST
VIRGINIA

DE

VIRGINIA

NORTH CAROLINA

EXTENT OF ALASKA
OIL SPILL, MARCH 24-
JUNE 30, 1989

Figure 4.4. The size of the Exxon Valdez *oil spill relative to the east coast of North America.* (Source: Exxon Valdez *Oil Spill Trustee Council, pers. comm.*)

on the eastern coast of North America, it would have stretched from Connecticut to North Carolina (Fig. 4.4). Imagining the ecological and economic damage to an area this large was nearly impossible.

The accident in Prince William Sound was unique for many reasons: It was the largest U.S. accident; it occurred in a relatively pristine area; it killed outright thousands of birds, sea otters, and other wildlife; and it destroyed the subsistence lifestyle of native Alaskans. It is also the best example of a catastrophic oil spill that received intense economic, social, and scientific scrutiny and study of a wide range of organisms, including humans. Because of the relatively rapid settlement of government legal claims and the establishment of a trust for the oil monies, restoration activities can continue in Prince William Sound, improving subsistence hunting, fishing, and recreational activities, as well as wildlife populations.

In the wake of the disaster, federal and state agencies mobilized to contain the oil, clean the beaches, capture and rehabilitate wildlife, mitigate damage to subsistence hunting and fishing, and reduce the effects on the ecosystems in Prince William Sound. Thousands of volunteers flocked to Anchorage, hitched rides to Valdez, and were hired to work on beaches along with crews from federal and state agencies, Exxon, and its contractors (Fig. 4.5). Many beaches had several skimmers and barges working at once (Fig. 4.6).

The immediate goal of all of the crews was to contain the oil, reduce the fish and wildlife losses, and clean the beaches, all nearly impossible tasks. Given the rough waters, the cold weather, and the shallow and rocky bottoms in many places, it was difficult to even reach many of the oiled beaches. Even when the waters were smooth as glass, many beaches were unapproachable because the shallow waters were filled with sharp rocks, treacherous for small boats or floatplanes.

Another goal was to conduct damage assessments to be used in the legal case against Exxon. The legal reality imposed a harsher reality: The count of dead bodies and the accounting of lost fishing and hunting opportunities were essential to prove economic and cultural damages in the impending legal suit. The need for legal settlements created further difficulties. As each agency tried to obtain its own data from its own experts for its own legal cases, it became impossible to share information and specimens. The federal and state governments, conservation agencies, native Alaskan groups, and Exxon all amassed data for their own ends. Anyone who knew anything about the animals or plants of the Northwest was contacted by some agency or Exxon for the purposes of obtaining "expert witnesses," often very highly paid. An air of urgency and secrecy descended upon the proceedings. The bodies of dead sea otters, seaducks, and murres were collected and preserved for evidence, rather than being used to gather as much information as possible on the adverse effects of oil. They

Figure 4.5. Top and center, *cleanup activities at the* Exxon Valdez *on shore;* bottom, *offshore where skimmers waited to collect oil.* (Source: Exxon Valdez *Oil Spill Public Information Center*)

Figure 4.6. Skimmers and collection boats offshore. (Photo courtesy of D. Policansky)

were locked in freezers until after the settlement, when many were dispensed to various scientific laboratories to further our knowledge about Alaskan wildlife and oil. Finally, the remaining specimens were burned.

In the aftermath of the spill, over a hundred studies were initiated by the state of Alaska and the federal government under the Natural Resource Damage Assessment regulations, which outlined a process to determine proper compensation to the public for injuries to natural resources. These regulations were part of the Clean Water Act (passed in 1963), as well as the Comprehensive Environmental Response, Compensation, and Liability Act (CERCLA), also known as Superfund (passed in 1980).

In September 1991, two-and-a-half years after the oil spill, the United States and Exxon entered a criminal plea agreement. Exxon was convicted of four criminal offenses, assessed substantial fines, and ordered to pay restitution of $100 million to be shared equally between the state of Alaska and the United States. The monies were to be used exclusively within Alaska for *Exxon Valdez*–related purposes: restoration, replacement, and enhancement of affected resources; acquisition of equivalent resources and services; and long-term monitoring and research programs directed to amelioration of the spill.

Concurrently, the governments and Exxon arrived at a civil settlement that provided payment of $900 million over a period of eleven years (minus reimbursements of certain costs associated with the cleanup). These civil settlement monies were to be managed by a trustee council comprising the

Table 4.1. Impact of Exxon Valdez Spill on Selected Wildlife in the Oil Spill Area

Species	Number of dead bodies	Estimated number killed	% of Prince William Sound population affected	Estimated years to recovery	Status as of 1995 in Prince William Sound
Mammals					
Killer whales	None	7	19	Unknown	AB pod not recovered
Harbor seals[a]	19	300	43	Unknown	Population decline continues; not recovered
River otters	12	?	?	Unknown	Unknown
Sea otters	1,000+	3,500–5,500	35	Unknown	Generally recovered but still affected in some areas
Birds[b]	37,000	250,000	—	Unknown	Some species still affected
Common and thick-billed murre	22,200	185,000	50–70	Unknown	Recovering
Marbled murrelet	985	8,400	7[c]	Unknown	Not recovered
Pigeon guillemot	614	1,500–3,000	10–15[c]	Unknown	Difficult to monitor; not recovered
Harlequin duck	200+	?		Unknown	Not recovered
Bald eagles	151	250	5	Unknown	PWS populations recovered
Invertebrates	Thousands	—	—	Unknown	Limited recovery

[a]Carcasses sink, unlike those of other mammals.
[b]Ninety species: 74.0% were murres, 7.0% were other alcids, 5.3% were sea ducks.
[c]In overall spill area, not just PWS.

commissioners of the Alaska Department of Environmental Conservation and the Alaska Department of Fish and Game; the Alaskan attorney general; and the secretaries of the U.S. Department of Agriculture, Department of Commerce, and the Department of Interior. The settlement organization established the Restoration Planning Work Group, which in turn produced a restoration plan that included extensive public participation.

While the legal settlements were rambling on, biologists and conservationists were evaluating the real effects on a number of plant and animal communities and tracking population levels. For some species, there was little information on prespill population levels. However, biologists had been studying some species for a number of years, and for those species there were reliable prespill data. And, of course, there were body counts for a wide variety of animals (Table 4.1). Additionally, the native Alaskans had a very good idea of the damages suffered by the species they regularly hunted and fished.

Invertebrates, such as mussels, were severely affected because many of the beaches where they live were completely covered with oil. The high-pressure water used to clean these beaches further disrupted the invertebrates; many have not recovered even today, and others, such as mussels, still had substantial concentrations of oil in 1995. The fish stocks in Prince William Sound were damaged by the spill because it happened before the annual runs of pink and chum salmon. For eons the salmon have gathered in the sound before moving upstream to spawning grounds. The huge numbers of salmon attract bears, gulls, and other predators to the edges of the sound and the streams.

In 1989 pink salmon moved into the sound as usual. Some died, but many made it to their streams and laid eggs. Mortality of the eggs from oiled streams remained high in 1989 (67 percent), 1990 (51 percent), and 1991 (96 percent). The high mortality in 1991 was due to increased mortality in upstream spawning areas untouched by the oil in 1989, suggesting that there might be some genetic damage to the adult females who were hatched the year of the spill. Even today, mortality has not returned to normal, and salmon populations have remained low, especially in the sound's southwest district. The harvest of salmon, despite intense efforts by local fisherman, is still as much as 25 percent below prespill levels.

As is true with most oil spills, birds were heavily impacted by the liquid oil and mousse, a thick mixture of water and oil that floats on the surface like a blanket, that stretched for miles along the shores and fiords of Prince William Sound and the Gulf of Alaska. Dead and dying birds lay oiled in the sea, along the shore, and on the beaches. Over the course of the summer of 1989, over 37,000 corpses were retrieved and identified. Some 30,000 of the carcasses, of ninety different bird species, were probably killed by oil. The number that died at sea is difficult to calculate. One study set dead birds

Figure 4.7. Common murres nesting in Alaska.

adrift to see what percentage of the corpses floated to shore. Extrapolations indicated that perhaps as many as 250,000 birds were actually killed. There is some controversy about the calculations and models used to generate these estimates, but nobody doubts that the total mortality was much greater than the actual count of dead bodies collected. In any case, this is the highest toll of bird life ever known from an oil spill. More birds may have died in the larger spills, but such data are hard to collect.

The spill caused serious declines in local populations of a number of seabirds, some resident and some migrants, including common loons, horned grebes, Kittlitz's murrelets, marbled murrelets, pigeon guillemots, and harlequin ducks. Some of these species were relatively scarce before the spill, and the stress from the oil spill, not to mention direct mortality, took its toll. It could take from a few years to decades for some of these populations to return to prespill levels, assuming they do not face another stress of comparable magnitude. Some populations, such as marbled murrelets, were already on a downward spiral, and the stress of the spill dealt these populations another serious blow.

Common murres accounted for the highest percentage of the dead birds, one of the few things government and industry biologists could agree on. The dead murres accounted for about 7 percent of the entire northern Gulf of Alaska population and 41 percent of populations in some local colonies in the oil spill area.

Recovery cannot be rapid because of the life history pattern of this species, patterns that are typical of most seabirds. Murres are long-lived, fish-eating seabirds in the alcid family, which also includes puffins. They nest colonially in groups of thousands on rocky cliff ledges, mostly on offshore islands (Fig. 4.7). They lay only one egg each year, and under the best of circumstances, only 40 to 60 percent of the breeding pairs at an Alaskan colony raise a chick that successfully leaves the colony. Of these chicks, only about 10 to 30 percent will ever return at four or five years of age to breed themselves; the rest perish at sea over the years. There is little that can be done to alter their way of life: they never lay more than one egg; it is difficult to improve their fishing success, which might improve breeding success; and it is impossible to increase the percentage of chicks that make it to adulthood. All that can be done is to reduce death of adults on the colony or reduce mortality of young and adults at sea.

Some common murre colonies in the sound had complete reproductive failure in 1989, 1990, and 1991. In others, reproductive rates have gradually increased, but vacant nesting ledges remain to remind us of the damage. Eight years later, the common murre population appears to be recovering, but this may not be the case for other members of the alcid family, such as pigeon guillemots or marbled murrelets. Scientists, however, are not certain how much of the reduction is due to the oil spill and how much to other factors.

In September 1995 seabird experts from all over the world met near Anchorage to combine their expertise to aid the restoration of the seabirds particularly impacted by the oil spill in Prince William Sound. They unanimously agreed that for long-lived seabird populations that were not heavily exposed to predation, restoration of populations within the spill area could be most affected by increasing the reproductive success of populations in the larger northern Gulf of Alaska region.

Populations can increase either by increased reproductive rates and subsequent survival or by the addition of breeding adults from outside the sound through immigration. The populations within the spill area can recover at a slow but steady rate if there is no addition, or recruitment, of breeding adults from elsewhere. But if the reproduction of young in the colonies in the northern Gulf of Alaska can be increased, then excess young birds from these colonies will spread to the impacted areas when they reach adulthood and are looking for nesting colonies. Once they breed at their new colonies, they will continue to do so.

Many of the colonies of murres and other species that nest on islands in the northern Gulf of Alaska have low reproductive success because of the presence of predators, such as arctic fox, that were introduced to these islands in the past by fur traders anxious to increase their fur catch. By removing predators that are not native to these islands, reproductive success of seabirds could be greatly improved, and surplus young could disperse to find new breeding sites in nearby Prince William Sound. The principle of increasing the reproductive success and population number of animals outside of an immediate spill area as a method of encouraging recruitment within the spill area is one that I feel will be used increasingly in the future for a wide variety of animals. Animal populations throughout the world spread out from source populations into unused habitats. By making use of this natural phenomenon, we can help restore populations naturally.

This idea that reproductive success should be increased outside the immediate spill area poses a problem for the *Exxon Valdez* trustees, however, who think in terms of restoration only within the impacted area, as defined by a map showing the extent of the spill. But birds and other wildlife do not respect such boundaries, and if we are to restore these populations quickly, we must increase reproductive success in populations that can serve as a "source" for replenishing the depleted colonies in the spill area.

Marine mammals, including harbor seals, sea lions and killer whales, were also affected. Dead and oiled sea otters were a particularly pathetic sight during the days after the spill. Some 1,013 sea otters were found dead immediately after the spill, and thousands of others perhaps perished without a trace. Many sea otters were brought into rehabilitation centers,

Figure 4.8. Sea lions on rocks in Prince William Sound.

where workers tried to clean them and restore them to health. Some of these were tagged and released, but nearly 70 percent were found dead or were missing within a few weeks. Sea otter numbers in the oiled areas of Prince William Sound declined 35 percent in the year following the spill, and show no recovery in the areas hit hardest.

Harbor seals and sea lions especially were affected, because they swam through the oil and hauled themselves out on rocks covered with oil (Fig. 4.8). Few dead harbor seal carcasses were found, because they sink when they die, in contrast to most marine mammals. In the months following the spill, from 50 to 100 percent of the seals in the spill area were heavily oiled, and some were coated over their entire bodies. Many were obviously weakened and were unable to find food or maintain their body temperature. The few seal pups born in oiled areas were soon covered with oil. Adults became lethargic and grew less wary with the ensuing months, allowing close approach. Examinations of seal carcasses indicated that in mammary tissue and milk, levels of hydrocarbons from the oil were relatively high, and that there were debilitating lesions in the brains of some. The lesions—mostly in the thalamus region, which controls normal functions—make it more difficult for the seals to perform normal tasks. Three years after the spill, seal numbers were still 34 percent lower on the oiled beaches. Today, seal numbers in the sound are far below the prespill num-

Table 4.2. Overall Effect of the Exxon Valdez *Oil Spill on Wildlife in Prince William Sound*

Recovering	Recovery unknown	Not recovering
Bald eagle	Black oystercatcher	Harbor seal
Common murre	Clams	Harlequin duck
Killer whale	Cutthroat trout	Marbled murrelet
Mussels	River otter	Pacific herring
Pink salmon	Rockfish	Pigeon guillemot
Sockeye salmon		Sea otter

bers. In 1995 the harbor seal population continued to decline by about 6 percent per year, continuing a trend that began before the spill. Clearly the spill added another stress to an already-stressed population.

The starkly black-and-white killer whales are a regular sight in Prince William Sound, and some of the herds, or pods, are resident. Biologists have studied them for years and have learned to recognize individuals by the shape of their dorsal fin and white markings on their backs. Killer whales can be identified easily from photographs. After the spill, a number of individual killer whales were missing from one of the major resident pods. Usually, the annual mortality rate for killer whales in this region is about 2 percent, but nearly 20 percent disappeared in each of the two years following the oil spill. Annual mortality rate did not drop to prespill levels until three years after the spill, but it increased again in the mid 1990s. Estimates based on birth and death rates and on mortality suggest that the affected pod will not regain its former size.

River otters, the smaller and more terrestrial cousin of the sea otter, did not escape either. They feed in the shallow waters near shore, where the oil concentrated most heavily. Although only twelve dead river otters were ever found, more no doubt died in their underground burrows. Unlike seals, river otters and sea otters rely on trapping air between their fur and skin for insulation. This insulation layer is disrupted by oil. Otters also swallowed oil while trying to clean their fur. The result is that populations declined, did not eat as well, and were less healthy. The recovery of the river otter is unclear, even today, and this is true for a number of other organisms (Table 4.2).

The *Exxon Valdez* oil spread over water and onto beaches that native Alaskans had used for hunting, fishing, and food gathering for over seven thousand years. Subsistence hunting and fishing are an important aspect of the life and culture of the fifteen Alutiiq communities in Prince William Sound and the Gulf of Alaska in the oil's path. Before the spill, the residents of

Chenega Bay in the sound averaged a subsistence harvest of about 342 pounds of meat per person per year. This dropped to 148 pounds after the spill. As they saw hundreds of mammals and thousands of birds dying in the oil all around them, what could the Alutiiq harvest? Not only were the game animals depleted, but there was no guarantee that the shellfish, birds, and wildlife were safe to eat.

In response to the concerns of the local subsistence cultures, the National Marine Fisheries Service in Seattle tested levels of polycyclic aromatic hydrocarbons (PAHs) in edible tissue of a variety of fish and game. PAHs can cause liver toxicity as well as cancer. The expert panel concluded that the PAHs were low and posed no health concern. But the experts went on to say that shellfish such as clams and mussels are unable to quickly clean themselves of PAHs, and hence should not be eaten from oiled beaches. Such contradictory advice did not engender confidence in the local people, who could see that there was still oil on many beaches where the shellfish lived, and the fish lived just offshore.

In the year after the spill native Alaskans in Prince William Sound harvested only about half as many species as before the spill, and overall consumption remained low. Even though testing continued through 1994, faith in the results was not high. Laboratory results showed that the levels of PAHs in fish, ducks, and deer did not make these species unsafe to eat, but even in 1991 the PAH levels remained high in shellfish from Windy Bay on the Kenai Peninsula. PAH levels in the blubber of harbor seals stayed high for a number of years following the spill—and blubber is an important part of the Alutiiq diet and domestic economy.

Today, contaminant sampling of species of fish, birds, and marine mammals used by subsistence Alutiiq continues. The trustees are involving the Alutiiq, who collect many of the samples from their traditional hunting and fishing sites. With such help, the trustees hope to provide reliable information to the Alutiiq about the safety of their traditional foods.

To the native Alaskans the oil spill has done more than contaminate their food, it has spoiled their whole way of life. Their confidence in their ability—honed by millennia of experience and traditions—to survive in their harsh homeland has been sapped by seven years of uncertainty.

Arthur Kill, New York Harbor, January 1990

Sometime during the night of January 1, 1990, a pipeline connecting the Exxon Bayway refinery at Linden, New Jersey, to the Bayonne, New Jersey, plant burst, and no. 2 fuel oil began to leak into the Arthur Kill. A red warning light went off in the Exxon facility, but it was ignored because it had misfired many times over the previous few months. Workers on the night shift assumed that this red light was just another false alarm. Darkness covered the Arthur Kill, and all seemed quiet. They went home. The next morning, a multicolored film of oil covered the water off the pier, and concern turned to panic as crews tried to locate its source. Exxon was reluctant to admit to the oil spill so soon after the *Exxon Valdez*, and for hours, refused to take responsibility. The Coast Guard moved in to begin cleanup. By the time Exxon finally did admit to the accident, storm winds and high tides had carried the oil—567,000 gallons of it— far down the Kill, into the tidal creeks, and onto the nearby marshes.

Only fifteen miles in length, the Arthur Kill (the Dutch word for creek) runs between Staten Island and New Jersey. It is in one of the most highly industrialized and urbanized areas of the Unites States, and indeed of the world. Because of its location, it faces major environmental problems every day: sewage pollution, chemical and oil pollution, boat traffic, garbage, channelization, industrial effluent, habitat destruction, and human disturbance. There are some 14 oil storage facilities on the Arthur Kill, with another twelve in nearby Newark Bay, the Kill van Kull, and the Raritan River (Fig. 4.9).

In spite of human encroachment, many salt marshes remain, providing habitat for a complex food web that culminates in breeding colonies of herons, egrets, and ibises. Top raptor predators, such as the marsh hawk, breed here, and during migration a variety of hawks pass through, stopping to forage on the birds and fish in the marshes.

The spill was considered major by the Coast Guard because it involved more than 10,000 gallons. Cleanup efforts were conducted by Exxon, under the watchful eye of the Coast Guard, the Atlantic Strike Team (mandated by the federal government), the media, and the public. It took a while for cleanup to get underway, first because Exxon did not assume responsibility, and second, because the importance of the wildlife resources was not immediately obvious. To many people, the Arthur Kill looks like an abandoned wasteland.

The cleanup operations and subsequent legal settlement from the Arthur Kill spill involved two states (New York and New Jersey), several cities (notably New York City and Jersey City), and the federal government. The legal settlement was very quick and imposed no constraints on the flow of scientific information. Exxon was eager to avoid more bad publicity. But it also helped that the effects of the Arthur Kill spill could be measured quite precisely—thanks to ongoing studies of the resources of the Kill conducted by biologists from Rutgers University, Ramapo College, and the Manomet Bird Observatory.

High tides and westerly winds initially blew the oil into the creeks and

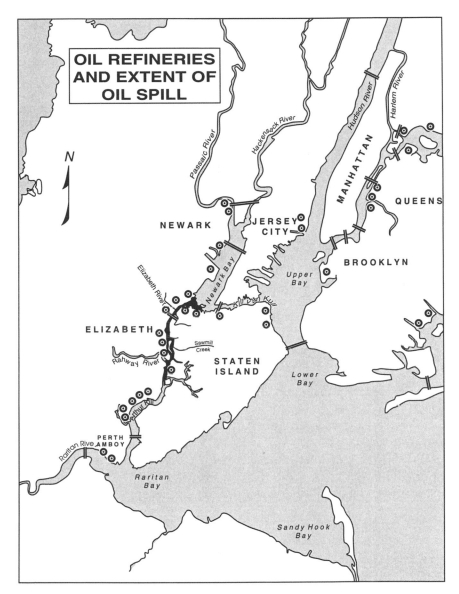

Figure 4.9. Locations of the oil refineries and the extent of the spill in the Arthur Kill. (Source: *Adapted from J. Burger, ed., 1994,* Before and after an oil spill: The Arthur Kill [*Rutgers University Press, New Brunswick, N.J.*])

onto the salt marshes of Staten Island, but with the next tidal swing, the oil dispersed to both sides of the Kill. Since it was winter, tides were particularly high, and oil was carried well up into the marshes. The delay in action meant that oil moved into all of the creeks before work crews could deploy booms to prevent more oil from entering the creeks.

Cordgrass, the main plant on the marshes, was particularly hard hit, and in all of the creeks in the vicinity the grass was smeared with a coat of black, sticky oil. Cordgrass grows in the peat from the low-tide line to the very highest tide. And it was all oiled. Even though the cordgrass was dormant in January and February, damage was obvious. Once the new cordgrass shoots began to grow in late April, they were usually sparse and short. Many creeks had no new cordgrass at all, only a bare fringe of oil-stained broken stems from the previous year's growth. By the end of the summer, everyone agreed that over 20 percent of the cordgrass had died, the 20 percent that fringed the creeks. Unfortunately, this 20 percent happens to be where most of the invertebrates live and where many of the marsh birds feed. In the summers of 1991 through 1993, more and more cordgrass grew out into the oil-stained mudbanks, but even today there are still bare peat banks where cordgrass once grew. Future studies will determine the longer-term effects to the vegetation and wildlife of the Kill.

As with most recent spills, volunteers worked alongside crews from Exxon and the state and federal governments to pick up injured and dead birds (over eight-hundred) and mammals that were oiled. Injured animals were carried to Tristate Bird Rescue and Research to be rehabilitated. Only about 20 percent of the birds were alive when they were picked up, and only about 40 percent of these ever recovered sufficiently to be released into the wild. Gulls made up 50 percent of the body count, and ducks 41 percent. They accounted for most of the mortality because the spill occurred in the winter, when these are the main species present. Had the spill occurred during the warmer months, many more herons, egrets, and ibises would have perished.

Some diamondback terrapins were also forced to emerge from their underground hibernation sites. Although only eleven were found, more no doubt perished underground, covered with oil. These deaths were particularly poignant because diamondbacks had only just returned to recolonize the Kill after being absent for many years because of pollution and low oxygen levels. Their recovery was set back by the oil spill.

The search-and-rescue efforts picked up twenty-eight dead muskrats covered with oil. Their populations were not affected because they are generally increasing in the region. No marine mammals live in the Kill, but oil that moved out into New York harbor and the Atlantic waters beyond affected some harbor seals that feed in coastal waters. Mammals, birds, and turtles were not the only casualties, however; hundreds of thousands of invertebrates died as well.

Figure 4.10. Fiddler crab dead in a sea of oil.

Many invertebrates live in the intertidal zones along the Kill, and most near the spill were covered with oil and died. Ribbed mussels, for example, normally grow in profusion along the creeks. Wherever a creek was heavily oiled, the mussels were all dead. In the following summers, some nearby creeks had no live mussels; in other creeks, only a few small ones survived. The closer the mussels were to the spill, the more severe the effect; but even several miles away some mortality could be detected.

Fiddler crabs—an invertebrate found on east coast marshes from Cape Cod to Florida wherever there is tidal flow—were huddled in underground burrows for the winter when the oil spill struck. The thick mud plugs at the top of their burrows could not protect the crabs from the oil that seeped down into the mud and into their burrows. In an effort to escape, many crabs came to the surface, where they were faced with more oil and freezing temperatures. Most died immediately from the cold and oil. Those that happened to emerge during sunny afternoons lay upside down, wriggling their legs, unable to turn over because of the oil.

Many thousands of crabs no doubt died in their underground burrows, unable even to make it to the surface. Crabs continued to emerge from their burrows, covered in oil (Fig. 4.10), for nearly two months (Fig. 4.11). In some creeks, nearly all of the fiddler crabs were killed; in others, fewer were killed, but in the following breeding seasons they were more aggressive, and spent less time feeding and engaging in courtship behavior. The crabs we took back to the laboratory were clearly impaired. They did not

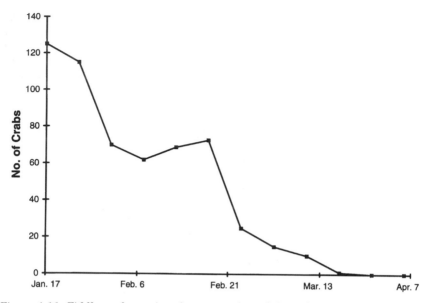

Figure 4.11. Fiddler crabs continued to emerge from their underground burrows for two months after the spill. They all died at the surface in pools of oil. (Source: *Adapted from J. Burger, J. N. Brzorad, and M. Gochfeld, 1994, Fiddler crabs* (Uca *spp.*) *as bioindicators for oil spills. In* Before and after an oil spill: The Arthur Kill [*J. Burger, ed.*] [*Rutgers University Press, New Brunswick, N.J.*])

dig burrows or feed appropriately. This was not due merely to being forced to the surface, because unoiled crabs that we dug up from Cheesequake, many miles from the spill, showed none of these aberrations. Indeed, the crabs from Cheesequake dug burrows immediately, fed avidly, and survived for many months in the laboratory.

People felt the effects of the spill as well. Many of the local residents fish or catch crabs or enjoy boating on the Kill. On any warm, sunny summer day hundreds of people are lined up here and there using string lines baited with chicken, the local method of capturing blue crabs. Children play along the shores, wander in the marsh, and paddle across the water in small, old, wooden boats. The needs of these people were largely ignored in the damage assessment because Exxon contractors interviewed only the large marina owners, who reported that all their customers merely used the Arthur Kill as a thoroughfare to the Raritan Bay beyond. In some ways, the people who actually use the Kill are like the native Alaskans: They are small in number compared with the rest of the urban New York area, they are relatively poor and without a vocal media presence, and many depend on fish and crabs to provide them with protein during the summer. They found the oiled creeks and mudflats upsetting, and curtailed their recreation and subsistence, perhaps better called "supplementation," fishing activities.

Table 4.3. Long-Term Effects on Organisms Following the Exxon Pipeline Leak in the Arthur Kill

Organisms	Immediate effects in 1990	Effects remaining in 1996
Vegetation	20% mortality	About 5% has not recovered
Blue crabs	Many dead and oiled	Recoverd
Fiddler crabs	100% mortality in some creeks; emerged from burrows and died of exposure	Population numbers generally recovered, but still behavioral differences
Mussels	High mortality in oiled creeks	Population numbers not fully back to pre-spill levels
Grass shrimp	High mortality	Did not recover for several years, still slightly depressed levels
Diamondback terrapin	Mortality, but effects unclear	Unknown
Gulls	300 died immediately; increase in oiled plumage for months	No long-term effects
Ducks	Over 200 dead	No long-term effects
Black-crowned night heron	14 died in oil; delayed timing of breeding	No long-term effects
Snowy egret	No immediate death; delayed timing of breeding; lowered reproduction success	Decreased reproductive rate for 4 years; population level and reproductive rate still lower
Muskrat	28 died; no effect on populations	No effects

As with other oil spills, there were long-term effects on the organisms living along the Arthur Kill (Table 4.3). Fiddler crab populations remained low across from the spill, and there were detectable behavioral effects for several years after the spill. Even today, some crabs in the creeks across

Figure 4.12. Great egrets nesting along the Kill were little affected.

from the spill site are more aggressive than those in unoiled creeks. Clams showed a higher incidence of lesions in several internal organs. Grass shrimp, an important component of the marsh food web, declined in numbers for several years after the spill. Several size classes of fish, such as mummichogs (a kind of killifish), were absent or reduced in number. These effects could be detected only because good baseline data were available.

Birds, however, were affected most obviously by the spill. Herons, egrets, and ibises, although not killed outright because they had not yet migrated back to the area, suffered severe reproductive losses in the 1989 breeding season (May and June). When they returned to nest in the trees and shrubs of Prall's Island and Isle of Meadows in the Kill, they were soiled by oil remaining along the shores. Species feeding in intertidal habitats were forced to switch foraging sites, and when they returned to their nests they transferred oil from their feathers to their eggs and young, some of which died. Snowy egrets were most affected, largely because they are tied to tidal marshes for their food, and these habitats were most oiled. The reproductive success of snowy egrets was abnormally low until 1993, and have remained at the low end of normal reproductive rates thereafter (Table 4.3). Other species, such as great egrets, that could switch foods, were not as affected (Fig. 4.12).

The Arthur Kill oil spill taught us one very important lesson: It is critical to be prepared. This includes having population data on sensitive, as well as common, species; having interagency and interstate coalitions that can act immediately when any environmental accident happens; having an inventory of local industries or transport facilities that might cause an accident; and having a well-thought-out list of indicator species that can be used to assess damage to natural resources. We also learned that it is critical to understand how the local people use the resources, and what they see as the existence values, that is, what the value is of merely having the resource and environment in a functioning and appealing state.

The Gulf War, Kuwait, 1990–91

Iraq forces invaded Kuwait on August 2, 1990. When they retreated in early 1991, they left in their wake burning oil wells and spreading oil slicks from terminals located along the coast. Videos of walls of flames rising several hundred feet in the air and of jet black smoke billowing above burning oil wells were watched on TVs in homes all across the world. Of the 935 oil wells in Kuwait, 650 were set ablaze. Plumes of black smoke from individual wells coalesced into one giant black cloud that moved ominously across the desert (Fig. 4.13). At the same time, the pipelines were opened at sea terminals at Al-Ahmady, Al-Shuaiba, and elsewhere, and oil flowed freely into the Gulf. We all feared the worst: massive death to fish and marine organisms, immense changes in air and water quality, and ultimately, global changes in climate.

As soon as the Iraqi army withdrew, the multinational armies that freed Kuwait moved in to stop the environmental devastation. Some twenty-seven oil spill teams from around the world converged on Kuwait to fight the burning oil wells. The work was dangerous and treacherous, but the teams worked tirelessly for months on end. First, they had to cap the oil wells to stop the fires, then they had to stop the oil flow from the terminals along the Gulf, and finally they had to clean up the oil spreading from the oil terminals and sunken oil tankers in the Gulf. With experience and increased logistical help, the number of wells that could be capped grew day by day. By early November 1991 all of the fires were extinguished. This was remarkable since everyone had predicted that it would take years to cap all the wells. The world collectively breathed a sigh of relief, and waited for the aftereffects.

By multiplying the average flow rate of oil per well, about 3,019 barrels per day, with the number of wells burning per day, it was estimated that the total amount of crude oil burned before the fires were extinguished was about 52.5 million metric tons. Assuming that the entire flow of crude was

Figure 4.13. View of the fires in the oil fields during the Gulf War. (Source: AP Wide World Photos, photo by Greg Gibson)

burned at the wellhead, this produced about 29.2 tons of black smoke per well, per day. Thus, over the nine months it took to extinguish all the wells, some 3.9 million metric tons of smoke were spewed into the air. To put this in perspective, this is equivalent to two-thirds of the smoke generated by all the forest fires in Canada for the same year.

Smoke can have several ecological and human health consequences: It can directly pollute the air over populated regions, it can rise in the atmosphere and cause changes in global climate, and it can contain toxic chemicals, which precipitate from the smoke and pollute cities and ecological systems. One of the chemicals of immediate concern was sulfur dioxide, since Kuwait crude oil is relatively high in sulfur. Sulfur dioxide causes respiratory irritation in people, and if severe, may predispose the lung to continued infection and disease. It also contributes to acid rain. The amount of sulfur released was 1.2 million metric tons, or an amount equal to two-thirds of the United Kingdom's annual emissions from coal-fired power stations. Other emissions from the burning oil included nitrogen oxides, oxygen, volatile organics, polycyclic aromatic hydrocarbons (PAHs), and heavy metals.

Several environmental protection agencies from different countries conducted air sampling in the burning oil fields and in the nearest populated areas. Analysis indicated that the pollutants were relatively low in the cities and near the oil fields. In general, except for the area immediately around the burning oil wells, ground-level air pollutants were within the allowable limits of most Western countries, for all monitoring stations. Most air pollution measurements were within the range of values found in any large Western city.

Many people worried that the smoke would pollute the atmosphere over a wider area, and could change global climate—as happens after massive volcanic eruptions. There was a clear effect on climate in the Gulf region, and Kuwait and Saudi Arabia experienced a drop in temperature of up to 18°F. Salt in the smoke from Kuwait might have contributed to the unusually heavy precipitation in Bangladesh and China, since salt serves as an excellent cloud-seeding agent. If climatic effects occurred elsewhere, they were hard to distinguish from the normal variations characteristic of global climate patterns.

The other major environmental concern in the wake of the Gulf War was the marine oil pollution from sunken tankers and destroyed oil terminals. The slicks spread out in the Gulf, soiling beaches in its path. Winds in the region normally cause the water to move counterclockwise around the upper Gulf, so the oil came ashore on the fertile tidal flats along the coast of the Eastern Province of Saudi Arabia. Of immediate concern was the possibility that the oil slick would reach the major desalination plants farther to the south and disrupt the flow of drinking water for southern Kuwait and Saudi Arabia, but this never happened.

As is true for the burning oil wells, it is impossible to determine the exact amount of oil that leaked into the marine environment. Best-guess estimates are that between two million and four million barrels leaked into the Gulf. The Iran–Iraq conflict of 1983 had spilled about two million barrels into this same region, but little attention was paid to the ecological consequences then.

The oil spill in this region was catastrophic because the oil continued to flow into the water for so long, affecting a wide range of organisms, including both migrant and resident birds, marine mammals, fish, and invertebrates. Where the oil washed ashore, it seeped into the sandy beaches, and sank deeper and deeper into the sands. As lighter fractions evaporated, the residual oil formed asphalt several inches thick. Even where the beaches appeared clean, oil was found in a grayish layer just below the surface, where it continued to affect invertebrate populations. Even today, several years later, oil still oozes out of the sand at high tides and makes its way into the sea.

On many oil-stained beaches, all the sand hoppers and annelid worms were killed, as were many shellfish. Only a few mollusks survived. The diversity of invertebrates in the Gulf is normally low because of the high salinity and wide fluctuations in water temperature, and continued oil pollution on top of these stresses severely reduces populations. Even today, the abundance and diversity of invertebrates on the oil-contaminated beaches remain lower than on nonpolluted beaches. Because oil persists in some subsoils, invertebrate larvae are discouraged from settling on these beaches, and burrowing invertebrates are unable to recover.

A variety of wildlife was affected immediately. Although the Gulf has a remarkable diversity and abundance of nesting seabirds, there are no endemic species. It does hold a large proportion of the world's Socotra cormorants, and a fair share of the sooty gull. However, lack of information on populations both before and after the spill makes assessing the effects on these species difficult. The world will not forget, however, the image of a socotra cormorant frantically trying to pull itself from a mass of thick oil. Ornithologists estimate that over 20,000 birds were killed in the spill. The birds most affected were great-crested and black-necked grebes, great and socotra cormorants, and dunlin. Injured birds were brought to rescue centers, and although about 65 percent of the cormorants survived, only 5 to 10 percent of the grebes lived.

Many of the shorebirds that winter in the area had already started their northward migration, making it difficult to determine mortality, since many no doubt died after leaving the area. The following winter, however, the number of wintering shorebirds in the oiled area fell from the usual count of 250,000 to 100,000, suggesting that many shorebirds died during migration following the spill. Landbirds were not immune, for many were migrating through the area when the vast plumes of smoke blackened the sky. About 10 percent of the birds caught by scientists on the coast of Tanajeeb, ninety miles south of the Kuwait border, were covered with soot. Many of the unsooted birds caught had lost a fifth of their normal weight, suggesting that they might not have had the strength to make it to their northern breeding grounds. This information is extremely interesting because it indicates that birds that are migrating through a region with an oil spill are severely impacted. Usually, it is impossible to know what happens to these birds.

Birds are the flagship victims of oil, but they are not the only migrants that were affected: Hundreds of migrating dragonflies were oiled when they tried to drink, feed, or rest, and many died in pools of oil and water. This pattern was also noted in the oil spills following the Iran–Iraq War ten years earlier.

Possibly the most potentially serious assault on wildlife was the oiling of a series of islands off the eastern coast of Saudi Arabia, where there are large colonies of breeding terns and nesting populations of green sea turtles.

Although there was some oiling, it could have been much worse. Some young birds died from exposure to oil, but the sea turtles apparently escaped. Some seabird nesting islands suffered additional stress on habitats from construction of new oil terminals to handle the oil diverted from the injured terminals in Kuwait. The long-term consequences of this construction will need to be evaluated, particularly if the new terminals remain in operation.

There has been remarkable recovery in the Gulf region considering the massive insult it received from the Gulf War, as well as the Iran–Iraq war of 1983. Although recovery is far from complete, there are several reasons for why it has proceeded relatively quickly. These include previous adaptation of organisms to low levels of oil from natural seeps; high ambient temperatures, which accelerate evaporation of the more toxic light fractions of oil and increase the speed of biodegradation; and the shallowness of Gulf waters, which allows sunlight to penetrate to the bottom, causing photooxidation of precipitated oil on the seabed. The region has been exposed to oil pollution for thousands of years because of massive natural seeps of oil and tar on the bottom of the Gulf. Thus the organisms living there have partly acclimated and adapted to low levels of hydrocarbons.

Even so, the chronic low-level exposure from both natural seeps and accidents makes oil spills in the Gulf region problematic as well. Massive oil spills on top of the chronic exposure to oil could cause severe damage to some vulnerable populations. For example, if a massive oil spill happened farther south in the Gulf, near the breeding center for the world's population of socotra cormorant, it could devastate the entire species.

One other aspect of this spill bears consideration: All the other spills discussed in this chapter were accidents, but the oil in Kuwait was spilled deliberately. The political and social instability of the Middle East may continue to produce wars or skirmishes, with more burning and spilling of oil.

As long as the Middle East has most of the world's known oil reserves, large oil terminals and gigantic supertankers will continue to operate in the Gulf. Because of the continuous potential for accidents, special precautions may be required to prevent chronic oil pollution from reaching toxic levels for the fish and wildlife living there. This is important both for the animals themselves and for the communities all along the Gulf that depend upon fishing and fish consumption.

Komi, Russia, 1994

With the change in political and social climate in the USSR, and its subsequent breakup into independent countries, there is an opening up of

Siberia in northern Russia, with new development, exploration, and exploitation of natural resources. The first surprise to Westerners was that Siberia is not the last pristine frontier in the Arctic, but that it had been grievously exploited and environmentally degraded. Vast areas are polluted with plutonium from nuclear reactor wastes, and with sulfur and heavy metals from a complex of smelters.

In some places in this huge land, 20 percent of the territory has oil and gas deposits that could make it the Saudi Arabia of the north. Oil companies from several Western countries are setting up joint ventures to tap the enormous reserves. One of these, the Timan Pechora basin above the Arctic Circle, has at least four billion barrels of oil reserves.

Siberia is the newest frontier where free trade and exploration of oil reserves will proceed with very few safety or environmental controls. It is in this atmosphere that the recent Komi oil spill happened, the result of a leak in the Kharyaga-Usinsk oil pipeline, about a thousand miles northeast of Moscow. The event was shrouded in secrecy, and scientists and anxious environmentalists searched the newspapers and surfed the Internet in search of information. By spring the World Bank was trying to raise money— approximately $140 million—for cleanup and containment of the Komi oil spill. The costs are higher than usual because of the uncertainty surrounding the amount of oil that may contaminate the Arctic river system and the Barents Sea.

It is impossible to estimate the exact amount of oil spilled, although some people believe the amount equals that of some of the largest spills. Over 100,000 tons—about 29,400,000 gallons—were still trapped in bogs and creeks, and when the area thawed, the oil was released into the wider environment. The nearby Pechora River basin was heavily oiled during the warm summer.

The bigger problem is that Russia has about 40,000 miles of unreliable and aging pipelines, more than half of which need to be replaced. Unless the pipes are replaced, these oil spills will continue to happen. Given Russia's economic difficulties, the pipeline will likely be replaced only with outside funding, difficult to raise in today's global economy.

Sea Empress off Milford Haven, Wales, February 1996

On February 15, 1996, the 147,000-ton tanker *Sea Empress* went aground at Milford Haven, Wales, near some of Britain's most treasured wildlife sanctuaries. There was nothing technically wrong with the ship; the cause of the grounding was human error. The Liberian-registered ship carried 130,000 tons of light crude oil. Once again, the problem of ship ownership and the laws governing ships arises. The ship was built in Spain, but owned by a Norwegian corporation that changed its port of registry to Liberia to save money by hiring a Russian crew, save taxes, and avoid regulations. The *Sea Empress* was a single-hulled ship, and much of the damage could have been avoided if it was double-hulled.

After running aground, the *Sea Empress* was battered by high seas and gale force winds, and nearly 30,000 tons (about 9 million gallons) of oil leaked almost immediately. The winds forced the slick out to sea, and hopes ran high that ecological damage could be averted. Salvage workers were hampered by the year's highest tides and strong winds, and attempts to refloat the tanker failed, but the danger of a breakup was still low. In the hopes of reducing damage to the 100,000 or more birds that live in Milford Haven, thousands of gallons of dispersants were sprayed over a twenty-five-mile long slick trailing from the stern. Even so, red-throated divers, a very rare species, and guillemots were coated with oil. Rehabilitation centers reported receiving up to 500 oiled birds a day for treatment. Thousands of birds died in the initial days after the spill.

Nearly a week later it took twelve tugs to free the crippled tanker from the rocks and tow it to St. Ann's Head, Pembrokeshire. By then, however, well over 65,000 tons (about 24 million gallons) had leaked into the sea. Lightering operations to remove the remaining oil were still hampered by high winds. Hopes to save the *Sea Empress* were fading as salvagers realized that twelve of its seventeen cargo tanks were ruptured. Even though the ship was removed from the rocks, it continue to leak oil, which continued to drift offshore, near the Pembrokeshire Coast National Park, one of Britian's most sensitive areas. Although skimmers were used to remove the oil as it reached the beaches, their efforts were hampered by low tides, which stranded the oil. In the end, the oil was so thick on some beaches, it could be shoveled off (Fig. 4.14).

The effects of the *Sea Empress* were less severe than those of the *Exxon Valdez*, even though it spilled over twice as much oil. The oil from the *Sea Empress* was lighter and tides dispersed it sooner. Even so, the oil reached Skomer, Skokholm, and Grashold Islands, putting 500,000 migrant birds at risk. As the oil reached the shores of these islands, crews tried to clean it up, but dozens of seabirds were affected, including guillemots, razorbills, cormorants, hawks, and manx shearwaters. Seals, porpoises and dolphins suffered immediately as their coats and eyes were covered with the oil. When they preened, they injested the oil, leading to immediate death in some cases. Biologists estimate that the damage will be felt for two or more decades.

Two months later there was a second wave of mortality of seabirds—and this continued for weeks. Although the obvious signs of oiling had disappeared, some 120 miles of Welsh coastline were still affected. Birds brought

Figure 4.14. Cleanup on the beaches after the Sea Empress *grounding in 1996.* (Source: *AP Wide World Photos, photo by Max Nash*)

to the local rehabilitation center suffered from oil-contaminated internal organs or starvation. The biggest problem was that their food supply of small fish and mollusks was gone or contaminated with oil.

The problem of contaminated fish was not restricted to seabirds. Fishermen were still forbidden to catch fish or shellfish in the three hundred-square-mile zone off the coast where the accident happened. Oil continued to wash up on Skomer Island, home to half the world's nesting population of Manx shearwaters, as well as many other seabirds, for three or four months. By three months after the spill, volunteers had counted 7,000 birds either already dead or completely covered with oil. Scientists estimated that for every dead or oiled bird found along the shore as many as 9 more may have perished but not been recovered.

This second wave of mortality was followed by additional losses due to reproductive failure. There were reproductive losses as the seabirds transfered oil from their own feathers to their eggs when they incubated, and even moderately oiled eggs had lower hatching rates. Once chicks hatched, there were lower survival rates and growth rates due to decreased and contaminated food supplies.

This spill illustrates, to some degree, the failure of government to respond to such environmental threats. When the *Braer* ran aground near the Shetland Islands in 1993, a commission recommended that the government provide adequately powered tugboats near crucial oil ports in case of future disasters. Environmentalists claimed that if such tugboats had been available, the *Sea Empress* could have been floated from the rocks much sooner, and oil could have been removed from the injured tanks to decrease the amount spilled.

In the wake of the spill, fisherman and merchants scrambled for a share of the estimated $85 million available from the insurers of the *Sea Empress* and the International Oil Pollution Compensation Fund. The monies, however, did not restore the habitat for the millions of birds returning to breed, or for the intertidal and other organisms living in the region.

The oil spills described above were all catastrophic for the local ecosystems they affected. Whether the spill was relatively small or massive, most of the oil was eventually washed away, but some remains on the beaches and in the marsh peats even today. Several lessons are clear from these spills, and bear repeating:

1. The most serious damage from spills usually occurs in the first hours or days after the spill. At this time the most toxic and carcinogenic compounds are released, and birds and mammals that encounter the initial oil plume are likely to die quickly if they cannot escape. At all of the spills described in this and the previous chapters, hundreds or thousands of birds and other wildlife perished.

2. The more high-energy wind and wave action at the site of the spill, the less long-term damage there will be. The oil is quickly dispersed and the lighter fractions volatilize, so the remainder is less toxic. To some extent this happened following the *Exxon Valdez* spill. The most severely affected habitats are quiet marshy areas with little tidal flow or wave action; thus, the Arthur Kill pipeline rupture caused long-term effects.

3. The more pristine an area, the greater its capacity for recovery. Although death tolls may be high initially, the organisms were healthy before the spill, and nearby populations that were unaffected by the spill can move in and colonize.

4. Heavily oiled areas, particularly in places with low-energy wave action, will show lingering effects. This was true of the *Amoco Cadiz* and the Arthur Kill spills, as well as some locations affected by the *Exxon Valdez* spill.

5. Regions with low levels of oil from natural seeps may have species that can live in these environments, and many have microorganisms that biodegrade oil. This was true for the Persian Gulf, where there are numerous natural seeps and vents.

6. Some cleanup efforts can be as harsh on the environment as the oil spill itself. This was particularly true for the *Exxon Valdez* spill, where

untested high-pressure, hot-water, sprays blasted rocks, dislodging and harming invertebrates and causing long-term damage.

7. The effects on organisms living on the sea bottom are largely unknown.

8. Although the greatest impact from oil spills occurs in the footprint of the spill, airborne pollution can affect local and global climate, producing secondary effects on agriculture.

9. The environmental damage of many of the recent spills could have been reduced greatly if the ships had double hulls. Nonetheless, many of the recent spills, such as the *Exxon Valdez* and the *Sea Empress*, were due in large part to human error—and we shall continue to be human!

Chapter Five

Oil Spills in an Environmental Context

● ● ●

The oil that spills from ruptured pipelines, disabled tankers, and faulty storage facilities enters terrestrial and marine habitats that may already have a number of naturally occurring chemicals, including oil, and may already be polluted by a number of factory-produced chemicals such as pesticides and PCBs (polychlorinated biphenyls). Some habitats have been disrupted by physical means, such as logging or bulldozing. We cannot study and evaluate the effects of oil spills if we regard them as incidents isolated in time and space. Instead, we have to consider them in a larger environmental context.

In this chapter I describe the other toxic chemicals that are common in the oceans and estuaries, consider the prevalence and effects of natural oil seeps, and examine the differential vulnerability of various organisms and ecosystems.

Pollutants Other Than Oil

Oil is just one of a number of pollutants that plague the planet. The other pollutants that are ever present in the marine environment include a number of synthetic chemicals such as pesticides, solvents, PCBs and dioxins, and other polyaromatic hydrocarbons (PAHs). Heavy metals, such as mercury, lead, cadmium, arsenic, tin, and chromium, are a particular problem in oceanic environments. Heavy metals come from a variety of manufactured products, as well as from natural processes such as erosion of bedrock and volcanic activity. Some mercury and other heavy metals have always been in the marine environment, but industrial activities have drastically increased their amounts.

Other important sources of contamination include volatile organic compounds such as benzene, nitrogen dioxide, and sulfur dioxide from automobile emissions and smokestacks, and the greenhouse gases such as methane and carbon dioxide. These latter compounds primarily are airborne, and when they enter the aquatic environment in the form of acid rain, they change the pH of water, which in turn affects how animals respond to other environmental stresses, including oil. When acid rain falls on water, it decreases its pH, causing fish to take up higher levels of mercury (often present in oil, especially used oil) in their bodies than they do at higher pHs. Mercury has a variety of effects on fish, weakening their resistance to oil pollution. Mercury then increases, or "bioaccumulates," as it moves up the food chain, and can render large fish, such as shark or swordfish, unfit for human consumption.

The problem of pollutants in the oceans has reached such proportions that the United Nations Environmental Program held a conference late in 1995 to seek global treaties on toxic ocean pollutants. Cleaning up the ocean is a global problem, and must involve shared responsibility, particularly among the industrial nations. Although the 1982 Law of the Sea treaty and other international agreements regulate ocean dumping and other forms of direct pollution, the recent conference focused on land-based activities that contribute indirectly to pollution of the oceans. Chemicals that are used for agriculture or industrial processes eventually make their way to the ocean via streams and rivers. Furthermore, although some chemicals are banned for use in the United States and some other countries, they are still commonly used in many others. Indeed, some pesticides are made in the United States for export to developing countries even though these pesticides cannot legally be sold in the United States.

The chemicals of concern for the UN conference were pesticides, DDT, toxaphene, chlordane, heptachlor, endrin, aldrin, mirex, and dieldrin, as well as byproducts of industrial operations such as dioxins, furans, hexachlorobenzene, and PCBs. These chemicals are a particular problem because they persist in the environment and remain in the bodies of animals for a very long time. Thus, long-lived animals such as some birds, sea mammals, and humans are particularly vulnerable.

The oil from oil spills is not the only oil that reaches the oceans. Land-based activities leak oil onto the land, and it flows into creeks, streams, and rivers to the seas. This oil, unfortunately, often contains other contaminants such as heavy metals. The U.S. Environmental Protection Agency estimates that 175 million gallons of used oil ends up in landfills each year just from people changing the oil in their cars. There are also underground spills from gas stations and tank farms, and this oil can contaminate groundwater. Eventually it flows to the sea.

It is on top of an oceanic environment already exposed to a variety of chemicals that oil has its greatest effect. Organisms stressed by toxic chemicals as well as heavy metals are at an extreme disadvantage when faced with oil pollution. This is particularly true if organisms are exposed to oil for long periods of time.

Natural Oil Seeps

As discussed at length in Chapter 2, since prehistoric times, natural seeps of asphalt and tar on the earth's surface and vents of natural gas or oil provided a treasured resource. These seeps, however, were also part of natural ecosystems, and plants and animals living near such seeps adapted to the oil, much like certain deep sea creatures thrive near hot water vents that would boil other species.

Today, nearly 10 percent of the oil that enters the oceans comes from natural seeps and vents. Like oil fields that lie beneath impenetrable bedrock, natural seeps and vents are unevenly distributed through the world. Seeps are associated with regions of high tectonic activity, where the plates of the earth are moving slowly beneath the sea and continents, the same places that have high volcanic and earthquake activity. Thus, natural seeps tend to be concentrated along the Pacific Rim, in central North America, in central Europe, and along the northern Mediterranean (Fig. 5.1). This map represents the known seeps, but it seems likely that many have not yet been discovered. Since seeps can represent substantial oil fields, this map also suggests places for petroleum geologists to explore. Exploration is sometimes disappointing, however, because many seeps do not contain sufficient oil for commercial exploitation, at least by present technology. Vents occur in the same region as oil fields, and in many cases have been used to locate wells.

Using data on the amount of oil that leaks from a few well-studied seeps, geologists estimate that between 250,000 and 600,000 metric tons of oil seep into the oceans each year. This estimate is based on rock structure, recent earthquake activity, and sediment thickness. It is also based on the over five hundred or so million years that oil has been seeping from the oceans. The Pacific Rim contributes about 40 percent of the world's total, not surprisingly, since this is a region of high volcanic activity. The estimate of oil entering the oceans from natural seeps may well increase as more are discovered, particularly in arctic and antarctic regions.

Seepages do not occur in all types of rock, but are limited to sedimentary

Figure 5.1. Locations of natural seeps. (Source: *Adapted from J. T. Stowe and L. A. Underwood, 1984, Oil spillages affecting seabirds in the United Kingdom, 1966–1983,* Marine Pollution Bulletin *15*)

rocks and to metamorphic or igneous rocks closely associated with sediments. Seeps on the surface happen because an oil reserve is breached— there is a fault line through which the oil moves toward the surface or fractures that allow the oil to seep upward.

One area with a high number of natural seeps is just off the southern coast of California. The geology here is highly complex, several fault lines run to the surface, and oil escapes. The one thousand-square-mile area from Point Conception to Point Fermin may spew upward of nine hundred barrels per day into the ocean from over fifty seeps, although the oil flow varies seasonally. Even so, the effects seem to be small, since hydrocarbons, indicative of exposure to oil, are not being concentrated either in the water or sediments. A good community of bottom-dwelling marine organisms is associated with these seeps, and populations of some species are higher in seep areas compared with areas free from oil.

Seepages should decrease over time, both because less oil is available in the underground oil fields, and because, with human efforts, oil is being removed from these fields. Diminishing oil seep rates in the Santa Barbara Basin, offshore of California, are directly related to commercial drilling in the area. As more oil is extracted, less is available for seeping. In Trinidad, a sticky stream of tar fifteen to eighteen feet wide flowed into the sea before asphalt mining. Now, none enters the marine environment. Thus, humans are also reducing the amount of oil that enters the marine environment from natural sources.

Oil can also reach the oceans naturally through the process of erosion from the continents. Based on the organic carbon content of sediments in rivers, geologists have calculated that about fifty thousand metric tons of oil are eroded each year and reach the oceans.

Oil seeps in marine environments are a natural part of many ecosystems, and presumably plants and animals have adapted to this oil over evolutionary time. There are a number of key differences between natural underwater seeps and oil spills, however. Oil from natural seeps comes from the ocean floor and makes its way through the water column, settling to the bottom, and dispersing slowly through the water. Thus, the thick, gooey mousse often present after an oil spill does not occur with natural seeps. In any given area, the amount of oil from a catastrophic spill far overshadows the oil coming from natural seeps.

Understanding how plants and animals adapt to low-level exposure to natural oil seeps may help us identify the species that are less vulnerable to spills and that can survive under conditions of chronic oil pollution. One piece of evidence that some organisms have adapted to the presence of low levels of oil is the occurrence of microorganisms that are capable of biodegrading or breaking down oil. These organisms have turned out to be extremely important in the development of biological controls for oil spills (discussed further in Chapter 7).

One ecological system exposed to natural oil from seeps is the Persian Gulf region of the Middle East. Karo Island was named for the tar ("kar" in the local dialect means "tar") that oozes from the sea bottom near the island. Oil also seeps from several other nearby underwater vents. A number of microorganisms that live in this region are acclimatized to the oil and actually promote the hydrocarbon biodegradation and photooxidation processes. These organisms not only aid in biodegradation of natural oil, but are present and can function when an accidental oil spill occurs. Microbiologists have cultured and bred such microorganisms for use in biodegradation elsewhere. A whole new field—bioremediation—has developed around the discovery and culturing of microorganisms that can be used to degrade oil.

Species Vulnerability

Animals and plants, as well as the nonliving parts of ecosystems, are not equally vulnerable to environmental changes. Some plants are fragile and have narrow habitat ranges, and they grow only on isolated sites. Likewise, some animals are very specialized, living in only a few places or eating only a few kinds of foods. Other species are generalists, with wide tolerances for different environmental conditions. They eat a wide range of foods, live in many different habitats, or live in water that changes from fresh to salt depending on the tides and rain. Such animals and plants are very adaptable and often can recover quickly from any disturbance, including an oil spill.

A number of factors determine whether an oil spill has devastating effects on plants and animals, including the size of the spill, type of oil, time of the spill (particularly in relation to the life cycle of the organisms), vulnerability of particular plants and animals, and the vulnerability of particular ecosystems.

The size of the spill—the number of gallons and the rate of flow—determines whether the oil covers large sections of land or ocean, whether the oil actually reaches the shore, and how much shoreline the spill covers. Small spills simply cannot cover as large an area, and the oil can evaporate or be washed away sooner by the forces of nature. Also, organisms from surrounding areas can recolonize small areas more quickly. In contrast, a massive spill may create a large area in which no plants and few of the microorganisms that form key links in the food chain survive. Plants whose seeds are carried by the wind may colonize barren soil, but those whose seeds fall to the ground or that spread by underground roots may take years to march across the soil.

The type of oil can make a big difference in the extent of ecological damage. How much oil evaporates; how fast the oil can spread over the surface of the water; how easy it is to remove, contain, or burn; how fast it moves toward sensitive beaches; and whether it can be cleaned from beaches and rocks—all these depend on the particulars of the oil. All oils are mixtures of many different hydrocarbons. The smaller and lighter molecules are volatile, and over time they will evaporate, leaving behind a dense, tarlike mixture. Heavy, thick oil coats rocks and boulders along the shore and eventually forms thick, viscous masses of asphalt that solidify and cling to the rocks.

The timing of a spill may be critical in determining whether a spill can be contained, whether oil can be removed from the surface of the water, what types of animals or plants will be affected, and how severe the effects will be. When spills happen during high winds or storms, as typically occurs during the winter months throughout the Northern Hemisphere, it is difficult or impossible for work crews to reach a spill. It may be hours or days before it is safe enough for professional oil spill response teams to move in. Even then, operations are slowed by the cold. During extreme cold, both humans and machines have trouble operating, and with thin ice or icebergs in the water, cleanup operations may be impossible. Severe storms often are helpful, however, in breaking up oil slicks and dispersing the oil through the water column.

Whether the spill occurs in winter or summer is another aspect of timing that influences which animals and plants are most affected. In the Northern Hemisphere, many species of vertebrates leave their breeding places as cold weather sets in and move to warmer climates. The degree of movement varies with the species, and with the latitude. Some species may be absent at the time of the spill and escape immediate injury. In the northern tundra, most species of birds clear out as cold winds sweep across the barren lands, and they migrate to more temperate regions, even to South America. The hordes of shorebirds that breed in the arctic tundra all around the globe begin to migrate south in late July or early August, when insects become less abundant. Only a few hardy species such as snowy owls, ravens, and some gulls remain when the heavy snows come. Even snowy owls wander southward when the snow is deep, and the lemmings are hard to find. The birds do not return until June when the ground begins to thaw, and insects are available for food. From June to the end of July, however, the tundra is teeming with shorebirds, owls, and other wildlife.

Winter provides its own stresses, of course, with the result that an oil spill then can be very harmful to the few animals that remain. Caribou and reindeer may shift a bit south to find food, but if the snows are very deep they may be unable to move far. Smaller animals like mice may have particular difficulties in winter if their food is oiled and they are unable to escape to areas where their food is not contaminated.

The fragile vegetation of the tundra is particularly vulnerable to oil spills. These plants cannot survive being covered with oil, and the very short growing season allows little time for recovery. Even if the spill occurs in winter, when the ground is frozen and plants are covered with snow, the oil will sink onto the delicate vegetation as the snows melt. The damage to the plants, of course, then affects the animals that depend on the plants for food and shelter. Migratory birds that miss the worst of a winter oil spill may come back to a wasteland and be unable to breed.

In temperate regions, timing of a spill is also important, for the activities of most species change with the season. The effect on plants is less catastrophic if the spill occurs in the late fall or winter when vegetation is dormant. Many invertebrates bury in the mud and sand along the shore as winter approaches. Species such as fiddler crabs dig their burrows deeper and finally plug the opening with a mud ball. They climb to the very bottom of their burrows, reduce their metabolic rate so that they require no food, and wait out the winter months. Many fish migrate out of the bays and estuaries, remaining several miles offshore in deeper water, or moving south along the coasts to warmer climes. Other fish go into the bays and estuaries to overwinter in the beds of vegetation or under the ice. Sea turtles migrate south just off the coasts, and species such as diamond-back terrapin burrow down in the mud to spend the winter in hibernation. Most birds migrate south to the southern United States, or fly farther to Central or South America. Similar migrations take place in Europe and Asia. Some birds remain throughout the year, while others that bred farther north, such as gulls and seaducks, migrate into temperate regions to spend the winter. In the winter, ducks and gulls may be the predominant birds affected by a spill; during the rest of the year, shorebirds, herons and egrets, terns, skimmers, alcids, cormorants, and other resident birds will be harmed.

If an oil spill occurs during the bird's breeding season, breeding activities may be curtailed or reproductive success reduced. Not only will the adults be subjected to oiling when they forage for food, but they will bring back oiled food for their young. Oil may be transferred from oiled plumage to eggs, preventing adequate gas exchange and reducing hatching success. Little oil is required to create problems: a few drops of oil applied to the surface of herring gull eggs will keep them from hatching. In some cases, reproduction can come to a standstill if food is unavailable or heavily contaminated.

If a spill occurs during the migratory season at a critical stopover area, a large proportion of the entire breeding population of a species can be affected. For example, the Copper River Delta in southern Alaska is where most of the shorebirds breeding in the western Arctic pause to stop and refuel before they migrate farther north. Each June, several million shorebirds gather there in dense flocks to feed on invertebrates and eggs. They gather again in the fall, just before migrating thousands of miles to their wintering grounds farther south. Delaware Bay in New Jersey is another critical stopover area, and each spring over a million shorebirds converge during a three-week period in late May–early June to feed on the eggs of horseshoe crabs. Upward of 90 percent of North American's red knots move through Delaware Bay at this time. Both areas are vulnerable to oil spills: The Copper River Delta is very close to an offshore oil exploration lease just east of Prince William Sound, Alaska; and Delaware Bay is one of the primary oil ports on the East Coast, and supertankers travel up Delaware Bay to docks near Camden and Philadelphia.

Most invertebrates are also vulnerable during their spawning season. Horseshoe crabs come in droves onto the beaches of Massachusetts, New Jersey, and Delaware to lay their eggs at the tide line in May and June, and an oil spill then could be devastating. Not only would the nesting females be covered with oil, but the eggs would as well, and they would not hatch. Since females do not breed until they are nine or ten years old, they have a slow recovery time. At other times, the horseshoe crabs are farther out in the bay, or in offshore waters, where they are less vulnerable because they are dispersed and remain on the bottom muds.

Tropical ecosystems are vulnerable for the entire year since most species are nonmigratory, remaining throughout the year. Moreover, many birds from the Northern Hemisphere migrate to tropical habitats during the winter, increasing the number of species at risk from an oil spill. All of the species of sea turtles return to tropical beaches to lay their eggs, and both they and their nests are vulnerable then. Even after egg laying, oil washed ashore can percolate through the sand, killing the embryos in their soft, leathery shells.

Life history characteristics of an animal or plant also determine whether it will be severely affected by an oil spill. These include how long it lives, how often it has offspring, how many offspring it can have at once, how much parental care it devotes to its offspring, and whether it is a generalist or specialist. Generalists are more apt to survive any catastrophic event because they are less dependent on only a few food items and are not restricted to particular habitats. For example, after the Arthur Kill oil spill, the breeding birds that were most affected were those that relied on only a few prey species for food and fed in only a few habitats. Snowy egrets, which rely heavily on small fish in intertidal creeks, suffered reproductive losses for many years because these prey populations were also affected. Great egrets, which feed on a variety of fish in deeper water, were not affected because they could move to other habitats.

Species with low clutch sizes and a long prereproductive stage generally have a slow recovery rate. If a high proportion of the breeders in an area are killed off, it will be many years before the young hatched there will return to start new colonies. In Prince William Sound following the *Exxon Valdez*, seabirds that lay only one egg and do not breed until they are eight to ten years old, such as common murres, have not yet recovered.

Some stages of the life cycle are more vulnerable to oil pollution than others are. For many species, the egg or developing embryo is particularly vulnerable to oil contamination. Following the *Amoco Cadiz* accident off Brittany, it was the first-year age classes of fish that were severely affected. No young finfish survived during the year of the spill, and that age class was forever missing from the populations. Following the *Exxon Valdez* oil spill, there was an increase in mortality and abnormality in eggs and larvae. There is some evidence that when surviving pink salmon returned to breed two years later, they seemed to have been genetically altered by the oil while they were in the egg or young fry stage.

Ecosystem Vulnerability

Usually when we think of damage from oil spills, we think of particular birds or mammals. But when many different plants and animals are affected, the whole ecosystem ceases to function well. Ecosystems are not equally vulnerable to oil spills. Even without the seasonal aspects discussed above, there are differences in vulnerability among ecosystems. The less complex the ecosystem, the greater the potential for long-term effects.

Less complex systems are generally those with fewer species and with less variation in the structure of the vegetation. With less structural variation there are fewer habitats for different animals. With fewer species, the food chain is shorter, and damage to any one link adversely affects many of the other links. The diversity in food types is also less, and the loss of any one species may result in wholesale starvation of the predators that rely on it. The ability of these systems to recover is lower because every species must recover or return before the system will function properly.

A recent United Nations document, the Global Biodiversity Assessment, stated that human activities such as logging, commercial fishing, and farming are endangering plants, animals, and entire ecosystems at a much higher rate than ever before in recorded history. Species are becoming extinct at fifty to one hundred times the average expected natural rate. Today, at least 4,000 plants and 5,400 animals are endangered and threatened with extinction. This rapid rate of placing species at risk further increases the potential for catastrophic effects from severe oil spills, particularly when they happen in regions already stressed by other human activities.

The ecosystems that are most vulnerable are arctic systems, desert systems, and closed marine systems that receive little direct wave action. Arctic and desert systems are particularly vulnerable because very few species reside in these systems. Food chains are short, and there is little diversity or variability in the prey base. Arctic systems are at risk for another reason: The growing season is very short, and the decaying season is short. Oiled vegetation has little time to grow and recover from an oil spill. Any vegetation that dies as a result of oiling may lay on the ground for years before it decays, and during that time the nutrients are lost from the system. For example, the small wooden stems of dwarf willows may take over one hundred years to decay. Animals may take years to move back into the arctic tundra if there is massive death following an oil spill. Some insects have a particularly long recovery time, as many are not long-distance fliers. Birds and mammals can migrate in, and the habitat may soon be filled, assuming the vegetation is healthy. However, if the insect prey base is not available, birds will leave before they set up territories and lay eggs.

Furthermore, since the growing season is so short and the cold winters so very long, the oil itself takes much longer to break down in arctic ecosystems. There are far fewer microorganisms capable of breaking down oil in arctic ecosystems, and the ones that are there have very little time each year to act. Hence, it may be decades before there is any recovery from the recent oil spill in arctic Russia.

Desert ecosystems are also vulnerable because of the low number of species and the stress of low water availability. If the few pools become fouled with oil, there may be no other option for the animals. They may be forced to drink the fouled water, and thereby die from exposure to oil.

Another factor that affects the vulnerability of a given ecosystem is its exposure to tidal flow. Any system that regularly receives tidal flow directly from the ocean will have a shorter recovery time because the oil can be removed rapidly by wave action, and the tides can bring in organisms for rapid recolonization. Similarly, oil spilled into a fast-flowing river can be removed by the action of the water. Oil spilled into backwaters with no outlet and no through-flow are much more vulnerable, as are relatively closed estuaries, lakes, or small streams far from the ocean.

Recovery after the Arthur Kill oil spill and after the barge *Florida* accident was relatively slow because the oil reached marshes that are not exposed to frequent tidal inundation. The oil remained in the Arthur Kill marshes for longer than would be expected for a spill this size, largely because tidal waters enter at both ends of the short river, and the water sloshes back and forth in the Kill for days without being washed out to sea. At West Falmouth, the oil moved far up on the marshes, and twenty years later there were traces of it in the peat. A lack of tidal flow and force meant that the oil was not washed away, and it slowly seeped into the marsh mud.

Chapter Six
Initial Responses to Oil Spills

● ● ●

Oil spills can happen anywhere; on the high seas, off the continental shelf, in bays and harbors, in inland rivers, and at a variety of transfer and use locations. At sea, it is the crew that responds, directed by a captain trying to save the ship and its cargo. The time comes, however, when outside help must be called in, officials notified, responsible parties informed, and containment and cleanup started. Whom the captain notifies depends on where the oil spill happens, be it on land, or on rivers, estuaries, the continental shelf, or in the open seas. If it happens on land, the spill is reported to the U.S. Environmental Protection Agency. In U.S. waters, the captain must notify the U.S. Coast Guard. Once informed that there has been an oil spill, government officials, conservationists, scientists, and the public become involved.

In this chapter I explore the initial responses to oil spills, including who responds, who makes the decisions, how different interests are protected, and the legal ramifications of cleanup actions. For the most part, I examine procedures within the United States, although some other nations have similar oil spill response plans. This chapter is on the mechanisms in place to deal with oil spills; the actual cleanup of spills is discussed in the next chapter. The legal aspects of damage assessment are discussed in this chapter because provisions of many of the laws that govern the initial response to oil spills were formulated with an eye toward damages suffered by humans and ecological resources.

Legal Considerations

Many laws govern the unintentional release of oil and its byproducts. The laws reflect our ambivalence about the threat to ourselves and the environ-

Table 6.1. Major Federal Laws or Acts Governing Oil Spills

Clean Water Act (CWA) (1968)
Clean Air Act (CAA) (1970)
Comprehensive Environmental Response, Compensation, and Liability
   Act (CERCLA, also known as Superfund) (1980)
   Type A rule for natural resource damage assessment
   Type B rule for natural resource damage assessment
Oil Pollution Act of 1990 (OPA)
National Oceanic and Atmospheric Administration regulations for
   damage assessment, under the National Marine Protection, Resources
   and Sanctuaries Act (NMPRSA) (1972, Title 3)

ment, balanced against the centrality of oil to our lives and economy. We are heavily dependent on oil, yet major spills can harm delicate habitats; destroy fisheries and shellfisheries; and threaten the way of life of fishermen, shore communities, and subsistence cultures. With the increasing size and number of supertankers, the aging of the tanker fleet, and this country's growing reliance on foreign oil, the risk of catastrophic oil spills increases. The rash of high-profile oil spills, including the *Exxon Valdez* and those during the Gulf War, has alarmed the public and stimulated federal and state agencies to tighten controls to reduce oil spills and mandate legal remedies when they do happen.

The control of oil pollution is largely a federal responsibility, although many states have additional laws that govern chemical spills, including oil (Table 6.1). Before 1990, the main federal law that applied to oil spills was the Clean Water Act, first implemented in 1968, and reauthorized in 1972 and 1990. Although the act's overall goal was to ensure cleaner water, it was enacted as a response to the horror of spreading oil from platforms off the coast of Santa Barbara, California.

The Clean Water Act allows the government to clean up an oil spill, unless the responsible parties will do so to the satisfaction of the government. If the government does the cleanup, it can recover the costs of the cleanup from the owners or operators. In some states, such as New Jersey, if the company does not assume that responsibility but is later found responsible for the spill, it can be assessed three times the actual cost of cleanup. Since the companies feel that they can clean up the oil at a lower cost than the government can, they usually choose to clean up the spill themselves. Often the owners and operators are willing to assume responsibility because the magnitude of the fines is partially dependent on how the courts view the responsiveness of the spiller. Companies that do not clean up the oil themselves often face high monetary penalties. The public, of course, also becomes angry with the unwillingness of an oil company to clean up its own spill, which can have a negative impact on sales. This clearly happened with Exxon, even though it did assume immediate responsibility for the *Exxon Valdez* accident. Angry customers cut up their credit cards and purchased gasoline elsewhere, and to this day, some people still avoid Exxon stations.

The Clean Water Act was later amended to include a provision whereby the federal government could recover the costs of replacing or restoring damaged natural resources, such as fish, shellfish, wildlife, public and private property, and shorelines and beaches. This was a remarkable provision, but it was many years before this clause was ever used. Damages were not sought because of the difficulties of assessing the value of damaged resources.

In 1980 the Comprehensive Environmental Response, Compensation, and Liability Act (CERCLA, also known as the Superfund legislation) was passed. CERCLA included a clause for recovery of damages to natural resources, but this clause was also seldom used. CERCLA specifically excluded oil, except when the oil included other hazardous substances such as mercury. Although CERCLA did not directly affect most oil spills, it had a great effect on the Clean Water Act by clarifying what costs for damaged natural resources can be recovered. As often happens with the law, legislation that applies to one problem (in this case hazardous wastes) has the potential to be invoked in other legal cases.

CERCLA more clearly defined the meaning of "natural resources" and identified who has responsibility for collecting damages. It stated that "authorized representatives" of the federal or state government that could seek these damages are the trustees of natural resources. This provision cleared the way for several state and federal agencies that directly manage or regulate natural resources to be responsible for damage assessment, including the U.S. Fish and Wildlife Service, National Park Service, and National Oceanographic and Atmospheric Administration.

With the Clean Water Act and CERCLA, two principles were firmly established: The federal government has the right to recover monies it spent to clean up an oil spill, *and* federal and state governments have the right to collect money to compensate the public for injuries to natural resources. Just as monies collected for cleanup must be spent at the site of the spill, monies collected for compensation of damaged natural resources must be used for the affected natural resources. These monies cannot be spent to clean up another site a thousand miles away or to restore natural resources outside of the spill area.

In addition, CERCLA provided two different ways to assess the damages as a result of a spill, called Type A and Type B rules. Type A refers to assessments that are done with a minimum of field work: the likely biological or other environmental injuries are determined using mostly computer analysis of the extent of the spill. Type A assessments are normally performed for small spills that cause minimal damage. Type B assessments use a variety of methods and extensive field work to assess the actual damage to resources, including economic and "lost uses." Lost uses are really difficult to evaluate, and there is a lot of argument about whether these should be included in damage assessments. Nonetheless, they are legally mandated, and will be discussed further later in this chapter.

The Oil Pollution Act of 1990 (OPA), partly a response to the *Exxon Valdez* and other spills that occurred in 1989 and 1990, replaced many of the previous acts. The *Exxon Valdez* (11,000,000 gallons) was followed in short order by the *World Prodigy* spill (Narragansett Bay, 290,000 gallons), the Houston Ship Channel spill (250,000 gallons), the *Presidente* spill (Delaware River, 300,000 gallons), the Exxon Bayway pipeline break in the Arthur Kill (567,000 gallons), and finally, the *B T Nautilus* spill (Kill van Kull in New Jersey, 260,000 gallons). In total, these spills spewed 12,667,000 gallons of oil into coastal waters in just over a year. The United States had never experienced such a rash of oil spills, and Congress was finally ready to deal with oil spill legislation, even according it a high priority.

OPA was passed to regulate all oil spills that occurred after that date. The Clean Water Act still applies to spills that happened before 1990, since many have not been fully resolved legally. But after 1990, oil companies and owners fall under the new regulations. OPA applies to all spills in navigable waters, on adjacent shorelines, or in the "exclusive economic zone," which extends two hundred miles offshore. Congress recast the Clean Water Act when writing OPA, enabling state and federal governments to recover damages and response costs far more easily. It also made possible the imposition of substantially higher civil penalties for spilling oil and increased the criminal penalties. Several provisions were added that apply to the construction of vessels that carry oil and to the construction of facilities handling oil. Congress increased the amount of money in the oil spill trust fund so that money would be available for cleanup if no one assumed responsibility, or to augment monies spent by companies or owners. This was extremely important because now the fund is large enough that cleanup can be started immediately, and more than one spill at a time can be handled.

OPA also identified the allowable trustees, the ones who can assess and claim damages. These include state and federal trustees of natural resources, Indian tribes, and foreign governments. Under this act, more groups of people are allowed to make claims for damages. Subsistence users of natural resources, as well as people who have lost personal property or suffered loss of profits, can sue for recovery of their losses. Although there are limits, they do not apply if the accident is caused by gross negligence, misconduct, or a violation of federal safety or operating regulations.

This last provision was very important in recent cases. For example, part of the basis for the *Exxon Valdez* settlement was the issue of misconduct on the part of the captain and safety violations on the tanker.

In sum, currently, the legal liability for owners and operators who spill oil is very clear: They are responsible for the costs of cleanup and for natural resource damages, regardless of fault. They are also liable for large fines if there is any indication of misconduct, the vessel being unsafe, or improper procedures. The damages that can be recovered include cleanup costs paid by agencies other than the owners or operators who were responsible for the oil spill, and the sum of the costs for restoring or replacing damaged or destroyed resources, and the value of lost resources (Table 6.2).

Table 6.2. Legal Costs to Owners and Operators of Vessels or Facilities That Spill Oil

Cleanup costs not paid for by owner or operator
Restoration of damaged or destroyed resources
Replacement of damaged or destroyed resources
Value of lost uses until resources are replaced or restored

Note. Damages are equal to the sum of the four costs listed.

Responses to the *Exxon Valdez* Spill

Since the *Exxon Valdez* spill was the largest in U.S. history, it is useful to examine the chain of events following that spill as an example of a real-world response. The confusion following the accident was partly responsible for the congressional enactment of OPA. It was obvious from the initial actions following the *Exxon Valdez* spill that clear procedures were not in place and that a central command must be part of a national oil spill response plan.

At the time of the *Exxon Valdez* oil spill, in 1989, only the Clean Water Act and the National Environmental Policy Act were in effect. The Clean Water Act mandated that the oil be cleaned up and that costs associated with the cleanup and restoration be paid by the spiller, in this case, Exxon. The National Environmental Policy Act required that an environmental impact statement be part of any significant federal restoration plan that followed the oil spill. It was clear, however, that the Clean Water Act did not provide a firm enough foundation, and that consequently, confusion reigned over lines of command. To some extent, the appearance of confusion came from the fact that there simply was not enough equipment available for the cleanup, the Coast Guard was coordinating rather than running the operations, and it took over a week for top governmental officials such as the governor and federal officials to take command. They made public statements within a couple of days, but the line of authority was unclear. Both the state and federal governments ultimately agreed that the on-site response by industry was slow and inadequate, equipment was unavailable and performed poorly, and cleanup was often haphazard. The public became confused over who was running the show, and why the decision-making process was so cumbersome, slow, and decentralized.

It eventually became clear to all that Exxon was running the show, not the Coast Guard or other government agencies. Exxon told cleanup crews where to go and what to do. Ironically, many people were angered that the company responsible for the spill was controlling the cleanup.

At the time of the spill, a number of institutional procedures were in effect. One was the National Contingency Plan. However, this plan got lost in the process, and in any case, the Coast Guard did not retain the authority it needed to control the process. Once the governor and federal officials became involved, the president, cabinet-level officers, and the U.S. military got involved. The sudden appearance of so many different officials further muddied the water.

The state of Alaska had several plans for response to oil spills, one of which was the Department of Environmental Conservation statewide plan, another being the Oil Spill Contingency Plan, Prince William Sound, also called the Alyeska Plan, which was in effect for this region. Developed between 1984 and 1987, this plan spelled out how the local Alyeska Pipeline Service Company response was to occur, but it had planned for a spill of one million gallons, not eleven million gallons. The plan could not be implemented immediately because the response barge in the port of Valdez was out of service, equipment was buried under several feet of snow, and skimmers and other boats were delayed six to eighteen hours. In short, the plan did not work.

Even though the Alyeska Plan was put into effect immediately, very shortly thereafter Exxon said it was assuming control and was going to run the response its own way, regardless of the plan. In theory, once the responsible party assumes responsibility, it should run many of the operations. But it is supposed to be responsive to a central Coast Guard command and is supposed to follow the established response plan, in this case the Alyeska Plan. Neither of these happened. This was a problem because the premise of the response plan was that all parties were supposed to be working from the same set of plans and instructions.

Exxon's unilateral decision on the second day to take complete control from the Alyeska Plan threw several years of planning and expectations to the wind. This was troubling to both the state of Alaska and the federal government, as well as to the public. Furthermore, on March 24, Exxon's chief executive officer, Frank Iarossi, announced that Exxon intended to fight the spill with dispersants as the first line of defense. This was not part of the Alyeska Plan, and it upset the fishing vessel owners and local residents who had taken part in the long process to arrive at an oil spill plan that was agreeable to all parties involved. Dispersants—detergentlike materials that allow fine droplets of oil to be distributed through the water column—were controversial and potentially dangerous, and the state of Alaska excluded their use in some of the areas of the sound, although it allowed them in others.

Two years later, when questioned by state and federal attorneys, Iarossi stated that he had not read the Alyeska Plan, did not know that Alaska had regulatory oversight, did not know that Exxon needed concurrence from the regional response team to use the dispersants, and did not understand why an Alaskan official and the Coast Guard were accompanying Exxon on the assessment overflights. Much of the confusion stemmed from the lack of knowledge on the part of Iarossi and Exxon: In direct contrast to the familiarity on the part of the fisherman and government officials with the response plan. Exxon's approach was dictated by the availability of equipment and contractors rather than by a series of well-thought-out management procedures. The use of dispersants continued to be controversial, as was the use of bioremediation and high-powered water spray to clean some sensitive beaches.

It was not until nearly two weeks after the spill that a clear team approach began to develop. The Coast Guard formally took on the job of federal on-scene coordinator, and President George Bush backed up this role by authorizing the Department of Defense to provide whatever resources the Coast Guard needed. Exxon cooperated with this procedure and remained involved in the cleanup. At this point, Exxon, the state, and the Coast Guard agreed to work together, and to let Exxon take the lead in performing the cleanup.

What emerged after years of analysis is that there was an established plan for the region, the responsible company took over the initial containment and cleanup without following the regional plan, the executive officer of Exxon did not know or understand the established procedures—and, further, seemed not to care—and confusion reigned over both the methods and the locations of cleanup. No clear-cut lines of authority were established initially. Massive social and economic problems compounded the response. The kinds of upheaval and displacement caused by the spill and the response were more like a natural disaster than was ever expected: People were clearly psychologically and culturally affected. All the regulations that were in place dealt with pollution control, not with the social and economic aftermath of such a disaster.

It was this mass confusion, lack of clear lines of authority, and frustration with Exxon for ignoring the established Alyeska Plan that led directly to the formulation of the Oil Pollution Act of 1990 by the U.S. Congress. This act clearly gives the command to the federal government under the Coast Guard, although the responsible party must pay for and provide the cleanup equipment and personnel. The decisions are no longer made entirely by the responsible party.

Cleanup Guidelines in the Wake of the *Exxon Valdez* Spill

The confusion that reigned during the *Exxon Valdez* spill response made it very obvious that legislation was needed to make the lines of command clear, and the OPA was in direct response to this confusion. Now there are clear procedures to be followed when an oil spill occurs. Following enactment of OPA, the National Response System was set up to accomplish the immediate and effective cleanup of an oil or hazardous substance discharge. It had taken twenty-three years from the time of the *Torrey Canyon* spill for the United States to develop a comprehensive oil spill law, with a coordinated system for responding to chemical spills.

The National Response System is a three-tiered response mechanism that mandates the formation of an oil spill committee to coordinate the actions of national, state, regional, and local government, industry, and responsible parties following a spill. The responsible party is the owner or operator of the vessel or facility from which the spill occurred. When an oil spill occurs, the National Response Center must be notified, a unified command system takes over, and one committee is formed locally to deal with the spill. The main function of this oil spill committee is to provide one unified command, where all major decisions are coordinated among the interested parties. This is extremely important, because oil spills sometimes involve two states, several local governments, and several federal agencies in the cleanup and damage assessment. At the very least, one oversight committee is essential to make sure that human lives are not endangered in the cleanup process. Many oil spills have the potential for chemical exposure, explosions, and fires. The unified command committee usually breaks up into a number of subcommittees that are responsible for different aspects of the cleanup (Fig. 6.1).

The oil spill committee has the ultimate responsibility for cleanup operations, and one person—the federal on-scene coordinator—is at the top. The committee is responsible for a number of functions, such as dealing with the media, assuring the health and safety of workers on site, and reducing the likelihood of further releases from the injured tanker. The com-

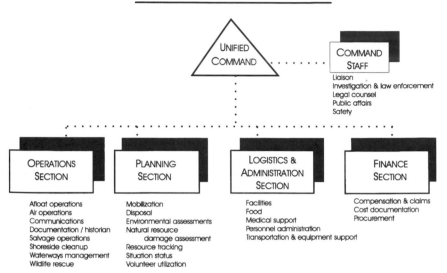

Figure 6.1. Unified command for responding to oil spills, as established by the oil spill committee. (Source: Adapted from Federal Register, OPA 1990)

mittee relies on a variety of local, state, and federal agencies to help in this task. The importance of having one small committee that can make decisions in the first critical hours following an oil spill cannot be overestimated.

Federal regulations clearly put the Coast Guard in the position of organizing the oil spill committee and being in charge of the cleanup operation when the spill is in navigable waterways or coastal waters. The U.S. Environmental Protection Agency fulfills this role for spills on land. Members of the committee include state representatives, a representative for the responsible party, and the marine safety officer. In most states, each agency that has responsibility for natural resources has designated a particular person to serve as the contact, and that person is ready to join the response committee whenever an accident happens. This person is usually on call twenty-four hours a day so that a response can be immediate.

Damage Assessment

Even before the cleanup operations are underway, the trustees responsible for natural resources begin their damage assessment. Several federal and state agencies are responsible for natural resources. The two federal agencies with primary responsibility are the U.S. Fish and Wildlife Service, for terrestrial resources including birds; and the National Oceanic and Atmospheric Administration (NOAA), for marine resources.

NOAA has set up a damage assessment and restoration program whose primary goal is to act on behalf of the public for injuries to natural resources from the discharge of oil or other hazardous chemicals, and to restore, replace, rehabilitate, or acquire the equivalent of the injured resources. This is a tall task given the scope of natural resources that could be damaged, such as all life stages of fish, endangered and threatened marine species, tidal wetlands, and other critical habitats. The goal is to place trained damage assessment scientists and economists at the spill site within six hours of a decision to assess lost or damaged resources. This usually includes all spills over 10,000 gallons, or smaller spills near particularly sensitive resources or commercial fisheries.

The U.S. Fish and Wildlife Service has additional procedures for evaluating the dangers to the fish and wildlife under their care. In many cases, there are existing census data for bird and mammal populations, and these can be used to evaluate changes in population levels following a spill. Service personnel in each region are familiar with the endangered and threatened species, as well as the resources of special concern.

A Simulated Spill: Predicting the Future

Having the National Response System is extremely important, but it is equally critical that federal, state, and local agencies within the spill area are ready to act. To see whether the system would really work during an oil spill, Larry Niles of the New Jersey Endangered and Nongame Species Program, and New Jersey state oil response officials organized an oil spill workshop in 1995 to examine what would happen if an oil spill occurred in Delaware Bay. The Delaware Bay was of particular interest for this exercise because it is an important migratory stopover area for over a million shorebirds that pass through in a three-week period each spring, it is the primary breeding ground of horseshoe crabs, and it has one of the busiest oil transport routes on the East Coast, entertaining between one thousand and three thousand supertanker calls each year. Moreover, the shipping lanes are narrow, and the bay is often choppy and can be treacherous during storms, which may last for several days.

Because of the sensitive resources, those of us involved in the workshop felt it would be useful to get the people who are interested in natural re-

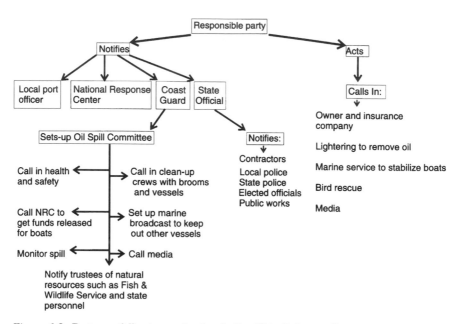

Figure 6.2. Response following a simulated oil spill in Delaware Bay.

sources together with the people who respond to oil spills. This included the state and federal officials, owners and operators of oil transport vessels, the cleanup companies, scientists, and conservationists. Participants and an audience were prepared for a simulated spill.

We sat in a room, far from any phones and faxes, with about twelve people at the table. A local captain of an oil transport vessel agreed to be the "responsible party" whose ship was leaking oil. Only those at the table could respond, and they were to respond as if the spill were happening at that moment. We generated a hypothetical oil spill on a computer map of Delaware Bay and simulated the trajectory of the spreading oil by the minute. The people sitting at the table had to explain what they would do and when. Our collective response is shown in Figure 6.2. The table captures the initial actions, but later responses were hard to follow, because everyone was talking at once. The excitement that reigned within only a few minutes cannot be captured.

The responsible party immediately notified the National Response Center, the local port officer and the Coast Guard, who successfully set up a unified command that consisted of the responsible party, state representatives, and a federal representative. But by now, others were chiming in with their responses. The responsible party then called in cleanup vessels, performed a lightering operation (the process whereby oil remaining on board is removed to prevent further spillage), called in the local bird rescue and rehabilitator, called a marine wrecking service to stabilize the boat, and dealt with the media. The responsible party also sent a person to be on the oil spill committee.

Meanwhile, the Coast Guard called the National Response Center to ask about funding, called the federal and state officials responsible for natural resources, and called a Coast Guard duty team to be on site in case there was a need for search and rescue of crew; sent out urgent marine broadcasts to warn the public and all ships to stay clear of the area; and called the U.S. Navy to supervise salvage (in coordination with the responsible party) and marine safety in Washington, D.C., to inform them about the problem. The Coast Guard has the primary responsibility for the oil spill, and although others are performing many of the cleanup operations, the Guard must oversee all these operations.

The response people for the state (in this case, one person from Delaware and one from New Jersey), said they would notify the governor if the spill was large, call their department of health to respond to problems within the community or on the water, notify the state marine police to stand by with helicopters, and inform the other state divisions responsible for natural resources. Both states planned on calling in the people who head the conservation departments to find out about critical resources at risk.

The people in Fish, Game and Wildlife immediately began to assess the damages to natural resources and to contact scientists already working in the bay. Their first concern was to find out which creeks and beaches are the most sensitive. An immediate conflict broke out over the potential use of dispersants which would be good for shorebirds but bad for fish. Conservationists and others present suddenly felt they were not represented by the central command, but nonetheless they assumed responsibility for providing the media with information about sensitive species and vulnerable habitats. They also mounted a campaign to solicit volunteers to search for oiled birds and other wildlife. This set up a bit of conflict between the rehabilitators called in by the responsible party and the volunteer conservationists. These two groups needed to be coordinated.

The exercise was fun and exciting, and everyone was very enthusiastic about the spill response, but several problems were obvious. Oil spill cleanup equipment cannot be everywhere at once; time is required to get the equipment from the storage warehouses to the closest dock by road, and then by boat out to the accident. The quickest the cleanup companies could get equipment to a spill site was three hours, under fair weather. If they were required to obtain additional booms (long, sausage-shaped strips of absorbent material that soak up oil and limit its movement) from the federal response warehouses, it would take even longer. Once the booms arrive, a decision must be made regarding placement: Should the booms be placed around the tanker in an attempt to contain the oil, or near shores to keep oil off sensitive shores or from entering creeks and rivers? Booms can be used to keep oil in or out of an area, but there may not be enough booms to do both. Another problem that must be dealt with is preventing collisions of other boats with the grounded or injured tanker. Tankers are so large that there is a risk of collisions from other boats in the area.

Many of these decisions must be made in short order, often with imperfect information, and they require tradeoffs. One option is to burn off some of the oil. This may be advantageous for shorebirds feeding along the beaches and for invertebrates living in the intertidal zone because less oil will reach the shores. However, burning provides an immediate health hazard for people, and the smoke may drift to onshore communities. Burning is only preapproved by the National Response System for spills that are at least six miles off shore, so the area where burning could be used in Delaware Bay is small.

Dispersants may be used to disperse the oil, but this puts more oil in the water column. This may reduce the physical oiling that is visually depressing, but it can increase toxicity to finfish, shellfish, and bottom-dwelling organisms. This put fisheries people arguing against the use of dispersants, while "shorebird" people argued for them to prevent the oil from reaching the beaches. Furthermore, dispersants work well only if the water is at least thirty feet deep, and much of Delaware Bay is shallower than this. If the water is shallow, the oil does not have sufficient space to become dispersed.

As our hypothetical oil spill day wore on it became increasingly clear that if the spill were large we had no effective way of preventing the oil from reaching the shore, and if a spill of any size occurred in bad weather close to the mouth of the bay, it would be impossible to control. We were left with the best viable options being to acquire computer-based navigation and tracking systems for the bay to prevent collisions, to prevent old tankers from ever coming into Delaware Bay, to encourage local towns and communities to "adopt" a shorebird beach that they would be prepared to protect, and to preposition equipment near particularly sensitive beaches during the shorebird migration period. Prepositioning is also extremely important for sensitive resources such as colonies of birds; booms can be permanently deployed around some small islands or be held nearby for rapid response. In large or sensitive ports, response barges and skimmers can be stationed near sensitive natural resources. On my visit to Prince William Sound, I was heartened to note that several oil spill response barges were positioned around Valdez and some of the islands of Prince William Sound.

I believe that such simulation exercises are very important for most states because they assure that all interested parties know one another and understand how the process works. They also foster communication between the response people and those who protect natural resources as well as pointing out the limitations of current oil spill cleanup technology and illustrating the problems that are unique to local bays and estuaries. Our exercise taught us that we simply cannot prevent damage to shorebirds and horseshoe crabs if a large spill happens during the peak of migration.

Our prediction that we could not protect the shorebirds if a spill occurred during the spring migration turned out to be all too correct. On May 9, 1996, the 876-foot, French-owned tanker *Anitra* spilled Nigerian light crude oil into the mouth of Delaware Bay. The spill happened during a lightering operation at the Big Stone anchorage. Booms were immediately placed around the tanker, and about 10,000 gallons of oiled water were recovered before high seas broke the booms and the oil drifted free. Initially, the estimates of the spilled oil were 10,000 gallons; this was increased to 20,000 gallons within a few days, and further increased to 42,000 gallons a week later.

Two aspects of the oil spill are interesting in light of the simulation: (1) the lack of a clear line of communication led to confusion, and (2) the effects were far worse than initially predicted. Although the spill happened on May 9, the state of Delaware was not informed until a day later, and the Department of Fish, Game, and Wildlife of New Jersey was not informed until three days later. Since New Jersey's Department of Fish, Game, and Wildlife was informed on a Sunday, it was not possible to reach all the key people, with the result that the people responsible for the shorebirds were informed on Monday—four days after the spill.

Initially the oil drifted toward Delaware, but then the winds shifted, carrying the oil toward Cape May beaches (Table 6.3). Strong surf and high tides two days later drove tar balls onto the beaches from Cape May Point to the Cape May Canal. Cleanup crews descended to pick up the oil, but no machines were used; thus, the beach sands were not unduly disturbed. The shorebirds had just begun to arrive at the Delaware Bay shores, and oiled sanderlings and other species were noted. The damage, however, seemed to be minimal, as few birds were affected. Since due to unseasonable cold waters the bulk of the horseshoe crabs had not yet come up, the shorebirds were concentrated on the salt marshes rather than on the beaches.

A week after the oil spill, cleanup operations were being shut down, but just a day later it became apparent that the spill was much worse than feared. Surfers on the Atlantic shore beaches reported an oil slick two to three feet below the surface, and with the next high tide oil began to foul these beaches. Initially, the oil struck the sandy points and spits that jutted out into the ocean, but soon entire beaches were affected. A forty-block area around Avalon had an oil slick thirty to forty feet wide along the high-tide wrack line. In some areas, 30 to 50 percent of the beach was covered

Table 6.3. Timetable of events for the Anitra *tanker accident in Delaware Bay, May 1996*

May 9 Oil spilled during lightering

    10 State of Delaware informed, oil washes up on its beaches

    12 State of New Jersey informed, oil washes up at Cape May Point

    13 Endangered and Nongame Species biologists informed; some shorebirds and a few horseshoe crabs oiled; estimate of oil spilled is 10,000 gallons

    14 First reported in newspapers

    13–16 Beach cleanup from Cape May Point to Cape May Canal

    16 Cessation of cleanup operations

    17 Oil slick reported 2–3 feet below ocean waters by surfers, oil begins to hit spits and points; 10% of some birds oiled; estimate of spilled oil upped to 20,000 gallons

    18 Oil washes ashore from Avalon to Ocean City, forming a 30–40-foot-wide slick along wrack line, some beaches 30–50% oiled; some birds are totally oiled

    19 Oil slick much worse than feared; oil coming ashore farther north, threatening Brigantine; estimate of spilled oil upped to 42,000 gallons; some birds totally oil smudged

    21–23 Oil slick continues to wash ashore at Ocean City with each high tide, leaving tar balls as large as melon balls; workers pick up oil in shovels and dump it into plastic bags or front-end loaders; about 90% of sanderlings and semipalmated sandpipers have some oiling

    25 Cleanup operations largely suspended in time for Memorial Day weekend

---

with a sticky, viscous oil that looked like melted chocolate and was difficult to pick up. As night temperatures dropped, the oil hardened slightly, making it easier to pick up in the early morning. Over three hundred people walked the beaches picking up oil.

As the oil continued to wash up on the beaches, more and more birds were oiled. At first only about 10 percent of the least terns and sanderlings were oiled, but within a day this rose to nearly 50 percent; and three endangered piping plovers were heavily oiled according to Larry Niles, chief of the Endangered and Nongame Species Program. The following day, the oil drifted onto beaches farther north, threatening Brigantine. More and more shorebirds were oiled, and many continued to remain on the oiled beaches rather than fly to clean areas. They hung their heads and hunched down, remaining in one place. Estimates were that about 50 percent of oiled birds would die within a few days, and all heavily oiled birds would die.

On May 21, thirteen days after the spill, oil was still washing up on the south Jersey beaches, concentrating at Ocean City. A thin veneer of oil washed up with each high tide, leaving a deposit of pea-sized to melon-ball-sized tar balls scattered along the high-tide line. In some places a dark film two to three feet wide covered the sand at the high tide line. About 120 workers walked the Ocean City beaches picking up oiled sand with shovels and putting it into plastic bags or front-end loaders (Fig. 6.3). Large front-end loaders patrolled the beaches, picking up thick oil and carrying the oiled sand to way stations, from which trucks would carry it away. These operations continued until May 23.

The smell of oil was strong in some places, and a sheen of green and red on the water indicated floating oil. Nearly 90 percent of the sanderlings and semipalmated sandpipers had some oil on their bellies, a result of feeding in the surf. Some birds were completely oiled underneath and transferred the oil to their faces when they preened. Heavily oiled birds spent more time preening than lightly oiled birds, decreasing their ability to feed. The large number of trucks and workers disturbed the feeding shorebirds, and birds already stressed by oil were forced to fly often from trucks racing up and down the tide line. The trucks found it easier to move over the recently packed sand than the sugar sand higher up on the beach. Unfortunately, this is where the shorebirds feed.

The endangered piping plovers were particularly hard hit because they feed in the surf and had already laid eggs. Piping plovers continued to become more oiled, and eventually 9 of the 24 found were so oiled that they were removed to Tristate Bird Rescue and Research for rehabilitation; they also oiled their eggs during incubation, so the eggs were also removed in the hopes that the plovers would eventually re-lay clutches. Personnel from the U.S. Fish and Wildlife Service and the New Jersey Endangered and Nongame Species Program were hoping that when the birds were returned to the beaches they would be clean, and if the birds re-laid, the eggs might hatch.

Sadly, the oil spill happened during a heat spell, with record temperatures in the high nineties, and some people flocked to the beaches even while the bulk of the oil was drifting onto the beaches. It was not unusual to see women in bikinis basking in the sun, men and women jogging along the tideline, and children building sand castles in the oiled zone. The tension between wanting to report the severity of the spill but not wishing to discourage beachgoers for economic reasons was palpable. As Memorial Day approached, city and state officials rushed to remove all traces of the oil from the beaches, because tourism is the most important industry for the affected counties along the coast. Giant tractors pulling discs raked the remaining oil into the beach, while others pulled thirty-foot-long logs to smooth over the surface. In theory, the oil was sufficiently weathered so

Figure 6.3. Top, *cleanup crews at Ocean City removing oil-contaminated sand;* bottom, *cleaning up oil slick at Ocean City.* (*Photos by T. Benson*)
Opposite, *The oil slick from the* Anitra *stretched for miles along the Jersey shore.*

that burial was not detrimental; however, even weathered oil has been shown to be harmful to birds when they digest it. By Memorial Day, however, only a faint odor of oil remained, and the beaches seemed clean. Nearly all of the semipalmated sandpipers, sanderlings, and semipalmated plovers feeding along the surf, however, had oil smudges on their otherwise white underparts.

Again, the oil spill response team was disappointed, for onshore winds brought more oil onto the beaches following Memorial Day. Just three weeks after the initial oil spill, easterly winds continued to bring tar balls onto the beaches from Avalon as for north as Holgate, extending northward the zone of effect. The tar balls formed in lines at the high-tide line, and it was possible to see where every wave had extended up the beach. There was a tar-ball line at the highest tide, and at the secondary tide line. Although the beaches were not closed, they were unpleasant because of the odor. Again, nearly 90 percent of the sanderlings feeding along the tide line were oiled. Gradually, the small weathered tar balls ceased coming onto the beaches with the high tides, and fewer and fewer sanderlings were oiled. But for many, the oil lingered for at least two weeks after the last oiling.

Conclusion

With the passing of the Oil Pollution Act of 1990, the federal government finally consolidated legislation relating to the intentional and accidental release of oil. The act clearly defined the legal responsibilities of the owners or operators who spilled the oil. OPA made the responsible parties liable for cleanup costs, compensation for injuries to natural resources, and potentially liable for civil penalties. It also set up a federal oil spill fund for emergency response, and to make funds available for cleanup should no one assume responsibility for the spill.

The National Response System was established to assume control when an oil spill happens. It gives the U.S. Coast Guard the responsibility of overseeing the cleanup, including establishing an oil spill committee to coordinate the response. The procedures clearly provide a central command for oil spills, enabling a rapid response regardless of where the spill occurs, or its size.

OPA not only provides the legal basis for response procedures, damage assessment mechanisms, and civil penalties but it assures that the cleanup response is rapid, and the legal settlement timely.

Chapter Seven
Cleanup, Rehabilitation, and Damage Assessment

● ● ●

When an oil spill occurs, everyone's attention turns to containing the oil, salvaging as much as possible, and preventing damage to natural resources. Cleanup must begin. Either the U.S. Coast Guard initiates the process, or the responsible party does. Given the tough laws governing the costs of cleanup following the accidental discharge of oil into the environment, it is beneficial for companies that caused the spill to immediately assume responsibility and begin the cleanup. If they fail to do so, and subsequently are found to be responsible, then they not only have to pay the cleanup costs, but are liable for fines as well. In some states, such as New Jersey, they can be assessed three times the cleanup costs as well as fines. Furthermore, it is widely believed by the companies that they can conduct the cleanup more cheaply than can the Coast Guard, and their simpler procurement processes may result in quicker response.

Offshore Cleanup Procedures

When an oil spill first happens, the crew immediately begins to reduce the loss of oil by stabilizing the ship, stopping the flow of oil to the damaged pipeline, or repairing the oil well (Table 7.1). Once outside help has been summoned, a variety of means are employed to decrease the loss of oil and to reduce the damage from the spill. Usually, the most severe problems result from an oil leak in water, whether it be from a grounded or injured vessel, a leaking underground pipeline, or a sabotaged oil terminal. Containment options are described later in the chapter. Although an oil spill

Table 7.1. Possible Containment and Cleanup Procedures Following an Oil Spill from a Vessel

---

Initial action
    Leaving ship unmoved to reduce chances of making hole bigger
    Lightering oil from damaged or other compartments
Containment
    Placing booms around ship
    Skimming oil from surface around ship
    Bombing vessel to burn remaining oil
Immediate cleanup
    Placing booms around oil slick or near sensitive resources
    Using skimmers to remove oil from surface
    Using dispersants to break up oil before it reaches sensitive beaches
    Burning oil slicks before they reach sensitive areas
Secondary cleanup
    Cleaning beaches using power sprays
    Cleaning beaches using mechanical means
    Using bioremediation to speed up natural biodegradation of oil by microorganisms

---

on land is clearly damaging, the oil does not spread as fast, and it is easier to contain by physical means.

The first line of defense for cleaning up a spill in water is to repair the leak, remove as much oil from the injured vessel as possible, and place booms around the ship. Many supertankers routinely perform lightering, removing some of the ballast (either oil or water), when they enter some ports, so the barges, personnel, and equipment are already present if a spill should occur near these parts. It is critical to remove oil from a damaged hold because doing so prevents this oil from flowing into the water. Oil may also be removed from compartments that are not damaged so that the ship will not topple over and sink into the water. Imagine that a tanker three times as long as a football field is leaking oil rapidly from a torn compartment that makes up the front third of the boat. If all the oil leaks out of that part, the back third will outweigh the rest of the boat, and the ship might simply tip upward and slide under the water. If the oil is removed at the same time from the other end, the boat will be balanced and remain floating.

When a tanker has an accident, the captain of the boat has a lot of responsibility to make the right decision. For example, one of the legal issues surrounding the *Exxon Valdez* spill was whether the captain should have left the tanker grounded on Bligh Reef when it first hit, rather than try to dislodge it. Some experts felt that he should have left it alone, because by trying to dislodge the boat he ripped the hole bigger, allowing more oil to flow into Prince William Sound.

Once the oil is spilling from a vessel, it can be contained by placing booms around it. Booms are long rolls of absorbent material that look like giant sausages strung end to end. They float on the water, moving up and down with the waves or tide. They are about a foot or two in diameter, and must be changed periodically when they become soaked with oil. They can be used as a barrier, a deflection device, a corral for containing oil, an absorbent, and as a containment area when oil is burned off. Booms work only if they are put in place very quickly, before the slick has spread out over the water, and only if the seas are calm enough for the booms to actually contain the oil. In very choppy water, oil will slosh over the booms. The biggest problem is getting the booms to the vessel before the oil has spread, an impossible task for most accidents, as it might be hours before booms can be brought to the site from mainland warehouses.

At the same time that booms are placed around a vessel, they may be put around sensitive resources such as an island used for nesting by birds, spawning creeks, mussel or oyster beds, or nursery areas for fish (Fig. 7.1). This requires that the response teams know where the critical natural resources are, and that Fish and Game departments or the Fish and Wildlife Service be called in for advice soon after the spill occurs. Again, however, the booms must be put in place before the oil reaches these areas, or they will only prevent the oil that is already on the beaches or mudflats from being washed away by high tides. Moreover, the booms must be changed with nearly every tide, or they will become so oiled that they will act as a wick to introduce oil to the creeks and beaches (Fig. 7.2).

If the spilled oil is a heavy oil, and it has formed a thick, slow-moving slick, then some can be removed from the water with oil skimmers (Fig. 7.3). These boats have giant vacuums that scoop the oil into holding tanks. Skimming works best when the oil is still thick and localized. It will not work when the oil is in a very thin film, in shallow water, or in creeks or on mudflats. Oil skimmers are used when the oil slick has moved to the far side of a bay or is trapped near an island, where it becomes concentrated in quantities large enough to skim. Most skimmers have a shallow draft and work best in protected areas such as inshore or nearshore waters rather than the open ocean.

Skimmers can be a valuable tool to recover some of the spilled oil, and ship owners are anxious to use them whenever possible. Their effectiveness also depends on their storage capacity, both on board and nearby. Since skimming is a system, not just a boat, it needs good containment possibilities, such as booms. Furthermore, support vessels to help transfer the oil from the skimmers to the storage barges are required. It is also difficult to

Figure 7.1. Top, *booms are placed around spawning creeks to contain the oil in an effort to protect sensitive resources;* bottom, *booms are placed around tidal creeks to prevent oil from coming in.* (Source, top photo: Exxon Valdez *Oil Spill Public Information Center*)

Figure 7.2. Booms must be changed often, sometimes with small boats.

Figure 7.3. Skimmers are small boats that skim oil from the surface, recovering it for further use.

see the oil clearly from deck, and many skimming operations need spotters in helicopters to work effectively. In the *Exxon Valdez* operation, as many as fifty skimmers were operating at one time, and helicopters were the factor limiting their effectiveness. Storage capacity was another limiting factor.

Skimmers also work best early on, when the oil is free-floating. However, with time and weathering, oil emulsifies and clogs gears and suction hoses, making both the skimming operation and the transfer of oil to barges difficult. Later, booms can be used to corral oil being washed off beaches, and skimmers then collect the oil.

Burning is another method of removing oil, but its effectiveness is highly dependent on the freshness of the oil. The light volatile fraction that can readily ignite usually evaporates within twelve to seventy-two hours of the spill. This window of opportunity varies with the type of oil, but is relatively short. Without this light fraction, the heavier oil beneath cannot be ignited. A decision must be made quickly.

Although we think of oil as a fuel designed to burn, burning is a tricky method to use for a number of reasons. When winds rise, compact slicks break up, and the oil mixes with water, making it difficult to burn. The national oil spill response guidelines permit burning only if the spill is more than six miles away from shore; otherwise special permission is required. The six-mile limit is mandated to protect shore communities from the smoke and fumes of burning oil. Burning oil is difficult to control, and if winds shift, smoke can drift over vulnerable wildlife resources and shore towns. One of the major concerns during the Gulf War was the great plumes of smoke that drifted from the burning oil wells. It was a particular danger for the work crews trying to cap the wells, as well as to surrounding villages.

Burning oil also creates problems for personnel doing the burning. Special equipment must be available for the response teams if burning is used, and additional fire and safety personnel must stand by. Intense winds and storms make this an impossible method, even when oil spills happen far from shore. In sum, burning is advantageous because it removes the oil immediately; however, it is relatively difficult to use technically, has human and ecological health consequences, and must be used within a few days of the spill.

Dispersants are sometimes used when there are critical resources along the shore that require protection, and dispersing the oil before it reaches the shore is essential. Dispersants are used to control oil during a spill, but they do not clean it up. To some extent, using dispersants is a tradeoff between reducing the likelihood that oil will reach sensitive beaches and harming open-water organisms. Dispersants are chemicals that break up the oil into smaller droplets and spread it throughout the water column. They do not change the oil and do not render it harmless. Dispersants work best in about thirty feet of water, but many oil spills happen in bays that are generally shallower than that, except for the shipping lanes. Furthermore, with large spills, dispersants simply cannot do the entire job.

Dispersants also have negative effects on fish and invertebrates that live within the water column as they increase and prolong these creatures' exposure to the oil. Another concern with dispersants is their relative toxicity to a variety of organisms. The early dispersants used in the 1960s and 1970s were quite toxic to plankton and other organisms living in the water column. In controlled laboratory experiments using algae, abalone, and smelt, the abalone were the most highly sensitive to dispersants. A variety of similar experiments have been conducted, and in general, invertebrates and vertebrates living in the water column are affected by dispersants. Those living near the surface are particularly vulnerable because they get the highest exposure when the finely divided droplets begin to disperse. There is still a risk to some organisms from present-day dispersants, although this is greatly reduced and remains for only a short period of time. Nonetheless, dispersants should not be used near very sensitive resources or during the time of spawning of fish and shellfish.

Some ecosystems are much more vulnerable than others to the effects of dispersants, so special consideration must be given to where the dispersants will end up. We need much more information, however, before we can understand the tradeoffs between sensitive areas and the open ocean.

Shoreline Cleanup

Initial efforts are concentrated on keeping oil from reaching sensitive shores or beaches. Eventually, however, oil from a large spill will wash ashore, and attention will shift from prevention to removal. For many people, oil covering the rocks or clinging to mussel beds is far more disturbing than a thin sheen of oil drifting over the bay. A shoreline cleanup program usually starts a few days or weeks after efforts to contain, skim, burn, or disperse the oil.

Several methods are used to clean beaches, such as picking up oil and asphalt manually, vacuuming up the oil, washing away the oil with hot water and high pressure, and using solvents and chemical cleaners. Oil-soaked sediments or asphalt can be picked up by hand, or with the use of front-end loaders and bulldozers. Using machinery to pick up large pieces of asphalt has many advantages, with few of the disadvantages of destroying the intertidal organisms, as the loaders remain fairly stationary, placed where workers cleaning the area by hand can dispose of oiled material, and bulldozers are used on flat areas. Vacuuming works on beaches with large rocks and

Figure 7.4. High-pressure cleaning of beaches following the Exxon Valdez *spill.* (*Photo by D. Policansky*)

few small rocks or sand, but it is very time-consuming and often disturbs organisms living there. Use of any of this equipment requires the ability to deploy it at the site, which can be difficult in a wilderness area far from roads.

Another method of cleaning beaches is to use high-pressure water to wash the stones (Fig. 7.4). Water for washing beaches must be hot, since cold water solidifies the oil, making it harder to remove. However, hot water cooks the organisms that reside there, and may do more harm than good. Some scientists have even suggested that washing a beach with hot water and high pressure damages the plants and animals living there so they will recover more slowly than if they had been left alone. Hot water may result in complete loss of mussels and rockweed, which provide cover for a large array of small intertidal plants and animals. Others argue that removing the oil from the beach and high-tide line actually puts more oil in the zone between the tides, where there are more sensitive organisms. Cleaning beaches may oil intertidal organisms that are less able to adapt to the oil.

In retrospect, it is conceivable that the pressure cooking of the shores of Prince William Sound was a bad thing to do, at least for the intertidal organisms. It created an illusion of aggressive response and cost Exxon a lot of money—a fitting penalty—but it may have been ecologically unsound. However, there is still disagreement between NOAA and the state of Alaska regarding the hot-water cleaning. The state of Alaska maintains that the harm done to intertidal organisms by the high-pressure cleaning must be balanced against harm to organisms that are higher on the food chain, such as fish, seals, and seabirds, which would have been much more affected had the method not been used. Furthermore, according to the state, damages to commercial fishing, tourism, and other human uses of the shoreline would have been greater as well.

Some companies have used solvents, essentially kerosene mixed with some detergents, to wash oil from beaches. These are similar to terrestrial dispersants, breaking up the oil and dispersing it farther into the substrate of the beach. This procedure has not been field-tested, however, and it seems imprudent to me to add another oil product to an already-oiled beach.

In the end, any cleanup decision has both ecosystem and public policy issues. Possible damage to intertidal organisms must be balanced against harm to other organisms and to human uses. Intertidal organisms often have the ability to recover by immigration of organisms from nearby unaffected areas, but the harm to fishing and tourism communities and to subsistence fisherman may linger for decades. Moreover, all of the people using Prince William were affected, whereas not all invertebrates living in Prince William Sound were affected—many areas of the eastern shore were not heavily oiled.

Bioremediation

A relatively new technique for enhancing the natural breakdown of oil in the environment is the application or encouragement of microorganisms that can degrade oil. These microorganisms break oil down into by-products that are no longer hazardous for other organisms. The microbes pull carbon out of the chains of molecules that make up the different parts of oil, the chains fall apart, and they break down into their basic units. A new field has emerged: the location and enhancing of microorganisms that are capable of breaking down the toxic chemicals humans introduce into the environment. It was easy for scientists to locate microorganisms that could break down oil, for many bacteria have evolved near natural oil seeps. Over eons, they became adapted to a relatively high and constant exposure to oil or natural gas that seeps into the oceans. Indeed, they began to make use of the oil as a source of energy, and to thrive in these environments.

Bioremediation can take two forms, the first being the introduction of oil-consuming microorganisms into an oil slick; the second, providing nutrients to enhance the natural biodegradation process of microorganisms already present on site. In this second method, fertilizers are applied to speed up the natural process of oil breakdown.

The first large-scale use of this technique was in 1967, when the cruise liner *Queen Mary* needed to get rid of 800,000 gallons of oily waste water in its bilge off the coast of Long Beach, California. Normally, bilge water is clean and can be released once the oil cargo is off-loaded at is destination. Then the bilge water is dumped to balance the empty cargo compartments. However, oil had leaked from the cargo hold to the bilge compartment, fouling the bilge water. Bioremediation techniques were used on the water in the ship, and after about six weeks, permission to release the water was received.

For the next twenty years, bioremediation work was conducted within confined or controlled systems. Scientists and engineers tinkered with the conditions, varying temperature, nutrient levels, and other physical factors, trying to improve the rate of degradation of oil. These experiments showed that oil can be divided roughly in thirds, with the lightest third being made up of volatile gases that evaporate fairly quickly. The middle third of oil is made up of hydrocarbons that can be broken down relatively easily by natural forces, but the last third is made up of compounds that are more resistant to quick degradation, and include waxes and asphalts.

Applying bioremediation technology to large-scale, outdoor systems has been slow. Extensive bioremediation was first tried on the beaches of Prince William Sound following the *Exxon Valdez* oil spill. This method was especially appealing because of the large number of beaches to clean, the impossibility of reaching many of them, and the very real limits of time, money, and personnel. The EPA invested about five million dollars to try a bioremediation program, Exxon committed funds, and the state added staff support, all aimed at a high-speed, high-profile research program.

The EPA rejected the idea of inoculation, the unleashing of bacteria to the Sound. This was fortunate, as the public was concerned about the release of genetically engineered bacteria as well as nonnative ones, and their effect in a wild system. Instead, the EPA chose to boost the overall bacterial population by adding nitrogen and phosphorus fertilizer. Nearly 5 percent of the population of bacteria in Prince William Sound are oil degraders, providing an adequate population to stimulate with fertilizers.

Even though such a wide-scale fertilization program was new, it took only three months to obtain the necessary approvals. There were no public hearings, no opportunity for independent scientific review, and no accepted guidelines for its use in the wild. This was an interesting experiment, with a lot at stake. The state was still cautious and worried about the outcome. Fertilizers were first added to the beaches in June of 1989. Gradually, the response crews added fertilizer to between 74 and 110 miles of shoreline. It was nearly two years before the toxicity testing indicated that, indeed, the fertilizers were not acutely toxic, and that the pulses of ammonia released by the fertilizers did not jeopardize water-quality standards.

Everyone agreed that the fertilizer increased the populations of microbes, but oil removal was the primary objective. The data are still coming in, and relative levels of oil are being compared on fertilized and unfertilized beaches. The results are mixed: The treatment significantly reduced the oil on some beaches, but it didn't work as well on others.

The work with the *Exxon Valdez* spill made it possible for other states to tentatively try their own experiments with bioremediation in the field. When oil leaked from the underground pipeline in the Arthur Kill, a small-scale bioremediation experiment was tried near Prall's Island, which harbors a sensitive heronry. No fertilizer was used for some time, and then fertilizer was added, allowing for a comparison of oil before and after treatment, on an experimental as well as a control beach. Within three weeks of fertilization, the average concentration of petroleum hydrocarbons dropped more on the fertilized than on the unfertilized beach.

These two sets of experiments indicate that bioremediation may provide another tool for cleaning beaches, particularly those that are otherwise unreachable. Over the next few years, more data will accumulate to give a broader picture of the best situations to use bioremediation.

Wildlife Rescue and Rehabilitation

Whenever an oil spill occurs in an estuary, bay, or ocean, birds and marine mammals become oiled. Dead and dying birds, sea turtles, seals, and even whales may drift to shore, awakening the compassion of even the most callous of observers. The sight of oiled birds or seals floating in a thick, black mousse, sinking amid a layer of multicolored oil, or dragging themselves on shore is more than many can stand, and hordes of volunteers descend on the site of the spill to aid the injured wildlife. This usually means combing the beaches, bays, and estuaries for oiled animals, walking the salt marshes, and bringing them to checkpoints for pickup (Fig. 7.5).

In the aftermath of most major spills, a search-and-rescue operation for wildlife is mounted. Such efforts may be coordinated by the responsible party or the government, but usually they are conducted under the direction of a contractor employed by the responsible party and approved by the relevant state agency. This is as it should be, for there must be some order. Everyone cannot be picking up oiled birds and bringing them home to

Figure 7.5. Oiled brant sitting in salt marsh following pipeline break in Arthur Kill. This bird died in a rehabilitation center.

nurse back to health. Injured wildlife should be brought to an approved facility where trained personnel know how to deal with each species.

During search-and-rescue operations dead birds and mammals are also picked up, and these are very important in the damage assessment process. Although different parties can argue about exactly how many murres or seals died in a given oil spill, no one can dispute that the number of dead and oiled bodies in the freezers died from the spill. The number of a given species that died in a spill can be used as a minimal restoration guide and can help biologists understand the effect of oil on migrant or resident populations in the succeeding years. Also, picking up the oiled carcasses removes the source of another problem: the carrion on which eagles, bears, or other predators might feed can result in ingestion of oil.

Normally birds or mammals are brought to a facility where trained professionals take over their care. For most injured wildlife, the first line of defense is to stabilize them by treating for the internal effects of oil. Animals receive a complete physical with a blood sample, including recording the location of all oil on their bodies. Their eyes are flushed with a sterile saline solution. Since many oiled animals are dehydrated, with compromised kidney function, they receive aggressive fluid therapy, including adding liquids intravenously. In some cases, they receive oral supplementation by gavage, inserting a tube into the crop for a bird or the stomach for a mammal. This is an old and established practice—I have lingered over the paintings on the walls of the tombs of the nobles outside Cairo, intrigued by the ancient Egyptian's use of gavage on ducks, dogs, and other mammals. Their intent, of course, was to fatten the animals for food just as the French farmers do for foie gras today. The procedure is the same for debilitated wildlife.

When many animals are injured at once, triage is required. Experts quickly examine them to determine which are doomed, which will survive with minimal care, and which will survive with aggressive treatment. The next process is cleaning the feathers or fur of oil. Lots and lots of warm water is required for each animal: one hundred gallons of 103°F water over a twenty-minute period. If the water is 2° cooler it will not remove the oil, but if it is 4° hotter it will injure or kill the bird. There is not much room for error. The washing phase is the most critical for the animal, and it is the one that amateurs most often handle improperly. Some cleaning agents may be used to remove the oil from the fur or feathers, but it must be rinsed off quickly or it will destroy the insulative properties. After all the oil is finally removed, the animal is rinsed in warm, clear water. Thorough rinsing is the most important step in the washing process. The animal is then placed in a holding pen to dry off, and heat lamps or hair driers may be used to dry and warm the patients.

Following cleaning, the animal is allowed access to a variety of foods and water. Most facilities provide birds and mammals with easy access to water for swimming, preening, or grooming. The water must be changed periodically to remove any oil still clinging to the animal or present internally. Months after the Arthur Kill oil spill, captive terrapins were still fouling their water with oil after each change of water. The oil was being voided from their digestive system.

Some animals may also be ill, as well as oiled, and they receive individual care. Once cleaned, others can be released within a few days. Depending upon the spill, between 30 and 60 percent of birds may be released following rehabilitation, but the number may be far smaller for heavily oiled birds and for oiled mammals.

Rehabilitating wildlife clearly has advantages for endangered or threatened species, for which every individual is worth saving. It is also important for people who feel that they must do something in the face of such wanton and unnecessary destruction. Nearly everyone feels better when they see a cute, cuddly seal being cared for and eventually returned to its homeland. However, there are several issues of concern with rehabilitation. One of these is whether the released wildlife survive in the wild, or whether we are merely prolonging their life to die of other causes a few days or weeks after they are released. Recent information with rehabilitated seabirds that were banded and released indicates that well over 50 percent are recovered dead after only a few days or weeks. Surely many more die at sea, where they are not found or are eaten by predators. Except in the case of an endangered species, the number of animals that can be rehabilitated and released is very small relative to the population as a whole. Their importance to the population is usually small, and their loss insignificant. This is particularly true given that rehabilitated animals may be released far from their original home, into the territories of others who now have to cope with them.

Released wildlife also pose a danger because of the potential for introducing disease to otherwise healthy wild populations. In many cases, injured wildlife picked up after an oil spill are taken to temporary quarters or to facilities not meant for them. Several species may be mixed together, allowing for the transfer of diseases. After the *Exxon Valdez*, hundreds of injured sea otters and harbor seals were taken to makeshift places or to animal hospitals filled with dogs and cats. It was impossible to determine whether these marine mammals picked up any diseases from the other animals, diseases that released animals could carry back to their native populations. This is not an idle concern. The California desert tortoise is endangered because the wild populations are suffering from a respiratory tract infection caused by bacterialike organisms called mycoplasma, apparently derived from released animals that carried the disease back to the few individuals remaining in the wild.

This last point, the potential for transmission of disease to wild populations, argues very strongly for allowing rehabilitation only in approved facilities with trained staff. There are a number of such facilities throughout the United States, and usually they specialize not only in rehabilitation but in research on the care and maintenance of a variety of species. Facilities such as Tristate Bird Rescue and Research have markedly advanced our knowledge not only of animal husbandry but of the natural rates of disease, lesions, and other abnormalities. Birds or other animals brought to such facilities serve a useful scientific purpose, and those that cannot be rehabilitated will not have died in vain, oiled on a fouled beach. Finally, the great cost in time and money devoted to the rehabilitation of injured wildlife that may not survive in the wild, and that may introduce diseases to an otherwise healthy population, may exceed the potential benefits, particularly when performed by untrained personnel in untested facilities.

Rehabilitation is, however, very important in the case of endangered and threatened species and for species of special concern. In this case, every individual, and particularly every breeding individual, is important to the population as a whole. When numbers are small, each individual may harbor genetic diversity that is vital to the species. Special attention and additional monies should be spent to rehabilitate such individuals and to learn the biological requirements for the husbandry of these species. Such information may become critical to maintaining wild populations or to working with captive populations for the purpose of introducing young to the wild.

Finally, I do not underestimate the importance of the very human need to feel that we are doing something in the face of environmental disaster. I too have carried an injured bird or sick snake home to nurse back to health. I am not arguing that we abandon them all but that instead we channel this desire to encompass the truly endangered and threatened species for which our efforts can make a real difference to population stability, that we leave the care of such animals to the professionals, and that we accept the fate of some to die in the aftermath.

Damage Assessment of Natural Resources

Both the Clean Water Act and the Oil Pollution Act of 1990 mandate that trustees for natural resources may recover damages for lost or damaged resources, as well as for replacement or restoration costs for these natural resources. Claims must, however, be substantiated by evidence, which is not always an easy task. The need for documentation led directly to several state and federal agencies formulating damage assessment procedures that could be used in the case of oil spills. Damage assessment has become big business, both for the injured parties and for the responsible parties, since there can be disagreement over exactly what the losses of natural resources actually are. Following an oil spill, both the injured parties and the responsible party hire "experts" to evaluate the damage to natural resources.

The process of damage assessment involves gathering evidence of injured resources, including dead bodies and counts of oiled but living animals, and counts or estimates of commercial, recreational, or subsistence hunting and fishing losses. In a perfect world, this would also include direct counts and estimates of wildlife population levels, estimates of lesions or tissue levels of oil, and estimates of reproductive success both before and after an oil spill. However, comparable information from before a spill is rarely available.

The most important aspect of damage assessment is determining how natural resources have been affected, both directly and indirectly, and in terms of actual as well as lost resources. Direct losses are those deaths that are due to the oil; indirect losses include deaths or impacts due to changes in behavior as a result of the oil. For example, when fiddler crabs become oiled they suffer behavioral impairments that include reduced reaction time and decreased digging ability. Their reduced reaction time leads to an increased potential to be eaten by predators such as night herons, and their decreased digging ability means they do not dig their winter burrows as deep, and many freeze over the winter. These changes were documented after several spills, including the one in the Arthur Kill, New Jersey, and at Falmouth, Massachusetts. In both cases populations declined for months or years after the spill.

Lost resources are natural resources that would have been available had the oil spill not happened. For example, a fisherman who depends on the capture of fish for his livelihood can recover damages for the fish he might have caught if there had been no oil spill.

In cases where more than one oil spill has occurred, or where there is chronic oil pollution as well as a major accident, the injured parties usually have to show that the oil on the dead birds is oil from the accident. With the use of chemical fingerprinting, it is now possible to determine the source of the oil. This was used after the Arthur Kill oil spill to prove that the damage was caused by the oil from the ruptured Exxon pipeline, not from a combination of the frequent small spills that plague the Kill. However, for most major spills there is no question of the identity of the oil. Usually only one major spill occurs at one time in a given place, and the identity of the responsible party is not in dispute.

Fingerprinting is done through a process called gas chromatography. This technique separates the various hydrocarbon components of petroleum according to the size and structure of their molecules. The oil in the sample of tissue or soil is extracted with a solvent that isolates the hydrocarbons. Each component or fraction can be separated and measured, and a recorder graphs the pattern of hydrocarbons, creating a chromatogram. Since each source of petroleum yields a product with a unique composition, each will yield a different chromatogram. The fingerprint of the spilled oil is compared with many possible source fingerprints, until the best match is found. This is then the fingerprint that identifies and distinguishes the type of oil.

Body counts are useful in damage assessment because they indicate the animals that certainly died from the oil. They can also be used to estimate the number of likely deaths. It is never possible to find all the bodies that die in a spill, so drift experiments and computer models are used to extrapolate to the real mortality. For example, after the *Exxon Valdez* spill, ornithologists set banded, dead oiled birds adrift, combed the beaches, and recorded how many marked birds beached on the shores. They then used the percentage of birds that reached shore to calculate the number of birds that likely died in the oil spill and were not recovered. Using this method, they estimated that although only about 37,000 birds were recovered after the oil spill, nearly ten times that many died from the spill. This estimate, that only a tenth of the birds that died were ever recovered, varies by oil spill. When spills happen closer to shore, a greater number of bodies are recovered; when they happen farther from shore, fewer are recovered. Few dead oiled birds might be expected to beach on shore when an oil spill happens far out in the open ocean.

Another way to estimate damages is to examine population levels before and after a spill. For example, after many oil spills there are fewer nesting birds at colonies within the oil spill area, with the number of birds nesting in the vicinity around the perimeter of the oil spill remaining the same. This usually indicates mortality of the breeding population. A similar method was used with harbor seals in Prince William Sound. Although few dead seal carcasses were found immediately after the spill, breeding populations in the area were severely depleted. Carcasses were not found after the spill because harbor seals sink almost immediately upon death, unlike other marine mammals, which float for days.

Another method of damage assessment is to estimate the death rate of a subset of the population and then extrapolate to the whole population. For example, at the time of the *Exxon Valdez* spill, scientists had been studying one pod of killer whales that lived in Prince William Sound for many years. They could identify each individual by its color pattern. After the spill they recorded how many individuals were missing, calculated the percentage of the pod that had perished, and extrapolated that to the whole population.

Damages can also be assessed by comparing the reproductive success of birds from the same breeding colony, or marine mammals from the same haul-out sites, from before the spill with success after the spill. After the Arthur Kill spill, snowy egrets had significantly lower reproductive success than they had over the previous several years. These reproductive deficits lingered for at least three years.

Injuries to fisheries or shellfisheries can be assessed by comparing the pounds of catch before and after a spill. Given the same effort, the catches should be the same. In France, the local fisheries suffered a 25 percent reduction in catch after the *Amoco Cadiz* spill even though they increased their effort. The native Alaskans suffered a decrease in the amount of fish, shellfish, and marine mammals they harvested after the *Exxon Valdez* spill, as well as a decrease in the diversity of the harvest. Although the effect on the French fisherman could be documented by the records of the local fisherman, this is not always the case with subsistence or recreational fisherman. This does not diminish their losses, however.

The losses suffered by other people who depend on coastal resources may be difficult to document as well. For example, the small, picturesque fishing villages along the French coast were wonderful tourist destinations before the *Amoco Cadiz*. However, after the spill, few tourists came to the small fishing towns; yet the extent of the losses to hotels, restaurants, and shops was never documented. Although recreational losses can be determined when they are measured in terms of boat rentals, boating field gear, bait shops, boat fuel, and birdwatching paraphernalia, it is much more difficult to account for losses for people with less money to spend. For example, many children and unemployed parents fish and crab along the Arthur Kill, and they could not do so after the oil spill. Yet almost no one considered the losses for these people.

Even more difficult to deal with are the losses of existence or aesthetic values. These are the damages that are most contested. Some oil companies claim that the only legitimate damages they are responsible for are monetary ones that can be measured. Existence or aesthetic values are difficult to value, yet are critical, particularly for native Americans, whose very culture is intertwined with them. How can we value our losses from no longer being able to visit a pristine shoreline, or our losses from this shoreline no longer existing even if we never expect to visit it? Many Americans value highly the mere existence of a rocky shoreline along the California coast, an unspoiled sea of salt marsh vegetation along the Massachusetts shore, or great wilderness in Alaska. Yet in the past twenty years, each of these has been spoiled by spreading oil that seeped deep into the peat or rocks.

Chapter Eight
Effects on Vegetation

● ● ●

Eventually, oil from a spill reaches the shores, piles up on the rocks, seeps down into the crevices, and lodges in nooks and crannies on the high-tide line, waiting to be driven still higher by succeeding storm tides. Sometimes it forms a viscous mass that slowly hardens into an asphalt that clings tenaciously to the rocks. Along other shores the oil drifts onto sandy beaches or into tidal creeks and back bays, where it finds salt marshes in temperate regions, or mangroves in the tropics. In some tropical regions such as along some of coastal Central America, it brushes against the levees of shrimp farms, and in much of Asia it blackens the dikes of massive fish farms and lowland rice paddies.

Unlike many mobile animals such as marine mammals and birds, vegetation has no hope of escaping the advancing oil: It cannot move, and it cannot slide deeper into the water. Each tidal cycle brings more oil, or it may wash some away. Without intervention, it is only the forces of nature that can cleanse the shores, removing bits of the oil slowly, year after year. In this chapter I examine how oil affects vegetation and trace the fate of oiled vegetation over time.

Subtidal Vegetation

There is little information on the effect of oil on the plants that live below the tides, in the subtidal region, which is always covered with water. For many marine organisms, such as crabs, shrimp, and fish, the large algae that often dominate subtidal habitats are important nursery sites and act as a primary food source at least as important as single-celled algae blooms.

Although the algae themselves may be less susceptible than terrestrial plants, oil remains on their surfaces, clogging their pores and preventing gas exchange. And if they become completely oiled, they will die. Furthermore, they are eaten by other invertebrates, causing further oil contamination for animals that live there.

Mass dieoffs of algae happened in intertidal mangrove habitats in Panama after over a million gallons of oil leaked from the wreck of the *Witwater*. Large beds of seagrasses also died. The seagrass grew over extensive coral reefs, and mats of dead leaves and roots drifted onshore. The algae and seagrass beds provided habitat and food for populations of invertebrates and fish; and many amphipods, decapods, polychaete worms, bivalves and gastropods, and small fish perished both from direct oiling and from loss of habitat.

Importance of Salt Marshes and Mangroves

The vegetation that lines coastal shores is an integral part of that ecosystem and is vital to both the marine system and to the terrestrial system. It is the interface between the land and the sea, and as with all ecotones, its role far outweighs the space it occupies. It is the place that terrestrial animals come to fish or bathe, the place that marine animals haul out to dig nests or rest a bit, and the place that thousands upon thousands of birds use for resting or foraging on their migratory journeys to nesting grounds farther north or wintering sites farther south. The interface between the land and the sea is critical, providing the place where their young are born, even though they themselves may abandon the eggs after laying them.

There are transient animals that live here for brief periods of time but spend the majority of their lives elsewhere, either on dry land or in the estuaries or open oceans. For a myriad of other creatures this is home. Others spend a significant portion of their time here; either during their early life stages or for their breeding activities.

A wide variety of birds live in salt marshes of the temperate zone, building their nests on the wrackline of dead eelgrass and cordgrass, within the high marsh vegetation, or in the small bushes that grow on the higher places. Herring gulls, laughing gulls, and common terns nest along the east coast of North America; Forster's terns and black skimmers nest along both coasts and the Gulf coast; and a variety of herons, egrets, and ibises nest in colonies of hundreds or thousands of pairs all along the coastal shores of North and Central America. Usually, each species nests together in a colony. But sometimes they nest in mixed-species groups, such as the herons and egrets. Here there is competition for space within the small bushes, as each heron or egret tries to nest on the highest site that will provide cover from rain and storms, as well as from predators flying overhead.

In more southern regions, birds nest in the mangroves, or on levees built by man. The gulls and terns, more northerly species by nature, are gone. Herons, egrets, and ibises are even more common, often nesting in very large colonies of thousands of birds, and their noisy colonies can be heard far across the bays and estuaries. Anhingas nest in these mixed-species colonies, or nest by themselves in smaller groups.

In both habitats a variety of birds such as sparrows and blackbirds nest solitarily on the marshes or in the mangroves. Their strategy is to hide in the vegetation rather than rely on the presence of other birds to warn them of approaching predators and to help defend the nests. In any one place their numbers are small, but along the miles of coastline, their numbers add up.

Birds are visible reminders of the importance of salt marshes and mangroves, and they are often the first ones we think about when an oil spill or some other polluting event fouls the shore. But there are many other creatures who depend on the interface between the land and the sea; many spend their whole lives here and are unable to avoid the advancing oil.

A diversity of invertebrates live here, including many species of mussels, crabs, shrimp, and shellfish. Salt marshes and mangrove swamps are vital nurseries for the eggs, larvae, and juveniles of fish. Much of the life of the oceans is dependent on the salt marshes, for they provide habitat for small larvae to hide and grow. The entire food web starts here. Algae flourish, bathed in the tidal waters and the bright sunlight. Small invertebrates feed on the algae and become prey to larger invertebrates and small fish. The small fish are eaten by larger fish, which in turn become prey for still larger fish or for birds. A complicated web of fish feed on each other, including the very large sport or commercial fish caught by humans, and by sharks in the ocean beyond.

The salt marsh vegetation and the mangroves are the base for this complicated and diverse food web. They are some of the most highly productive regions of the world, producing more biomass per unit area than agriculture. Although not usually harvested today, early settlers to North America used the marsh grasses as hay for cattle, as mattress stuffing, and as garden mulch. However, most of the vegetation eventually dies, providing food for millions of decomposers, who break down the vegetation into nutrients that are reused, and the cycle begins anew.

Salt marshes provide the structure, the stability, and the safety for our estuaries. Without them, the land would wear away, moving farther and farther inland. The upland forests beyond, which seem so permanent and stable, are there because the salt marshes and mangroves take the brunt of winter storms and hurricanes. Year after year, century after century, they absorb the forces of nature, changing slightly with each passing storm, but remaining nonetheless.

General Effects of Oil on Vegetation

Salt marshes, mangroves, and other types of intertidal or estuarine vegetation are particularly vulnerable to oil and other chemicals because there is little strong wave action, at least at the landward edge. Although the leading edges of these intertidal habitats may face the full force of storms and tides, the forces quickly dissipate as they move over the marshes and swamps. In the back reaches the tidal flow may be sporadic, and is very weak even then. Most of the marsh is not directly exposed to the cleansing surge of the surf, so only the leading edge is exposed to daily tidal inundation sufficient to wash away pollutants. Oil and other pollutants that reach the back edges seep deeper into the muds or peat and remain for years or decades. There the toxins are available to cause low-level chronic effects for many years. Salt marsh vegetation thus acts as an oil trap for stranded spills.

The most devastating effects from oil spills often occur at the leading edges of marshes and mangroves because it is here that oil first reaches and concentrates. The most critical effect of oil in these regions is direct habitat loss or destruction, even though this may be temporary. For many spills, vegetation loss is not even mentioned; or when it is, only a cursory statement is made. When oil hits these regions, it covers the vegetation both aboveground and underground as the oil seeps into the peat. Vegetation that is completely covered with oil normally dies: It cannot take in oxygen or release carbon dioxide, and roots are unable to take in the necessary nutrients. Prop roots of mangroves are particularly vulnerable because this is the only way that these trees obtain necessary oxygen.

Information on the effects of oil spills on salt marsh vegetation, particularly *Spartina* species such as cordgrass and salt hay, comes from experiments conducted in the laboratory or in the marshes themselves in the 1970s and 1980s. J. Baker and her colleagues from England and Wales found that crude oils and their products differ widely in their effect on *Spartina*. Toxicity increases along the series, from paraffins (known as alkanes), cycloalkanes, olefins, to aromatics. Within a series, small molecules are more toxic than large ones. All this means is that all oils are not the same, and to be able to predict the effect, it is essential to know the type of oil that was spilled.

Baker's experiments indicate that oil on the leaves and stems of vegetation reduces the oxygen diffusion out of the stems and the roots, and oiling of aboveground parts affects the underground system, even if oil didn't seep down to cover roots. Light oils penetrate plant tissue and disrupt membrane structure, while heavy oils smother the plants and interfere with normal oxygen diffusion.

Spartina can survive a small spill if only the surface leaves and stems are covered, because it can sprout new growth from underground buds, much as it does each spring. However, it will not tolerate repeated spills, or spills where the oil covers both the stems and the roots. This suggests that vegetation can recover more quickly from an acute spill than from chronic spills. Yet many marshes are exposed to chronic oil pollution, and their overall productivity must be severely reduced. In extreme cases, vegetation may not grow as close to tidal creeks and mudflats as it might under pristine conditions.

Some experiments have been conducted on the effect of timing of an oil spill on salt marsh vegetation. Oiling has its most devastating effects on seeds; if oiling occurs when flower buds are developing, they do not produce seeds. Furthermore, if oiling occurs in the winter, oiled seeds rarely germinate in the spring. This has the effect of drastically changing the species present in a marsh, and with only one major oil spill, the marsh may revert to vegetation that grows entirely from underground rhizomes, with flowering plants gone from the marsh.

The above experiments were conducted mostly in the field, on salt marshes otherwise exposed to the elements. Other experiments have been conducted in laboratories. In the late 1980s, M. Leck examined the effects of oil on germination of seeds collected from marsh soil in New Jersey tidal freshwater marshes. These marshes are primarily freshwater because they receive freshwater from streams and rivers, but they also receive some tidal inundation. Leck's most interesting finding was that seeds are affected in different ways. Oil significantly reduced germination and growth of some species, but had less of an effect on others. Some species, such as arrowhead, experience enhanced germination and survival when exposed to oil, which may be a result of less competition from the seedlings of other species. This suggests that even within flowering plants there are differences in response to oil. Oil spills thus have the ability to change the species composition within marshes, changing the very character of the marsh. These changes may be permanent, since rare species or those unable to compete as well may never again invade the marshes.

Several experiments and observations in different types of marshes indicate a range of tolerances among plants. Very susceptible species are those with shallow roots or with no underground storage organs. They are usually annuals, and they are quickly killed by a single oil spill. This category includes seedlings of all types, as well as adult plants of species such as saltwort. Susceptible species are those which may be killed, but can recolonize a marsh quickly, including filamentous green algae and black grass.

Intermediate in their response to oil are perennial species that can recover from up to four light oilings, but decline rapidly if oiled more often or to a greater extent. These include some perennial grasses and the hardier marsh grasses. Relatively resistant marsh species include perennials that have a competitive advantage due to fast growth rate or mat-forming habit, and perennials such as plantagos, with a robust, rosette growth form that have underground storage organs such as tap roots.

While some experiments examined the direct effects of the oil, others examined how cleanup affects vegetation. Experiments conducted on the effect of dispersants show that they are not effective in removing oil from vegetation and may further injure the delicate vegetation. Dispersants sometimes move deeper in the soil and stress roots that may have escaped injury from the oil.

Cutting of oiled vegetation has been tried as a cleanup method since the early 1970s. Usually it is considered for sensitive wildlife areas where oil exposure should be minimized, either for animals that live there or for those that will soon migrate in, including waterfowl, wading birds, or fur-bearing mammals. Presumably, cutting and removing the oiled vegetation will decrease the chances of their exposure to the oil. Although this method may reduce oil exposure for wildlife, it may also lessen the survival or recovery of the vegetation. As with many oil spill decisions, this is a difficult situation for managers, who must choose between habitat productivity and wildlife resources.

A review of over twenty papers on cutting following oil contamination indicates that recovery or regrowth of the vegetation was positively affected in less than a third of the cases, and was unaffected in another third. Put another way, if vegetation is cut to save wildlife, there is a greater than one in three chance that there will be negative effects on the vegetation. The positive effects on vegetation were all associated with heavy fuel oil (such as no. 6) and heavy crude oil. The difference may well be that lighter oils, such as no. 2 fuel oil, have greater water solubility: When vegetation is cut the interior plant surfaces may provide a more direct pathway for the lighter oils to penetrate to the delicate roots.

When oil is in a thick layer, vegetation cutting may be good because it will open passageways for gas exchange with the roots; and with time, new shoots may grow from roots and rhizome energy stores. Several factors influence the effect of cutting on marsh vegetation, including oil type, degree of oiling, seasonality, repetitive oiling, natural flushing or tidal flow, degree of cutting, physical substrate disturbance, and other environmental stresses such as storms and other pollutants. Cutting has a more positive effect in the fall or winter when plants are dormant. During this time they are less vulnerable to toxic effects. Since translocation of carbohydrates and nutrients from aboveground parts to underground parts happens during fall, cutting might stimulate regrowth the next spring.

There are two other potential disadvantages of using cutting as a cleanup method. The physical disturbance to plant roots and sediments caused by people tromping across the marsh to cut and haul off the vegetation can be substantial. Other, more delicate plants that live amid the larger plants can be completely killed by physical disruption. And, of course, if there is another oil spill following cutting, the devastation may be complete, as the exposed stems will carry the new oil directly to the root systems.

To summarize, experiments with oil have indicated that salt marsh plants show a wide range of susceptibility to oil, ranging from some annuals that are killed by a single oiling, to others that can withstand repeated low-level oiling. The type of oil influences toxicity, with light aromatics causing the most acute toxicity. Most *Spartinas*, which form the basis for most salt marshes, can withstand some oiling, but not severe or repeated oiling. Competitive advantages are gained by tolerant species following oiling. This is particularly striking in upland reaches of the marsh, where a wide diversity of flowering plants usually abound. Marsh-cleansing methods, such as dispersants and cutting, do not decrease the damage done by oil pollution, and may actually increase the harm.

Salt Marshes

Salt marshes fringe temperate coastlines along North America, Europe, and much of Asia. These are all very vulnerable to oil spills because the vegetation is relatively short, usually only a meter or two high, and can be completely covered with oil from even a relatively small spill. This is particularly true if storms accompany the oil spill, and the tides are higher than normal. Whenever a spill occurs nearshore, oil eventually reaches the salt marshes, and in some places, the vegetation may be completely blackened with oil. In many parts of the world, oil wells are drilled either on these marshes, or only a short distance offshore. Such marshes may be exposed to long-term chronic exposure to oil, with occasional large spills. Oil exposure can directly kill the vegetation, but it can also delay growth in the spring, and decrease the height or stem width.

When oil leaked from the underground pipeline in the Arthur Kill, oil spread over the narrow river and immediately fouled the creeks and edges of the salt marshes. Although booms were placed over the mouths of many creeks to prevent oil from reaching the inner labyrinth of salt marshes, this was done many hours after the spill, and oil had already flowed into most of the creeks. In some cases, the booms held the oil in the creeks, but further contamination was prevented.

It was obvious to even the most casual visitor to the Kill that the oil covered the vegetation along the creeks and shorelines (Fig. 8.1). The effect of oil on vegetation in the Arthur Kill was examined following the oil spill by a contractor hired by Exxon, as well as by several scientists, including myself. This oil spill provides an interesting case because most marshes could be examined, tidal flow is relatively low, and the vegetation could be monitored for several years. Since the Arthur Kill has tidal flow at both ends, the water sloshes back and forth rather than simply flowing from one end to the other. Much of the oil just moved back and forth, unable to flow out to be diluted by the ocean waters.

The degree of oiling varied in the marshes (Fig. 8.2), but most were heavily oiled. Since the oil spill happened in the dead of winter, when the aboveground vegetation was brown and dead, the initial effect was to coat all the dead stems with oil. However, in the following growing season, 15 percent of the total salt marsh acreage was completely dead, and 6 percent was severely affected. In many places, there was a zone two to three yards wide where the *Spartina* was completely dead, with only the oil-covered stems from the previous year remaining.

Exxon, in its publicity, proudly announced that only about 20 percent of the marsh vegetation was affected, and the rest seemed fine. Unfortunately, the company failed to mention that it was the 20 percent adjacent to the creeks and shorelines, the 20 percent that harbors the highest abundance and diversity of invertebrates. It is this 20 percent that most of the young fish use, where most of the fiddler crabs live, where most of the birds feed, and where all of the mussels live. In short, the oil killed the critical interface between marsh and sea. Moreover, to lose 20 percent of a productive salt marsh with one oil spill is spectacular. Should another major oil spill happen soon, even more of the marsh would be destroyed.

It is seven years since the major oil spill happened in the Arthur Kill, and the vegetation in most areas has slowly recovered. Yet the vegetation in the most heavily oiled creeks is still dead or sparse. In some places, the effect is obvious to me only because I know every detail of the creeks and marshes. To the casual observer, the marsh looks healthy and vibrant; but I know that before the Arthur Kill oil spill, the vegetation grew lush and thick down nearly to the midtide line. Thousands of fiddler crabs wandered about the mudflat at low tide. Now the rich, dark muds in the creeks across from the spill have fewer fiddler crabs and mussels, and the marsh vegetation starts well above where it once grew.

Longer-term studies have been conducted in the marshes in Wales. Heavy fuel oil smothered the marshes near Martinshaven in 1971; recovery began during the first five years, but took fifteen years to complete. Even

Figure 8.1. Top, *oiled vegetation along the Arthur Kill;* bottom, *oil on rocks along the Arthur Kill.*

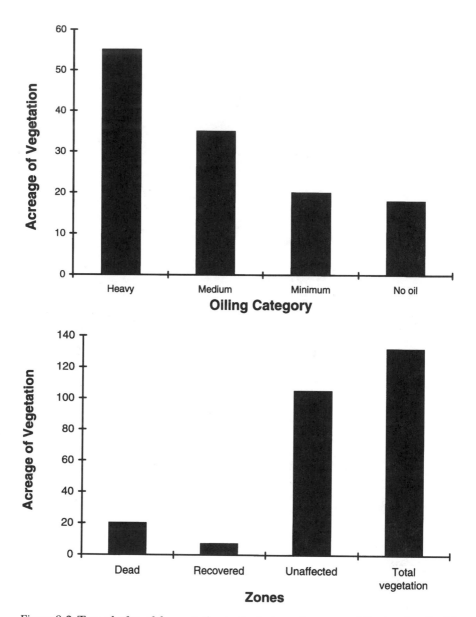

Figure 8.2. Top, *the fate of the vegetation in the first growing season following the oil spill in the Arthur Kill;* bottom, *acreage of marsh vegetation that was oiled.* (Source: *Adapted from J. Burger, ed., 1994,* Before and after an oil spill: The Arthur Kill [*Rutgers University Press, New Brunswick, N.J.*])

today, twenty-four years later, oil is still visible in core samples and may be exerting a subtle effect on overall growth and productivity of the grasses. An oil spill of light Arabian crude in the Strait of Magellan, Chile, in August 1974 fouled the marshes there. Over twenty years later the oil still remains on the surface, and the vegetation has not recovered at all. In some places, where the oil deposits are thinning, tiny bits of vegetation try to grow. It is clear from this spill that where oil deposits are thick, the natural recovery of vegetation may take decades.

Mangrove Systems

In tropical systems, mangrove trees replace salt marsh plants as the species that grow in intertidal zones. Mangrove trees usually have roots that grow upward, out of the mud and into the water and air. The tips of these prop roots are exposed to the air, and provide oxygen to the root system.

Oil can kill mangrove communities: A devastating oil spill in Panama in 1986 (50,000 barrels) killed miles of mangroves, leaving the organisms that depended on the mangroves marooned in a sea of death, and most died themselves. Everywhere that oil washed ashore there were dead and dying trees. In the end, the mangroves were completely dead along nearly twenty miles of shoreline. Reproduction in mangroves is either from underground roots or from the seeds that sprout while still on the tree, and then fall to the ground along with a leaf. The heavier seed smashes into the mud, with the leaf pointing upward, and the seed sprouts roots into the mud. Some seeds died on the tree before they were ready to fall, and others died in the mud, covered with oil. Seedlings in the area also died.

The mangrove trees in Panama slowly started to disintegrate, first the leaves fell off, then limbs broke off, and finally the trees collapsed into the bay. Even the trees that survived at the fringes of the spill were affected; they had fewer prop roots and did not grow as fast as mangroves in unoiled areas. When there are fewer prop roots, the habitat is seriously affected because they serve as settlement surfaces for a diverse group of organisms. These physical effects are now independent of any lingering effect of the oil; and they will continue to affect the habitat for decades.

Even small oil spills in tropical regions can have devastating effects on the vegetation. When a barge sank in the Bonny Estuary of Nigeria, nearly 30 percent of the mangrove prop roots and 32 percent of the seedlings were completely covered with oil. Within a five hundred-yard area around the oil spill there was partial defoliation of the mangrove trees, and most of the seedlings died. Just over a thousand gallons of oil spilled, yet it had an impressive local effect.

Overall, it is clear that oil of all types can affect the vegetation that lines our coastlines. The magnitude of the effect is only a matter of how much oil spills, how deep it is, what type of oil it is, what type of vegetation grows there, and what natural forces can remove the oil. When vegetation is completely oiled, it normally dies, along with seeds and seedlings that are coated. Depending upon the depth of the oil covering the vegetation and the muds, vegetation may not come back for years or even for decades.

Chapter Nine
Effects on Invertebrates and Fish

● ● ●

Mussels, clams, lobsters, crabs, barnacles, limpets, and polychaete worms—as well as a vast array of other invertebrates—live in the bays, estuaries, and oceans. Yet they, as well as fish, are often ignored by the media and the public following oil spills. For many invertebrates, there is no escaping an oil spill, as they are planktonic, floating freely in the ocean or bay currents, completely at the whim of the tides and winds. Others can move about of their own volition over short distances, while still others are relatively sedentary, remaining on the same sandy or muddy bottom or attached to rocks in the intertidal zone for most of their adult lives.

Invertebrates and fish vary in their response to oil, largely because of variations in life history strategies. In this chapter I describe the pelagic and benthic environment where invertebrates and fish live and examine the effects of oil spills in each of these environments. Although sea turtles, marine mammals, and birds also spend part or all of their lives in these environments, they are considered separately in the next two chapters.

Pelagic and Benthic Environments

Life in the seas can be divided into the pelagic environment and the benthic environment (Fig. 9.1). The pelagic environment occurs in the middle-depth and surface waters of the open sea while the benthic refers to bottom-dwelling organisms. Seabirds and marine mammals are usually pelagic, as they spend all or part of their life cycle within or above the open ocean. Planktonic environments are those of the open ocean and open

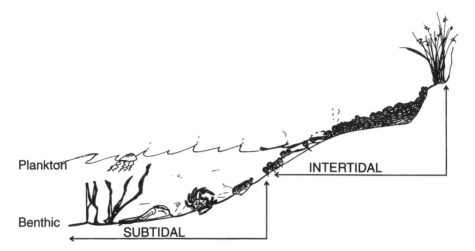

Figure 9.1. Schematic of habitats where invertebrates live.

waters in bays and estuaries. "Plankton" refers to a large variety of single-celled animals called zooplankton, many small crustaceans, the larvae of perhaps the majority of marine vertebrates, adults of a wide range of invertebrate groups, and the eggs and larvae of many fish species, as well as single-celled plants called phytoplankton. Plankton live in the upper layers of the sea, and they are free-floating, rather than attached to or crawling upon the bottom.

There are normally large changes in the abundance and species diversity in planktonic communities, and many undergo daily vertical migrations. They move up in the water column as night descends, when the threat of predation is less, and descend again at daybreak, when they are again vulnerable to predators from above and below.

Planktonic Organisms in the Pelagic Environment

Plankton that live in the upper layers of the sea are particularly vulnerable to toxic water-soluble elements leaching from floating oil, as well as to microscopic droplets of emulsified oil that sink in the water column, either from natural processes or from dispersants. A number of laboratory experiments indicate that oil has many effects on planktonic organisms: Oils with a high aromatic content are more toxic than others, fresh crude is more toxic than weathered oil, and oil causes mortality as well as a variety of sublethal behavioral effects. In addition, oceanic plankton seem more vulnerable than coastal species. Some species, however, such as barnacle larvae and copepods, can apparently swallow droplets of oil and excrete them in their feces, remaining unharmed.

Field experiments with plankton have been conducted by constructing large enclosures that contain plankton communities, and then introducing different amounts of oil to study the effects. These experiments show that with very low concentrations of oil there are few effects, but with higher levels, there are changes in species composition of planktonic communities. However, it is difficult to interpret these data, since even under normal conditions there are frequent and rapid changes in community structure. Plankton populations are patchily distributed in the oceans and bays because of changing water currents; it is very hard to detect changes as a result of an oil spill. Also, the long-term ecological effects are expected to be small on planktonic organisms, except for the very largest and most widespread oil spill.

Observations during oil spills are also difficult to interpret. Gross observations of plankton following the *Torrey Canyon*, the Santa Barbara blowout, the *Argo Merchant*, and the *Amoco Cadiz* showed no large changes in the abundance or species composition of plankton. However, following a spill of 1,000 tons of oil from the *Tsesis* in the northern Baltic Sea the zooplankton biomass decreased dramatically. It is difficult to determine if the organisms died or simply moved out of the area into adjacent waters.

Although the toxic components of oil or other contaminants can kill planktonic organisms, the losses usually are rapidly replaced because of immigration from outside the affected area and rapid reproduction by the survivors. Most plankton have a short life span and high reproductive rate, allowing populations to quickly build up to prespill levels, once the contaminant levels have decreased.

Effects on Invertebrates in the Intertidal Environment

The benthic environment can be divided into the intertidal zone and the subtidal zone (Fig. 9.1). The subtidal zone is always covered by water. Organisms that live in the intertidal zone are particularly vulnerable to oil, because it is here that oil concentrates, brought in by the tides, repeatedly, over many cycles.

Acute effects usually occur a short time after an oil spill. Death may result from the absorption of very high dosages; physical clogging, preventing normal feeding; or morphological damage to the animal's respiratory surfaces, causing suffocation. Bivalve mollusks, such as mussels and clams, suffer from depressed oxygen consumption over the gill tissues, as well as from decreased filtration rates, and they starve. Some bivalves try to compensate by switching to anaerobic respiration, but this reduces feeding rates and survival.

The soils beneath the intertidal zone are often anaerobic (lacking in oxygen) and contain organisms adapted to that condition, such as bacteria. One problem in the intertidal zone is that the oil may penetrate to the anaerobic environments through the burrows of worms, mollusks, and crustaceans, as well as through the stems and roots of plants that have died or been compromised by oil. These channels may also allow oxygen to penetrate to soils that would otherwise be anaerobic. Many of the organisms that live in these burrows then die, covered with oil, and the burrows collapse, trapping oil deep within the sediments.

Some invertebrates show few effects from oil spills; this is partly a function of their ability to eliminate oil rapidly. However, when covered with oil, most invertebrates cannot eliminate enough to avoid the effects. Some worms, however, do quite well when competitors are killed by oil. This is a recurrent theme with oil spills: Some tolerant organisms can increase in numbers, making it even more difficult for others to move back in. Laboratory experiments show a clear relationship between the amount of oil and the severity of the effect on intertidal invertebrates, known as a dose-response relationship. For example, there is an increase in severity of deficits in feeding, respiration, and growth in mussels. It is difficult, however, to relate these to conditions in the wild.

It is useful to examine the effects on invertebrates that live in the intertidal zone during specific spills. Mussels were profoundly affected by the *Exxon Valdez* oil spill. Mussels are very common in coastal Alaska and are an important part of the subsistence harvest. They live in the mid intertidal zone and were heavily oiled following the spill. Since most mussels live in high-wave regions, they were spared the high-pressure cleansing that occurred on many beaches. Although much of the oil was washed off the mussel beds by the waves, in some beds the mussels did not grow as fast and there were fewer of them. Furthermore, the mussels in some bays continued to have high tissue levels of oil even four years later, and mussels in some bays are inedible even today because of high levels of oil. Oiled mussels are potential pathways of contamination for species in intertidal areas including harlequin ducks and juvenile river otters.

In the first few days following the pipeline leak in the Arthur Kill there was devastation of the invertebrates living in the intertidal zone. Ribbed mussels, soft-shelled and other clams, and fiddler crabs suffered high mortality. Mussels and clams died, their shells gaping open and their bodies exposed to the water and air. Normally, they open only when covered with tidal waters, and remain tightly closed as the tides recede. The oil penetrated the mud, leaving other invertebrates such as mud snails, periwinkles, and bloodworms dead. The mud in areas near the spill was devoid of any bivalves or other invertebrates until the beginning of summer, nearly five months later, when recolonization began. On some particularly oiled creeks and mudflats, however, the mussels did not reestablish themselves until three or four years after the spill, and the process is not yet complete even seven years later. A similar response was noted in Massachusetts following the *Florida* barge accident.

Examination of soft-shelled clams from the Arthur Kill following the oil spill indicated that there was a marked increase in the number of severe sores or lesions in the digestive gland, gills, mantle, intestine, and kidney. Before the oil spill, only about 10 to 15 percent of the clams had lesions on their intestines, but this increased to about 75 percent after the spill. The number of lesions remained relatively high for three or four months. A similar increase in the number of lesions in clams occurred after the *Amoco Cadiz* oil spill, and they recovered less quickly, perhaps due to their lack of previous exposure to oil. The clams living in the Arthur Kill are chronically exposed to a low level of oil and have partially acclimated.

Fiddler crabs were another organism severely affected by the Arthur Kill oil spill. They are particularly useful as bioindicators of environmental degradation because they are widespread and abundant in estuarine habitats around the world, and are an important link in estuarine food chains. They are relatively sedentary, making them indicative of local exposure, and are susceptible to a variety of environmental pollutants. The effects of oil spills on fiddler crabs have been examined around the world. In the Niger Delta of Nigeria and at the West Falmouth oil spills there was high initial mortality of fiddler crabs. At West Falmouth the crabs suffered long-term effects that included reduced species diversity, reduced ratio of males to females, reduced juvenile settlement on oiled shores, locomotory impairment, and abnormal burrow construction. They suffered high overwinter mortality for several years, partly due to the fact that crabs with oil in their tissues dug burrows that were not quite deep enough, and they froze to death. Decreased populations were still evident in Falmouth seven years after the spill.

The Arthur Kill oil spill happened in the winter, when fiddler crabs were in underground burrows. However, the oil penetrated the mud and forced hundreds and thousands of fiddler crabs to the surface, where they died from cold stress, covered with oil. Their death was not solely due to cold, however, because oiled crabs brought to the laboratory and washed subsequently died. Death was also not due to forced emergence from their winter burrows, because I dug up some crabs from a pristine marsh at the same time, and they lived for months in the laboratory until I finally released them. The oil continued to seep into the mud for months, and fiddler crabs emerged prematurely for several weeks. They all died on the surface.

The oiled crabs I brought back to the laboratory were unable to dig normal burrows, and many never even started. In contrast, the unoiled crabs immediately began to dig burrows, and within a few moments were below the mud in their individual cages. The unoiled crabs also emerged periodically to feed on the surface, stuffing the food rapidly into their mouths, while the oiled crabs never fed.

Some crabs in the oiled creeks of the Arthur Kill, however, survived to emerge at the normal time when the weather warmed up. They were behaviorally impaired, however, and were more aggressive and less attentive to burrow construction and feeding than were crabs from unoiled creeks. There were far fewer burrows per crab in the oiled creeks, making it harder for them to find a nearby burrow when night herons and other predators approached. Population numbers were lower in oiled creeks in the years following the spill, and are still lower in the creek immediately across from the spill.

The physical cleaning of beaches by high-powered water spray is often problematic for intertidal organisms. Oil removal does not necessarily speed recovery, and, on the contrary, may prolong recovery if the cleanup removes living organisms and alters the habitat. The exception, of course, is in the case of beaches that are so completely oiled that it would take many years for the oil to be washed away by natural processes. This may have been true for many of the heavily oiled beaches after the *Exxon Valdez.*

Recovery of organisms within the intertidal zone ranges from one to ten years, and rocky shores recover more quickly than sand or salt marsh shores. Most organisms living in rocky intertidal zones show some recovery within about two years, but recovery can be much longer with heavily oiled shores, or where drastic cleaning injures the organisms. This is particularly true if there are deposits of asphalt or if toxic oil is trapped in anaerobic sediments. Asphalt can be three to five inches thick in the intertidal zone, and often develops a weathered crust, with viscous oil beneath. Gradually these asphalt pavements may be weathered, but they remain longer higher up on the intertidal rocks.

Recovery of invertebrates living in the intertidal zone is dependent on the natural removal and weathering of the oil over periods of time that range from one to ten years, or more. The time scale is influenced by the energy level along the shore, the size of the sand or gravel, the type of oil and its concentration, and the biological characteristics of the shore. Recovery for many invertebrates may also depend on the size of the oiled area, and the natural rate of recolonization. If organisms have to travel a great distance to resettle beaches and rocky shores, it may take decades to do so.

Subtidal Organisms

There is much less information about the effect of oil on invertebrates that live in the subtidal zone, largely because people are far less concerned about them and because they are far less visible and more difficult to study. Although the water protects subtidal invertebrates from the direct physical impact of the oil, the oil can be carried to the seafloor by transport on fine sand particles that sink, by the mixing of water-soluble fractions of oil, and by direct exposure from natural seeps and human-made leaks from underground storage facilities, wells, and pipelines. The impact of a surface oil spill, however, normally is delayed and reduced in the subtidal zone. It takes a while for the oil to filter down through the water.

As with intertidal organisms, there is enormous variability in the effect of oil on subtidal invertebrates. The impact depends upon the nature of the spill, the nature of the environment, and the species present. The extent and severity of the oil spill, as well as the speed of weathering, also affects these organisms. Certain bivalves are relatively insensitive to oil, while others such as the amphipods are particularly vulnerable.

Amphipods, small, shrimplike creatures with lots of legs and that swim on their sides (Fig. 9.2), are particularly vulnerable to oil spills. The *Amoco Cadiz* oil spill off the coast of France and the *Florida* spill off Buzzards Bay, Massachusetts, killed large populations of several species of amphipods. In the *Florida* spill many other crustaceans also died. In the *Tsesis* spill in the Baltic Sea in 1977, amphipods were also killed in large numbers, and some species almost completely disappeared. Recovery of amphipod populations can be slow following an oil spill, particularly if the spill covers a large area. Full recovery of amphipod populations after the *Amoco Cadiz* was very slow because of their nearly complete mortality in the area of the spill. It took nearly ten years for the amphipods to recover after the *Amoco Cadiz*.

Like the intertidal fiddler crabs, some subtidal organisms that are not directly killed by the oil spill die secondarily when they are forced from their burrows by the oil. Once they leave their burrows, they may be thrown against rocky shores by the force of waves, where they die from exposure. After the *Amoco Cadiz* many subtidal urchins and razor clams were killed during the first few weeks when they washed up on beaches.

Subtidal invertebrates were studied extensively after the *Florida* spill. The abundance and diversity of the subtidal organisms decreased immediately after the spill. The species with diverse diets, such as the polychaete worm *Capitella*, survived the best and increased in relative abundance for nearly a year following the spill. These opportunistic species have the ability to increase rapidly because they have large initial populations and early matur-

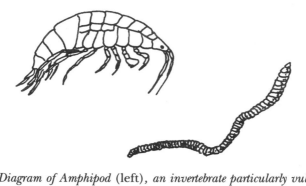

Figure 9.2. Diagram of Amphipod (left), *an invertebrate particularly vulnerable to oil spills, and a polycheate worm* (Capiltella) (right) *that increases in numbers following spills.*

ation. As the other the other native species began to reestablish themselves, the *Capitella* worms decreased in number. Five years after the spill, however, the normal balance of subtidal invertebrates was not yet restored.

A similar increase in the number of opportunistic polychaete worms occurred after the *Amoco Cadiz* accident. The species of polychaete worm that flourished depended upon the concentration of oil in the water. The increase in these worms was a direct result of an increase in the number of dead bodies, which decayed and made organic nutrients available. Polychaete worms, however, do not all respond the same way. Experiments conducted with sandworms showed that oiled worms emerge from burrows more often than those from unoiled sand, and are exposed to predators on the surface. Oiled worms placed on the surface of sand have impaired burrowing ability, and require longer to construct burrows. Although they recover after twelve hours, their aberrant behavior exposes them to increased predation rates while they are on the surface. Their decreased burrowing ability is similar to what I observed for fiddler crabs following the Arthur Kill spill.

Other subtidal organisms are also affected by oil spills. Shrimp populations in the Arthur Kill declined in the year following the spill and began to increase the second year after the spill. American oysters exposed to crude oil experimentally eat less food, use less of the food, and lose weight compared with controls; and with high exposure they die. With prolonged chronic exposure most also die. Clams also show severe dysfunctions with chronic exposure to oil, including decreased burrowing rate, increased respiration rate, and decreased growth rate, culminating in death. Over time, such effects lead to lower populations in the wild.

Lobsters and subtidal crabs are particularly vulnerable to oil when they are molting because the oil can penetrate their bodies rapidly. Abalone can

Figure 9.3. Female horseshoe crabs coming to lay eggs at tide line in Delaware Bay. Along with thousands of other shorebirds, laughing gulls come in droves to feed on the eggs.

suffer lowered reproductive success during oil spills because they rely on particular chemical cues from the environment to spawn, cues that are jammed by oil.

Several species in the subtidal zone are vulnerable because they move around, and may come into the intertidal zone to spawn. For example, horseshoe crabs normally remain on the bottom muds just off the Atlantic shores, but they come into the bays and estuaries in March to breed and thus are intertidal for a brief period. In late May and early June the females and males come up to the shore to spawn, and the females lay eggs at the tide line (Fig. 9.3). The horseshoe crabs can be covered with oil at this time, and their eggs will die if oil sinks down into the sand and covers them. Horseshoe crab larvae can die if covered with oil, and they are especially vulnerable to oil until they move out into subtidal waters at several months of age.

Following the *Exxon Valdez* several shellfish were severely affected. The spill occurred just prior to a critical time: The eggs that female shrimp and crabs had been carrying all winter were hatching and the young were being released into the plankton community. These young float about just below the water surface, where they can be covered with oil. Older crabs were molting, making them vulnerable because their soft bodies were completely exposed to oiled water. Oil-contaminated sediments were found as deep as 330 feet in Prince William Sound in 1989 and 1990, and over time, the oil moved deeper. Spot shrimp were less common in oiled compared with un-oiled areas, though prespill patterns of harvest make these data hard to interpret. King crabs, Dungeness crabs, and others were studied initially, but so few crabs were found that the studies were discontinued.

In some heavily oiled fiords of Prince William Sound there was almost complete devastation of the benthic community in 1989 and 1990, although a tremendous repopulation occurred in 1991. In the year following the oil spill, almost one third of the invertebrates declined at oiled compared to control sites. Invertebrate populations associated with eelgrass beds especially showed serious population declines in 1989, 1990, and 1991. There were decreases in invertebrate diversity and abundance in oiled sites when compared with control sites. The number of clams, crabs, sea stars, and amphipods all decreased.

Overall, subtidal organisms can be affected by oil, particularly species such as amphipods, which may take ten years or more to return to prespill population levels and species diversity. Most species suffer declines in their numbers, and they may take several years to recover. A few species are relatively unaffected, and may increase in numbers because of decreased competition with other species. It is apparent that once the physical and direct toxic effects of oil begin to decline, invertebrates can recover and some may even use the petroleum hydrocarbons as an energy source.

The declines in abundance and species diversity of a wide range of invertebrates in both the intertidal and subtidal environments has serious implications for marine communities as a whole, because these organisms form the basis for many complex food webs. For example, benthic amphipods are important prey for a variety of fishes and sea birds. Crabs feed on mussels and other invertebrates, and in turn serve as prey for fish, otters, and birds. The links are endless, and vary according to where the oil spill occurs, but they are critical to the fish, birds, and marine mammals that live and forage in coastal and oceanic waters.

Coral Reefs

Coral reef animals are a special case of subtidal organisms. Corals are colonies of tiny animals with tentacles that build a framework of calcium or other material for protection. Their tentacles gather microscopic plankton for food. Fortunately, the effect of oil pollution on corals has been relatively low because most of the oil transport occurs in temperate waters, far from tropical reefs. There are exceptions, for example, in the Caribbean, the Middle East, and in Asia. As more offshore oil reserves are developed in

Indonesia and other tropical countries, oil spill accidents near coral reefs will surely happen.

There are two regions where intensive oil-drilling and transport activity is currently being done near sensitive coral reefs: the Arabian Gulf and the Greater Caribbean region. The Gulf is one of the busiest oil transport arteries in the world—half of the world's oil passes through this region—and its reefs are exceptional and deserve protection. The Greater Caribbean area also has many oil refineries, tanker terminals, and oil fields scattered about, as well as active reefs. Coral reefs in both regions are exposed to low-level oil pollution, with negative impacts on coral growth. Coral reefs in both regions could be greatly harmed by a massive oil spill, particularly if dispersants are used. These would put more oil in the water column, where it could harm coral.

Oil can cause mortality, reduce growth, and reduce reproduction for individual organisms of coral reefs. Individual corals can also suffer tissue death, impaired feeding, changes in the rate of adding calcium to their bodies, and an inability of larvae to settle appropriately. These problems will then affect community structure on the reef, as some species of coral will do well while others will suffer population declines. Whole areas of coral may die, and the reef may whiten and then disintegrate, leaving the other fish and animals it shelters without habitat.

The 1986 wreck of the *Witwater* near the Smithsonian Tropical Research Institute in Panama spilled over a million gallons of oil. The oil quickly filtered down through the water to the algae and seagrass beds that covered the coral reefs. Platforms of fringing reefs form extensive intertidal flats in the region, and the algae, seagrass, and sea urchins suffered extensive mortality; dead leaves, stems, and skeletons littered the reefs. This reduced the sunlight that filtered to the corals, and the algae that lived within the corals died. Abundance of most common coral reef genera decreased by 50 to 96 percent, and total coral cover decreased by 76 percent at depths of about three yards. At depths of nine to twelve yards, the decrease in live coral cover was 45 percent. Most of the coral still alive at depths less than three yards showed signs of stress, including bleaching or swelling of tissues, and globules of oil were present in their tissues. In some cases, bleached or dead areas were surrounded by a black halo characteristic of bacterial infection. Where there was more oil, there were more lesions on the massive corals.

Fish

Fish can be exposed to oil throughout their life cycle, from the egg, to larva, to adult; and the damage from oiling depends upon the life stage. There is general agreement among fishery managers that oil spills are damaging to finfish by affecting the eggs and larvae, as well as by direct mortality of all life stages, including adults. However, there is little information on the effects of oil on fish, largely because good population information on fish is usually not available before a spill, information on age structure and sex ratios is unavailable, and information on size distribution is impossible to find. What we do know about the effects of oil on fish comes from experimental studies in the laboratory, as well as from a few observations following oil spills.

Experimental studies in the laboratory show that oil causes a number of pathological conditions, including fin erosion, skin sores, liver damage, and inflammation of the olfactory tissue. In experimentally oiled ponds, a few mullet developed caudal fin erosion within twelve days of exposure, but a day later nearly all fish had it. By thirty-four days there was some regeneration of the fins, which continued for several week until near-complete recovery. Fin damage, which occurs in the wild as well as in the laboratory, usually affects the tail fin of species such as mullet, or the posterior fin in bottom-dwelling flatfish. Fin erosion was evident in dab, sole, and plaice after the wreck of the *Amoco Cadiz*, but gradually most recovered. English sole and Atlantic croaker develop liver sores when exposed to oil for many weeks or months. Olfactory membranes of Atlantic silversides and sand soles also degenerate when exposed experimentally to oil.

Although laboratory studies are useful in identifying the types of problems that oil causes, it is only by following fish living in the oceans that we can determine the significance of oil spills to their populations. When there is an oil spill, fish often move out of the area unless they are too impaired to swim. However, fish near the spill can be killed in the hundreds or thousands. After the *Amoco Cadiz* several tons of fish died, although many moved away from the oil slick; scientists found a number of sublethal pathologies in mullet and flatfish. These fish had reduced growth, produced fewer eggs, and had lower recruitment of adults into the population for at least three years. Although some eggs hatched the year of the spill, none survived; and numbers were greatly reduced in the first-year age class in the following year as well.

The Arthur Kill oil spill is unique in that much baseline information on fish populations from before the spill was available. John Brzorad and I had been following prey fish as part of a study on food resources available for herons and egrets nesting nearby. We found that the oil had two primary effects on the mummichogs, the forage fish used by herons and egrets. The oldest and largest mummichogs were more abundant before the oil spill than in either of the two years following the spill. This change is a community response: The oil caused the death of the larger mummichogs, which decreased the predation rate on the smaller, young-of-the-year fish, which then could grow faster. Smaller fish were more numerous (Figs. 9.4 and

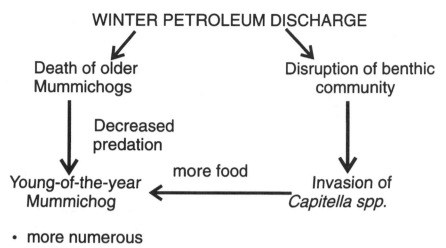

Figure 9.4. *Community effects of oil in the Arthur Kill. Oil kills the older mummichogs, allowing more young-of-the-year to survive.*

9.5). At the same time, there was an invasion of polychaetes, which provided additional food for the young mummichogs, and even more survived than usual.

Fish eggs, however, are particularly vulnerable to oil because they are immobile. After the *Argo Merchant* oil spill 20 percent of cod and 46 percent of pollack eggs were dead; following the *Torrey Canyon* 90 percent of the pilchard eggs were killed nearby, compared with 50 percent farther from the spill. Similar death rates of eggs of several fishes also followed the *Exxon Valdez* spill. Yet the eggs or larvae of other fish appear to suffer no adverse effects from oil. When eggs exposed to oil hatch, more abnormalities are present in embryos and larvae. Oiled eggs produce young with malformed jaws, problems with the vertebral column, reduced heart rate, loss of coordination and equilibrium, and degeneration of nerve cells.

Figuring out the importance of loss or damage to fish eggs and larvae is difficult because their normal mortality is colossal. Only a minute proportion of larval fish survive to adulthood under the best of circumstances. Usually with one oil spill, only one age class of fish is damaged or eliminated, and this would not be sufficient to cause a noticeable difference in adult population levels or commercial catches. However, the danger seems to me to lie in repeated spills or low-level chronic exposure to oil, which may injure or kill several age classes. This could affects population levels over the long run.

The *Exxon Valdez* spill provided an opportunity to follow populations of

Figure 9.5. Simple wooden box used to separate different size-classes of fish. Note absence of large fish from samples in the Arthur Kill following an oil spill.

fish from egg to adult. After this spill, biologists compared the eggs of pink salmon from oiled and unoiled streams. They found that eggs incubated in oiled streams had mortalities 67 percent greater than those in unoiled streams in 1989, 51 percent greater in 1990, and 96 percent greater in 1991. In 1989 and 1990 the increased mortality was confined to oil-contaminated intertidal areas. However, in 1991 the mortality also occurred upstream, where there was no oil contamination in 1989, indicating that genetic damage may have been responsible, since the females that spawned in 1991 had hatched in oiled streams in 1989. If there is genetic damage, several generations of pink salmon may experience low hatching rates.

Many juvenile pink salmon migrated through and grew in oil-contaminated areas. Young fish sampled in these areas had oil in their tissues, presumably from swallowing oil directly. The oil did not cause massive mortality, but the growth rate was slowed by 25 percent. Since growth rate correlates with survival, the decrease in size led directly to higher death rates of juveniles.

In 1990 and 1991 there were record harvests of pink salmon in Prince William Sound, higher than the previous ten-year average. At first, this suggested that there was no long-term population effect on pink salmon. However, the waters of the Alaskan Gulf were unusually warm in these years, and food was abundant, accounting for high survival rates. But more important, 85 percent of the harvest was from fry—baby fish—produced in hatcheries, where they were not exposed to the oil. The wild pink salmon were not in record levels. This is surprising and indicates that there may have been an effect on wild salmon since if they were not affected they should have prospered as well as the hatchery salmon. The classical argument goes that wild fish have higher survival rates than hatchery-raised fish, yet following the oil spill, the hatchery fish survived better. In 1992 the total run of pink salmon was extremely poor, as both food abundance and ocean temperatures were low during the 1991 rearing season. Both wild and hatchery fish survival was below anticipated levels, but the effect was greater for wild fish. Again, wild fish usually do better under stressful conditions, but they did not do so in 1992.

Two other salmonids in Prince William Sound are Dolly Varden and cutthroat trout. There was little prespill information on these species and only a few streams were sampled in postspill studies. However, survival and growth of both species were lower for fish from oiled compared with unoiled streams. Dolly Varden had a 37 percent lower survival of adults in oiled streams, and cutthroat trout had a 29 percent lower survival in oiled streams compared with adult survival in unoiled streams. Growth rates were similarly affected, with a 23 percent reduction for Dolly Varden, and nearly a 40 percent reduction for cutthroat trout. These growth-rate deficits continued in the following year. This is remarkable since these species were not in the sound until June, when levels of oil in the water column had declined to sublethal levels. Presumably they obtained their exposure from eating contaminated prey.

Another fish of commercial interest in Prince William Sound is the Pacific herring, and unfortunately the oil spill coincided with the spring herring run. Immense numbers, several thousand tons, of Pacific herring arrive in the spring to spawn eggs on intertidal and subtidal seaweeds. Seabirds and shorebirds feed on the eggs, and sea lions and humpback whales feed on the herring. Over 40 percent of the areas used by herring to spawn and deposit eggs, and over 90 percent of the areas needed for summer growth, were oiled. Adult herring traversed oil sheens and mousse to reach their spawning grounds. The young that did hatch had to move through oil or remain in oiled areas all summer.

For Pacific herring, egg and larval mortality and physical deformities were much greater in oiled compared with unoiled areas in both 1989 and 1990. The spawning biomass of herring in Prince William Sound has decreased every year since 1989, except in 1992. The estimated peak spawning biomass of Pacific herring in 1992 was at a record level, but only a year later, in 1993, the adult spawning population collapsed. Commercial fishing was curtailed, then closed entirely in 1994 through spring 1996. A virus and a fungus are likely agents of the collapse in 1993. Many of the adults returning in that year would have come from eggs laid in 1989, and the epidemic may be yet another example of oil-related stress.

I think that the data from Prince William Sound indicate clearly that there may be more severe damage to fish at all stages than we previously thought. These problems were evident only after detailed, long-term studies of fish in one area. Fish stocks all over the world are suffering severe population declines, so much so that fisheries have collapsed in many places. In others, stringent limitations on fishing takes are all that stand between viable populations and near extinction. It may be that oil pollution adds just one more stress to an already overstressed population.

Chapter Ten
Effects on Birds
● ● ●

Birds have always served as beacons of well-being for humans. In the early days of exploration, mariners on the high seas looked for albatrosses as an indication of trade winds, and for gulls and terns as harbingers of land. They searched for flocks of diving birds, for below the birds would be dense schools of tuna, bluefish, and other fish they could catch for their long journeys across the wide oceans. When humans began to dig deep into the earth for coal and other minerals, and precious metals, they took canaries below to warn them of foul or poisonous odors too faint for them to smell. Odors that could kill. They used canaries as an early-warning sign of toxic gases, and if the canary ceased to sing or fell over dead, they hurried from the mine. Since birds have so many air sacs, they absorb any airborne toxin quicker than mammals.

In our own time birds have served as an early warning for pesticides and herbicides (Fig. 10.1). As these chemicals built up to dangerous levels in the environment, birds suffered developmental and anatomical problems, and eventually their populations began to decline. In the 1960s the world was appalled to realize that populations of raptors and fish-eating birds had produced almost no young for a number a years—victims of DDT. When birds had high levels of DDT in their bodies, they laid eggs with thin shells, and when they incubated them, the eggs broke.

Today, they have warned us again, this time about endocrine disruptors. Over fifteen years ago, researchers noticed that nests of some gulls had six eggs instead of the usual three. After careful investigation, it was discovered that these nests contained two female parents instead of a male and a female. High levels of some chemicals such as DDT and PCBs had caused the feminization of males, and they were no longer interested in mating. In response, the females paired with each other, and copulated with

Figure 10.1. Gulls, such as this herring gull, serve as an early warning of environmental contamination.

neighboring males. Each female laid three eggs, in the same nest. Some of these eggs hatched and they raised young, although the percentage that fledged was less than for heterosexual pairs. This led to many other studies, and to the realization that other animals such as alligators can also suffer feminization when they are exposed to high levels of certain chemicals. Only now are we beginning to investigate the possible effect of endocrine disruptors on rates of breast and testicular cancer, and lowered sperm counts in humans.

Birds are used as indicators of environmental degradation because they are very sensitive to chemical and physical hazards. This makes them ideal indicators, but only if we are vigilant for early signs of defects. Because birds are so fascinating to people, as well as being useful to scientists and as ecological risk assessors, there is more information about birds than most other animals that encounter oil spills. It is also hard to ignore thousands of dead and dying birds as they lay oiled on beaches. Public empathy for birds and mammals is simply greater than for fish and invertebrates—except for economic interests.

In this chapter I describe the birds that are vulnerable to oil spills and examine the effect of oil on birds. Unlike most other groups of animals, there are accurate body counts of dead birds, and new techniques are making it possible to estimate the actual mortality from oil spills.

Birds at Risk

Seabirds are more at risk from oil spills than are most other birds. Seabirds are those species that spend a great deal of time in marine environments and have an active salt gland on the top of the skull near the base of the bill that allows them to drink salt water and then secrete the salt. Penguins, albatrosses, shearwaters, petrels, tropicbirds, frigatebirds, gannets and boobies, some cormorants, phalaropes, skuas, gulls, terns, auks, puffins, and murres are all seabirds. These birds are most at risk because they spend most of their time in coastal or oceanic waters where they can encounter oil.

The majority of seabirds nest in large colonies of hundreds to thousands of pairs. Many nest near the coasts on small offshore islands, while others nest on oceanic islands thousands of miles from the mainland. Some spend many years at sea before coming to land to breed. For example, sooty terns do not have waterproof feathers and must remain on the wing from the time they leave their natal colony at a few weeks of age until they return to breed as adults at seven or eight years of age. Most seabirds, however, water-proof their feathers by preening oil onto them from the oil gland located at the base of the tail. They can then land on the water without becoming waterlogged.

Other birds at risk from oil are grebes, loons, shorebirds, herons, egrets, and ibises, which either nest near coasts or migrate there during the winter. Some shorebirds nest along the shore, although the majority nest in tundra regions of North America, Europe, and Asia. Those that nest along the shore are vulnerable all year, and those that migrate and winter there can be exposed to oil for over half of the year. Shorebirds may gather in the hundreds, thousands, or even millions in some spectacular stopover and overwintering sites. Landbirds such as crows, marsh hawks, and a variety of songbirds, called passerines, may also be exposed to oil when they come to drink, but generally they are little affected by oil spills.

Birds are harmed by being covered with oil, by ingesting it, and by bringing it back to oil their eggs or offspring. External oiling can coat their feathers, bill, feet and eyes. When feathers are coated with oil, a bird's ability to maintain its body temperature is reduced because the insulating layer of air between the skin and feathers is destroyed. Furthermore, oil can clog the feathers, making it impossible for the bird to fly or swim. When birds try to remove the oil by preening they ingest it or further clog their bill and feathers. Oil on eyes can be an irritant, or when severe, can cause blindness. Birds can ingest oil directly from the water, from their food, or from preening their feathers. Some estimates, based on studying oiled birds in captivity, suggest that birds ingest 50 percent of the oil on their feathers within a week of exposure. Oil exposure from food can result either from the food being covered with oil or from prey items that have themselves ingested and accumulated oil.

Species Differences in Vulnerability

Different seabirds are affected by oil in different ways, largely because of differences in breeding schedules, foraging methods, and geographical ranges. Species that nest on tropical, oceanic islands, such as many petrels, albatrosses, and sooty terns, have relatively low exposure to oil spills because their nesting islands are far from any shipping lanes, and the oil dissipates before it reaches these shores. Although they can be exposed while foraging, most of these species fly long distances to find food, and can simply fly over an oil slick. Species that nest in arctic and antarctic regions have also been relatively free from oil pollution because there has been little oil exploration or development there. This is, of course, changing with arctic exploration in North America and Russia, but birds there have been little impacted so far.

The species that are most at risk are those that nest in regions of heavy oil exploration and drilling, and along transport routes. These include the North Sea; arctic Alaska, Canada and Russia; and the coastal import and export regions of North America, Europe, the Middle East, Japan, and other parts of Asia. Most of the major accidents have happened from the coast of France to the North Sea and in the Middle East, although smaller spills and chronic spills happen everywhere there are activities related to oil (refer back to Fig. 2.8).

Species that feed in coastal bays and estuaries and on the continental shelf are also at high risk because it is here that supertanker collisions, groundings, and other accidents occur. Any birds that regularly nest or forage along coasts are at risk. Few major oil spills happen in the open ocean because there is nowhere to ground and there is enough space to avoid collisions.

Some methods of foraging are more likely than others to expose seabirds to oil. Seabirds forage by a number of methods: flying above the water, then diving to the surface to snatch food from the surface; sitting on the water and grabbing food from the surface or just below the surface; or plunging into the water and diving below to catch prey. Some birds actually use their wings to "fly" under the water, diving tens or hundreds of feet. Coastal species, such as herons and egrets, normally obtain their food by standing on the mudflat or in shallow water and stabbing their prey. Other coastal

Figure 10.2. Diagrammatic representation of food chain. Lower levels on left, higher trophic levels on right.

species, such as shorebirds, run in and out with the tide, picking up invertebrates from the surf or wet sand.

Even with these differences in foraging method, all birds are exposed to oil on the surface of the water. Species that land on the surface or plunge through it can easily and quickly oil their entire bodies. This includes terns, gannets, and boobies, which dive into the water from great heights; puffins, auks, murres, cormorants, and others which sit on the surface and dive to great depths for food; and gulls and phalaropes, which sit on the surface to pick up items. Species that fly above the water and snatch prey from the surface obtain less oil because they never immerse their body in the water; this includes species such as frigatebirds and tropicbirds.

Finally, species that eat larger fish accumulate higher levels of oil through bioaccumulation. Bioaccumulation means that with each link in the food chain there is a magnification of the level of any contaminant in the organisms (Fig. 10.2). Levels of any contaminant, such as oil, are generally low in vegetation and in animals that eat vegetation, intermediate in animals that eat herbivores, high in animals that eat carnivores, and highest in those that eat large carnivores. That is, levels of any contaminant for marine animals are usually highest in birds and mammals that eat large predatory fish.

Death Tolls for Oil Spills

Birds have been dying in pools of oil since the turn of the century, when we began to transport oil around the globe, making accidents and chronic exposure commonplace. Before 1910 birds were reported dying from oil from shipwrecks near Washington, California, Rhode Island, Scotland, and the Scilly Islands off Britain. The pattern continued in the 1920s: There were reports of up to 900 wildfowl dying in one spill near Narragansett Bay, Massachusetts, in 1921; several thousand were killed near Puget Sound in Washington in 1924; and several thousand scoters were killed near Massachusetts in 1928 and again off the English coast in 1929. Similarly, in the early 1930s thousands of dead oiled birds were reported from around the English, Scottish, and American coasts.

It was not until the mid-1930s, however, that actual body counts of species were made. In 1936, 1,400 birds washed ashore along the Kent coast of England; and in March 1937 the *Frank Buck* collided with another boat off the California coast and 6,600 guillemots washed ashore, coated with oil, along with many western grebes and white-winged scoters. With the war effort, there were a number of spills along the east coast of North America, and 5,000 ducks were killed in one incident alone in 1942. In 1948, about 10,000 ducks died in the winter from oil in the Detroit River. These represent some of the first detailed counts of mortality.

With the increase in tanker size that occurred in the early 1950s, seabird destruction escalated. Tankers carried more oil, so accidents resulted in larger quantities of spilled oil, and higher seabird mortality. Partially this was due to a complacency on the part of the world community, and partly to a lack of techniques available to contain and remove oil by burning, dispersing, or skimming.

When the *Fort Mercer* and *Pendleton* wrecked off Chatham, Massachusetts, in a gale storm in February 1952, nearly 150,000 eiders perished, although this number is an estimate, not a body count. Over 30,000 ducks, mainly long-tailed ducks, were killed off Gotland in the Baltic in March 1952. Gotland was a particularly bad place for spills: the next year, nearly 10,000 ducks were killed there again by an oil spill, two years later another 10,000 died in a black mousse, and in 1957 yet another spill there resulted in 40,000 dead ducks. In 1955 a very heavy and thick slick from the wreck of

Figure 10.3. Oiled common murre off the coast of California in the late 1960s. (Photo by M. Gochfeld)

the *Gerd Maersk* killed an estimated 275,000 ducks, mostly common scoters, in the mouth of the Elbe River in Germany.

Massive dieoffs because of oil spills continued well into the 1960s before the world became alarmed at the death and destruction of birds and marine mammals. Despite the 1954 International Convention to prevent oil pollution of the seas, pollution continued to increase. In the 1950s and 1960s it was not uncommon to have 5,000 to 15,000 birds, mainly wintering waterfowl, die from oil spills in ports in Europe and the United States. At this time, oil was mainly being transported between the United States and Europe; Middle Eastern and Asian reserves were not highly developed, and Russia used the oil it produced. The first large spill reported for Japan occurred in 1965, when large numbers of kittiwakes and streaked shearwaters were killed by oil spills, but as yet, numbers were uncounted. The reports of such kills from Japan reflects that country's economic development and dependence on oil, as well as a growing environmental awareness.

Accidents continued into the 1960s. Hundreds of murres died in a blowout of an offshore well near Santa Barbara, California (Fig. 10.3). From June 1964 until April 1967 there were 19 tanker groundings (seventeen large spillages) and 238 supertanker collisions (with twenty-two large spillages) worldwide. More international meetings were held to discuss and

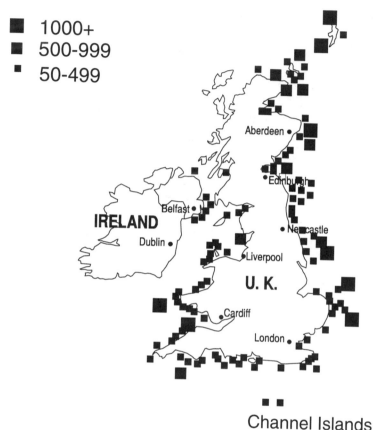

Number of birds affected:

■ 1000+
■ 500-999
■ 50-499

Figure 10.4. Effects of the oil spills on birds around the British Isles, 1971–1983. (Source: Adapted from Stowe and Underwood 1984)

control pollution in the seas. The environmental movement that swept the United States and Europe in the late 1960s extended to oil as well. When the Clean Water Act was passed in the United States, it attached clear responsibilities and costs regarding oil spill pollution.

The number of birds reportedly killed by oil decreased in the late 1960s and early 1970s, so that usual counts were less than 5,000, although 15,000 died in the Wadden Sea in the Netherlands in 1969, and over 9,000 died there in 1972. A report on birds that died from oil spills around the British Isles from 1971 to 1983 listed ninety-nine spills that killed less than 500 birds, nine spills that killed 500 to 999, and only eleven spills that killed over 1,000 birds (Fig. 10.4).

The decrease in mortality of seabirds in the 1970s and 1980s because of oil was due not only to the environmental movement but to the fact that many of the larger tankers were new and in relatively good condition, with communication and radar systems that could prevent some collisions. The 1970s and 1980s also saw increased attempts to count dead and dying wildlife and heightened rehabilitation efforts; but they also saw an increase in overall complacency that we had solved the oil spill problem.

Europeans were startled when 30,000 birds died—mostly guillemots, little auks, and razorbills—following an oil accident in Skagerrak Strait, between Denmark and Sweden, over New Year's in 1981. Americans were shocked when the *Apex Houston* went aground in central California, killing 834 birds outright and leaving 3,364 debilitated oiled birds on the beaches. Most of these died. However, it took the *Exxon Valdez* to wake up the American public and Congress to the dangers of large-scale oil spills: 37,000 dead oiled carcasses were collected along the beaches of Prince William Sound and the Gulf of Alaska. This was impressive for any oil spill, and represented the largest documented avian mortality from an oil spill. The actual death toll from these two accidents will be discussed below.

The Oil Pollution Act of 1990 set aside monies for oil spill cleanup and response, mandated a central control for oil spill response, tightened up the requirements for tanker safety, defined damage assessment, and stipulated claims on lost natural resources, at least within the United States. This made it essential to determine not only the direct mortality of birds during oil spills, but to ascertain the long-term effects on reproductive success and population levels.

In summary, the birds that suffered the highest mortality following oil spills over the last fifty years are auks, murres, guillemots, puffins, mergansers, eiders, scoters, oldsquaws, scaup, goldeneyes, loons, grebes, gannets, pelicans, and petrels. This will not change, as these are the species that live in coastal waters, dive below the surface for food, and spend a great deal of time on the water's surface, floating, resting and feeding. The species affected largely depends on where the oil spill occurs, the type and amount of oil spilled, and the time of the year.

The *Apex Houston* and *Exxon Valdez*: Estimating Actual Mortality

Most of the documentation of bird mortality from oil spills relies on body counts of individuals washed up on beaches. Since oil spills generally occur offshore, the actual mortality is unknown because many birds sink or are eaten by predators and scavengers before they ever reach shore. Factors that affect the relative percentage of oiled and dead birds that reach the

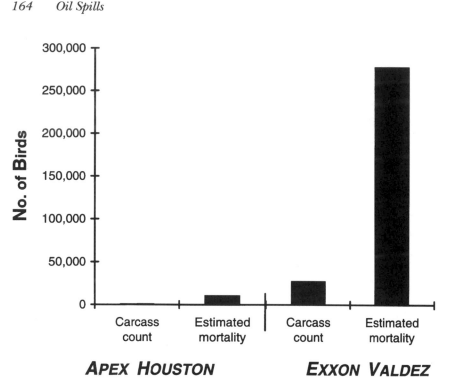

Figure 10.5. Relationship between the number of carcasses picked up along beaches and the estimated mortality following the Apex Houston *and the* Exxon Valdez *spills. (Sources: Adapted from G. W. Page, H. R. Carter, and R. G. Ford, 1990, Numbers of seabirds killed or debilitated in the 1986* Apex Houston *oil spill in central California,* Studies in Avian Biology *14;* Exxon Valdez *Oil Spill Trustee Council, 1995, 1995 status report [Exxon Valdez* Oil Spill Trustee Council, Anchorage, Alaska])

shore include distance of the oil spill from the shore, wind and tidal conditions, and the number of predators and scavengers. The relative persistence of dead birds on shore also affects how many bodies people pick up. It is of some significance to find a better way to estimate the real damage for the purposes of recovering losses due to damages of natural resources. This information is also essential for trustees of natural resources who wish to predict future population levels or make management decisions about which species should be targeted for restoration and what restoration actions may be necessary.

After both the *Apex Houston* and the *Exxon Valdez* elaborate computer models were developed to estimate the number of birds actually killed (Fig. 10.5). For the *Apex Houston,* scientists collected all beached birds and compared the number of live and dead for different species (Fig. 10.6). Using a constant at-sea loss rate of 15 percent per day of the spill, which was based

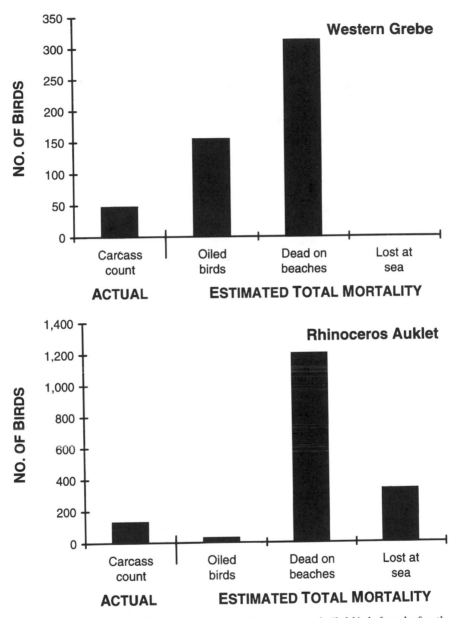

Figure 10.6. Relationship between the number of carcasses and oiled birds found after the Apex Houston, and the estimated number lost at sea. (Source: Adapted from G. W. Page, H. R. Carter, and R. G. Ford, 1990, Numbers of seabirds killed or debilitated in the 1986 Apex Houston oil spill in central California, Studies in Avian Biology 14)

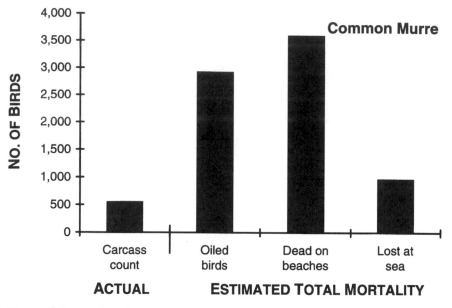

Figure 10.6. (continued)

on one study that released oiled carcasses to see how many reached shore, they considered how many were lost at sea and how long oiled carcasses remained on beaches. Overall, scientists estimated that 10,577 birds died in the spill, although only 834 carcasses and 3,364 live oiled birds were found. They believed that almost half of the birds that died were found. However, this oil spill happened relatively close to shore, and they did not take into account birds that flew or swam long distances before they died from the oil.

The *Exxon Valdez* provided another opportunity to determine the actual number of birds that died following a spill. There were 30,000 oiled carcasses of ninety species collected: 74 percent were murres, 7 percent were other alcids, and 5 percent were sea ducks. Biologists used the number of carcasses (including those that died in rehabilitation centers), information on populations in the spill area, and estimates of the number of birds lost at sea to determine the total number that probably died. They released 100, tagged, oiled, dead birds in Prince William Sound in May to determine the percentage that would be lost before reaching beaches. The birds they set adrift were representative of the carcasses they had stored in freezers: that is, 74 percent were murres, and so on. Using all the available information, they estimated that the total kill from oil pollution was 300,000 to 645,000 birds. Taking into account all available evidence, Piatt's and Ford's best estimates are 250,000.

Some controversy surrounds the use of computer models to generate estimated mortality from oil spills. The models are necessarily based on estimates of the number of birds that sink, are eaten, or never make it to beaches or that drift onto beaches that cannot be surveyed for logistical reasons, and local population estimates before the spill. There is the possibility of error in each of these factors.

Most of the estimates, however, clearly indicate that only 10 to 50 percent of the birds that die ever wash up on beaches. These estimates correlate very well with the studies of carcasses set adrift: 0 to 50 percent of those set adrift are never recovered. This estimate strikes me as fairly conservative, given that the only oil spills that are extensively studied are those that occur near the coast, where a higher percentage of birds could drift ashore. Recovery rates for oil spills that occur farther from land or in arctic regions, where winds and strong currents may carry carcasses far from shore, may be much lower. It also strikes me that with low-level oiling, birds may fly hundreds of miles away before they succumb to illness or death. We should be cautious in our estimate of the number of birds that actually die, and I would submit that these "conservative" estimates (i.e., that most dead birds reach the beach) are actually more tenuous than assumptions that a high proportion of dead birds never make it to the beach.

Sublethal Effects

Information on sublethal effects comes from observations of ill birds following spills, of birds experimentally exposed in the field, and of experimental birds in the laboratory. Birds are ideal for laboratory or experimental studies because many are small enough to be maintained easily, in contrast to sharks, dolphins, seals, walruses, and whales. Furthermore, studies of oiled eggs and young can be conducted either in the laboratory or in the field.

There are a variety of sublethal effects of oil on birds, including matting of feathers, loss of insulation, increased food needs because of thermal stress and decreased absorption, and internal injuries. They also suffer lowered reproductive success when eggs or young are oiled, including decreased hatching success and developmental abnormalities. When young chicks eat oiled foods they grow more slowly and never get quite as large as unoiled chicks. All of these effects can seriously affect bird populations.

When adult birds ingest oil, depending upon the amount, they can suffer acute poisoning or can develop a number of problems, from an inability to absorb food through the lining of the digestive tract to an increase in lesions in several organs. For seabirds, if the nasal salt glands located at the

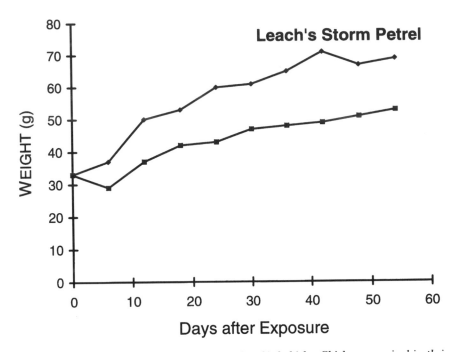

Figure 10.7. Growth rates of oiled and unoiled seabird chicks. Chicks were raised in their own nests by their parents. (Sources: Adapted from D. M. Fry, J. Swenson, L. A. Addiego, C. R. Addiego, C. R. Grau, and A. Kang, 1986, Reduced reproduction of wedge-tailed shearwaters exposed to weathered Santa Barbara crude oil, Archives of Environmental Contamination and Toxicology *15; R. G. Butler, A. Harfenist, F. A. Leighton, and D. B. Peakall, 1988, Impact of sublethal oil and emulsion exposure on the reproductive success of Leach's storm-petrels: Short- and long-term effects,* Journal of Applied Ecology *25).*

base of their bill get clogged, and they may be unable to handle the salt load from marine waters, which can create severe problems because they depend on drinking salt water. Oil causes changes in the amount of hormones secreted, which may lead to lowered clutch size in females. Ingestion of oil can stress birds so that they die months later: Birds already stressed by oil have a higher death rate than birds with no internal oil when very cold weather sets in.

Minute quantities of oil are sufficient to cause mortality in developing eggs. This was known as early as 1950, when oiling of eggs was used as a control measure for herring gulls that were usurping the habitat of native gulls and terns in Maine and Massachusetts. Decreased hatching rate as a result of oiling has been demonstrated in the laboratory for Japanese quail, herring gulls, great black-backed gulls, mallards, and eiders. When only a

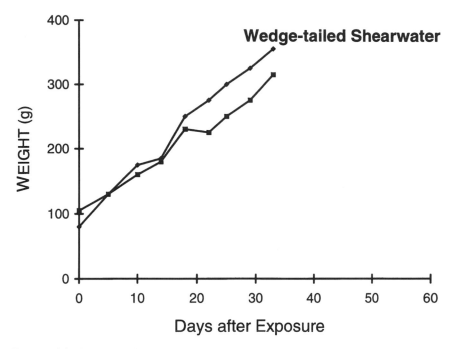

Figure 10.7. (Continued)

tiny amount of oil is added to eggs in the wild that are incubated by parents, the eggs also fail to hatch. These field experiments with the eggs of
black-backed gulls, laughing gulls, Louisiana herons, Leach's storm petrels,
wedge-tailed shearwaters, and sandwich terns clearly demonstrate that if
parents bring back oil on their feathers, hatching success can be severely
affected.

When developing eggs are exposed to small quantities of oil, the hatch-
lings can be born with deformed bills, incomplete ossification of some
bones, reduction in the size of the liver, and smaller overall size. Decreased
growth rate occurs with a number of young seabirds exposed to oil in the
wild, such as herring gulls, Leach's storm petrels, wedge-tailed shearwaters,
and black guillemots (Fig. 10.7). These kinds of effects must be demonstrated in the laboratory because they can be caused by contaminants other
than oil, and it is hard to determine cause in wild populations.

Reproductive losses due to oil on the eggs are indirect effects of oil on
parental feathers. Parents can transfer oil from their breast feathers to their
eggs. Parents, however, also ingest oil, and this can affect their reproductive
success. When chickens and mallards are fed oil they lay fewer eggs, and
when Cassin's auklets are fed oil they delay the onset of egg laying and
experience reduced hatching success. However, the auklet chicks that did

hatch did not suffer lower growth or development. Many young that are fed a diet containing oil grow slower than unoiled chicks, develop flight feathers more slowly or not at all, and have a number of lesions in their kidney, liver, stomach, and other organs. Delayed growth and development as a result of oil ingestion has been shown for herring gulls, black guillemots, fork-tailed storm petrels, and Leach's storm petrels—all species that encounter oil in the wild.

One experiment on herring gulls in the Great Lakes tried to establish what the effect of a real oil slick might be by exposing them to a simulated no. 2 fuel oil slick. Hatching success and chick survival were reduced, but the experimental slick was much thicker than a normal one. "Natural" experiments can thus be used to examine effects on reproductive success. Similarly, when wedge-tailed shearwaters in Hawaii were given oil in capsules or on their plumage, they suffered lower clutch sizes, lower hatching success, and overall reduced breeding success compared with shearwaters that were not exposed to oil. Although the oil was applied artificially to the feathers, it was similar to exposure the shearwaters might encounter in a spill.

One of the more interesting experiments involved fulmars. Crude oil was experimentally released in the Norwegian Sea: The fulmars deliberately avoided settling on the sea surface that was heavily polluted. However, about 5 percent became oiled when they were drawn irresistibly to food thrown from research vessels.

These observations from both the field and the laboratory suggest that seabirds suffer a variety of sublethal effects from exposure to oil. Lower clutch size, lower hatching rate, lower chick survival, and delayed growth rate and fledging times all influence reproductive success and ultimately affect population levels. Even if these effects are insufficient to cause noticeable declines in seabird populations, they are surely influencing evolution because they can alter which parents contribute genes to the next generation.

Chronic Effects

Although it is the spectacular oil spills that grab our attention, the ones in which hundreds and thousands of oiled seabirds and marine mammals die, the effects of low-level chronic exposure to oil can be enormous. Experiments in the laboratory with small amounts of oil suggest that it weakens the birds so that they may live for months or years without problems until there is an environmental stress such as extreme cold weather, and then they die at a faster rate than birds that had no exposure to oil. Carcasses found on beaches often have only minute quantities of oil on the plumage, demonstrating that small quantities may lead to death of a seabird when combined with extreme cold. Very low chronic exposure leads to depressed body weight, and this too renders birds less able to withstand extreme environmental conditions.

Effects on Avian Populations

Although the initial mortality of birds during oil spills is very distressing to us, the more important question ecologically is whether this form of pollution has an effect on population levels either regionally or globally. Although we can clearly demonstrate that thousands of birds die each year from oil spills, the effect on populations has been hard to determine, largely because doing so requires years of study, both before and after an oil spill. Without baseline data on population levels from before a spill it is difficult to prove that populations were affected.

There are many examples during the twentieth century of local seabird colonies that have either been destroyed or severely impacted by oil spills. When an oil spill happens near a colony during the breeding season, all the adults in the colony may die. Common murres nesting on the Farallones off the California coast may have numbered 40,000 at the turn of the century. Their numbers steadily declined as a direct result of repeated oil spills in the first half of this century, but began increasing in the 1970s, peaking at over 100,000 birds in 1982. But two oil spills in the 1980s, the *Puerto Rican* and the *Apex Houston*, caused high mortality. Breeding populations declined to less than 50,000 birds, and some of the small colonies became extinct. Although El Niño events and gill netting accounted for some of the decline, these same factors were present in northern California, yet that region did not experience a population decline during this same period.

Several species of birds suffered high mortality during the *Exxon Valdez* oil spill in 1990. The dead-body count for common murres alone was over 27,000, for marbled murrelets and pigeon guillemots it was over 800 each, and for harlequin ducks it was 400. These translated into mortality estimates of nearly ten times that number for each species. Over 30 dead bald eagles were picked up, but the estimated number killed was 900. Never before had this number of carcasses been picked up after an oil spill, and clearly the deaths had an immense effect on local populations.

Surprisingly, bald eagles recovered rather rapidly, and by 1996 there was no longer a population effect. That is, populations in Prince William Sound are as high now as they were before the spill. Harlequin duck populations, however, have not recovered, and there is concern about poor

Figure 10.8. Young birds, such as these black-crowned night herons, are particularly hard hit after a spill because they can be oiled by their parents and are often fed oiled and contaminated foods.

reproduction. Even today, seven years after the spill, there is low reproduction by these ducks in the oiled, western parts of the sound, though these data are hard to interpret given the poor prespill records on harlequin ducks. The ducks continue to eat mussels and other invertebrates that may still be contaminated. They are particularly vulnerable to effects because they eat whole mussels, including the basal thread that extends into the soil, some dirt, and the mussel shell, exposing them to any oil remaining.

Several seabirds—common murres, marbled murrelets, and pigeon guillemots—suffered population declines after the spill. However, only common murre populations in Prince William Sound were in good condition prior to the spill; the others were already declining for a variety of other reasons. Thus, common murres are a good example of a local population that was severely impacted by an oil spill. Half or more of the population in the sound was killed outright by the oil; and 10 to 20 percent of the population in the entire northern Gulf of Alaska was killed. These estimates do not come only from the dead murres picked up along the shore, but from declines at the breeding colonies.

In the years immediately following the spill, the murres that returned to northern Gulf of Alaska colonies laid eggs a month or more late and

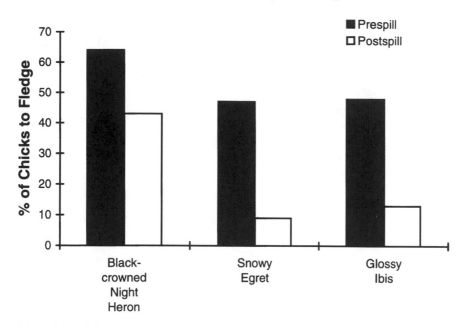

Figure 10.9. Effects of oil on nestlings following the Arthur Kill oil spill. Fewer young of these three species fledged after the spill than before the spill.

suffered lower reproductive success than they had in previous years. The oil spill perhaps affected the age distribution because it was the older, experienced breeders that returned to the colony early that faced the greatest oil pollution. Many of these died, removing the prime breeders from the population. It may take decades for the normal age structure to be restored. It is as if a war removed all the eighteen- to twenty-five-year-old males from the U.S. population; it would take a full generation to restore the population to normal. Fortunately, productivity seemed to have returned to normal by 1993.

The oil spill in the Arthur Kill provided another example of population effects. K. Parsons studied the herons and egrets nesting there for a number of years, and has continued to do so. When the pipeline broke in midwinter, there were no herons and egrets in the area, so none died. However, when they migrated back in March and April, they found oil-covered marshes and mudflats. For most of these species, breeding was delayed in the two years following the spill, although clutch sizes were normal. Perhaps the depleted food base resulted in delayed laying rather than reduced clutch size. The percentage of chicks that fledged, however, was significantly lower for black-crowned night herons, snowy egrets, and glossy ibises in the breeding season following the spill (Figs. 10.8 and 10.9). Snowy egrets were particularly hard hit, and the number of young fledged

Figure 10.10. Snowy egrets were the most affected by the Arthur Kill oil spill, largely because they fed mostly in the intertidal zone, the region most heavily oiled.

dropped from 1.5 per nest before the spill to less than 0.5 after the spill (Fig. 10.10). They suffered lowered reproductive success until 1993, and did not fully recover until 1995. Most chicks died of starvation due to reduced availability of fish. Snowy egrets are more dependent on tidal habitats than are the other egret species, many of which can feed in a variety of habitats. The other species are generalists, are less tied to tidal habitats, and hence recovered more rapidly.

The *Apex Houston*, the *Exxon Valdez*, and the Arthur Kill pipeline accident all indicate that local populations can be severely decreased by oil spills. The population effect can also encompass a larger region, as with the common murres of central California and the Gulf of Alaska. More important than the effect of one oil spill may be the ability of oil to weaken individuals and populations so that they are more vulnerable to other environmental stresses. Should another oil spill of the same magnitude happen within a short period of time, the devastation would be compounded. Populations already in decline, such as marbled murrelets and pigeon guillemots, may be dealt a deathblow by oil, and local populations may never be able to recover.

Recovery: A Measure of Effect

If oil spills have the ability to decrease populations of some species, at least locally, one important question is, How long will it take for populations to recover? Presumably, populations that take longer to recover have been more severely affected than those that recover within a year or two.

Several factors may determine how fast a bird population recovers following an oil spill or any other environmental insult. Populations can be rebuilt only by new reproduction or by immigration from outside the spill area. New reproduction depends on the degree of damage the adults have suffered, and on their normal rate of reproduction. If parents have suffered greatly, then reproduction might be curtailed because the adults will be unable to produce eggs or feed young. However, even if parents are not impaired, they can reproduce only as fast as their normal rate will allow. For example, gulls and terns normally lay three eggs, whereas auks, puffins, guillemots, and other seabirds normally lay only one egg. This means that gulls and terns have the potential to build up their populations sooner than most other seabirds. Immigration depends on the proximity of other source populations that can export adults to the depleted colony. If there are no other colonies within miles, it may take longer to recolonize a colony devastated by an oil spill. Moreover, if the nearby populations have also been affected by an oil spill, there may be few potential immigrants.

Recovery time, often determined with computer models using life history tables, may be a good indication of the relative damage of an oil spill. Recovery times have seldom been determined because the long-term studies at breeding colonies are required to do so have not been undertaken. Following the Arthur Kill, recovery time of the snowy egrets was five years, and these species have larger clutch sizes than most seabirds, allowing for rapid recovery. Furthermore, there were healthy egret colonies nearby in both New York and New Jersey to serve as sources. Recovery times for the birds affected by the *Exxon Valdez* may be much longer. Estimated recovery time for the common murres is 50 to 120 years, for the Harlequin ducks it is 15 to 50 years, and the prognosis for the marbled murrelets and pigeon guillemots is not good because they were in trouble before the spill.

The populations of seabirds discussed above are not limited to the regions where the oil spills occurred. Herons and egrets breed all over the world, and common murres breed all around the arctic in thousands of colonies. However, oil spills can also occur in regions where there are seabirds with very limited ranges. This occurred with the Gulf War and the Socotra cormorant, whose populations are limited to the Gulf region. Fortunately, their colonies were not impacted because the oil did not reach them, and few cormorants were in the oil spill footprint. The jackass penguin is limited to South Africa, and 75 percent of the world's population breeds along the southern coast of that country, in an area where the risk of oil spills is very high. Important shipping lanes pass close to the breeding and feeding areas. The probability of a single large spill having devastating effects on the entire species is increasing every day, with the increase in number and age of supertankers. This is not an isolated case; other seabirds also have limited ranges, and are equally at risk.

In Argentina, where Alexander Wetmore found oiled seabirds in the 1920s, the development of offshore oil is increasing. Several species of seabirds—Olrog's gull and a flightless steamer duck—are certainly vulnerable by virtue of small populations and limited range.

When recovery times are estimated to be in the decades to century range, it seems to me we have demonstrated that oil spills can have a devastating and permanent effect on local breeding populations of seabirds. Should another oil spill happen in the near future, these populations would be further at risk. This suggests that the dead and dying birds found along beaches are not just a temporary phenomenon, but represent a potentially severe population effect.

Chapter Eleven
Effects on Mammals and Sea Turtles

● ● ●

Seals, seal lions, sea otters, whales, and sea turtles are exotic animals that most of us see only occasionally, if we go far out to sea on a boat, stand on a rocky promontory in Maine or Alaska, peer off a high cliff in California, or watch from a sandy beach in Cape Cod, our eyes trained on the horizon. Yet we have a special kinship with them, as we somehow feel their intelligence, playfulness, and caring. Walruses are the most exotic, living as they do in the far north. Their odd appearance appeals to us, and they have played as heroes in books and songs.

Whales and seals figured heavily in survival for many cultures, who either hunted them for food or for lamp oil. Whale and seal hunting was an integral part of Inuit cultures and of the whalers of the 1700s and 1800s. For many centuries, the Inuit of the frozen north ate whale meat, carved whalebone knives and scrapers, and used the giant ribs for support for partially underground houses of mud. Many Inuit and other northern peoples still hunt whales as a central aspect of their lives even though they now do so with motorboats. Today, other seafarers from Russia, Norway, and Japan hunt whale for meat or for the oil, although the world community frowns on commercial whale hunts.

Sea turtles were also hunted for meat, and their shells were used as a form of "plastic" to make jewelry, hairpins, combs, and hairbrushes. These items can still be bought in many Caribbean countries, although sale of tortoiseshell items is illegal worldwide. Turtle eggs were an important food source for many coastal cultures. Today, most of the world's seven species of sea turtles are endangered, largely because of overhunting of adults, excessive poaching, predation of eggs on nesting beaches, and being incidentally caught in nets used for fishing and shrimping. Being air breathers, sea turtles die from lack of oxygen when they get caught in nets that are not hauled out for several hours.

In this chapter I discuss the reasons why marine mammals and sea turtles are vulnerable to oil spills, describe laboratory experiments on the effects of oil on them, and examine how marine mammals and sea turtles have been affected by specific spills. Although terrestrial mammals that come to oiled shores to drink or find food can be oiled, this is apt to be incidental, the numbers are usually small, and the degree of oiling is usually low. Few land mammals have perished in most spills, although freshwater animals such as river otters and muskrats can be affected, and they are discussed here briefly.

Freshwater Mammals at Risk

A number of primarily freshwater aquatic mammals can be harmed by oil pollution. And, of course, oil spills do happen in rivers, although these spills are usually relatively small, since large supertankers cannot pass through most rivers, and in most cases would not be allowed to do so even if they could. After the Arthur Kill oil spill, a number of muskrats and raccoons were found heavily oiled and dead. Both of these species, however, are extremely common within the metropolitan and suburban New York City area, and there was no cause for concern about population effects.

There is concern, however, about the fate of the river otters following the *Exxon Valdez* spill. River otters are misnamed—they do not feed exclusively in rivers, but in the shallow nearshore marine waters. They are not considered marine mammals, however, because they spend time on land, often in underground dens, and are not adapted for extensive underwater existence. After the spill, their environment was partially despoiled, since some of the beaches and rocky shores were covered with oil. River otters came across oil when they surfaced while feeding or swimming through the water, and they ate contaminated food.

Only twelve river otter carcasses were found, but most researchers felt that many more died in their underground dens, sick and ill, and covered in oil. By comparing the numbers of river otters in oiled and unoiled places, officials determined that there were fewer otters after the spill, and those that survived ate less food and were underweight. In oiled areas the otters stopped using the sites with shallow slopes leading to the water— usually preferred for feeding—and they avoided these sites for at least three years following the spill. They ate fifty fewer species of food items after the oil spill, which may partially account for their poor body condition. The lack of diversity in food items meant that the otters in oiled areas had to increase the area they used for foraging, called their home range. It takes more time and energy to search over a large home range for food than a normal, smaller home range. Otters caught in the oiled areas had elevated levels of hydrocarbons in their blood and other tissues at least until 1992, and even today may be suffering from immune deficiency diseases. The status of river otters in Prince William Sound is unknown.

Marine Mammals and Sea Turtles at Risk

Marine mammals and sea turtles are particularly vulnerable to oil spills because they spend most of their lives at sea and must come to the surface to breathe air. Unlike fish, which can stay well beneath the water while they move away from oil, marine mammals come up for air every few minutes. When they break the surface their whole bodies can become oiled, time and time again. Seals and sea lions haul out on rocks to rest, and this exposes them to oil on the water's surface, as well as on the rocks. Susceptibility to oil, however, varies according to the anatomy, physiology, and habitats of the animal.

Although when we think of marine mammals we think of seals, walruses sea lions, sea otters, and whales, the group also includes manatees and dugongs, which inhabit more tropical waters, and polar bears, which live in the tundra. The danger that these latter mammals will be exposed to oil is increasing with more oil drilling in subarctic and tundra regions and in offshore tropical waters.

Species Differences in Vulnerability

The different species of marine mammals and sea turtles can be affected differently because of their lifestyles and anatomy. The primary exposure of marine mammals is through direct physical contact with the oil. Oil can irritate the eyes, as well as coating the fur. Many marine mammals use their blubber for insulation from the cold, but some, such as fur seals and young animals, depend on a fur coat for warmth. Usually seals that are not heavily oiled can clean their fur within a few days or weeks. Sea otters are particularly vulnerable because they have very little blubber and depend on an intact fur coat to keep warm (Fig. 11.1). When oil breaks the integrity of the fur, the warm air trapped next to the body is lost, and the animal may die from exposure. The thermoregulatory abilities of whales and other marine mammals are not impaired by oiling because they depend on a thick layer of blubber for keeping themselves warm. Heavily oiled mammals with fur coats face another threat: They cannot swim well, and may drown.

Figure 11.1. Sea otters are particularly vulnerable during oil spills because they feed near the surface. Top, *otter resting on water;* bottom, *a dead, oiled otter* (*head is near the left, paws are folded over toward top edge of photo*). (Source: Exxon Valdez *Oil Spill Public Information Center*)

All marine mammals are vulnerable to inhalation or ingestion of oil, which may cause internal lesions in the liver and kidney. Inhalation or ingestion may also lead to secondary infections such as pneumonia. Thick slicks of oil pose an additional problem for baleen whales because it can cling to the baleen, lowering the flow of water and thus the amount of food they encounter. Thick globs of oil can also clog their breathing passages.

Sea turtles have a slightly different lifestyle than most marine mammals in that they come to land to dig nests and deposit eggs, although many marine mammals haul out. They also are exposed to oil while at the surface, where they can breath, float, and feed in it. Oil can affect their vision and retard swimming.

Experimental and Field Evidence

Many seals have very large eyes, which are particularly susceptible to oil, so irritation of the eyes and mucous membranes follows most exposure. This problem, discovered by exposing a very few seals, in experiments, is usually relatively short-term, since it is the volatile fraction of oil that irritates, and this quickly evaporates. Seals and others can be exposed to oil through inhalation, leading to high tissue levels of petroleum hydrocarbons, and eventually to lesions, kidney damage, and degeneration of the liver. When ringed seals are fed foods laced with oil in the laboratory, the oil concentrates in the blubber and liver. Seals can metabolize and excrete some of the oil that ends up in the liver and kidney, but this mechanism is less effective in young than adults, and is not effective with high exposure to oil. The storage of oil in fat or blubber may pose a problem during long migrations, lactation, or periods of low food availability, when fat stores may be used, releasing high levels of hydrocarbons into their bodies.

In large enclosures, some whales and dolphins appear to be able to sense and avoid oil slicks. Trained dolphins avoid oil by using visual, tactile, and echolocation cues. However, the ability to detect oil is different from avoiding it. Dolphins may choose not to leave the area of an oil spill because it is home, and the place they are currently foraging, resting, or having young. In contrast, sea otters do not seem able to detect or avoid oil slicks in captivity. In captivity, sea turtles exhibit some ability to avoid oil slicks, but this does not seem to be the case in the wild, where they will remain in oil-covered areas for long periods of time.

When exposed to oil in captivity, sea turtles show severe effects in several organ systems, including skin sores, digestive tract inflammations, and eye and nose injuries. The turtles seemed to suffer from an impaired immune system, which may suggest why sea turtles die from oil in the wild. The oil may simply weaken them sufficiently that they die from diseases. When turtle eggs are exposed to oil in the laboratory, they have lower hatching success. Thus, if beaches are heavily oiled during the nesting season, there might be little or no hatching that year.

We have a good deal of information on what happens to common marine mammals during oil spills, but we know little about what happens to manatees and dugongs during oil spills. There have been few large oil spills in tropical waters, where manatees and dugongs live, and when such spills have happened, they were not studied. During the Iran–Iraq War of 1983 and the Gulf War of 1991, however, some oiled dugongs were found dead. We know relatively little about the exact number that perished, or how they died. It was difficult to get into these areas to collect carcasses or perform autopsies. Similarly, there are no reports of the effects of oil spills on polar bears, so we do not know how they would fare in the event of a spill.

Sea otters are vulnerable not only because of their dependence on a thick coat of fur, but because they feed near the surface on foods covered in oil. The susceptibility of otters was recognized as early as the late 1970s, when thirteen European otters died following an oil spill in the Shetlands, north of Scotland. They had many sores and bleeding in their stomachs.

Following the *Exxon Valdez* spill, when the oil slick moved across Prince William Sound, sea otters were the most abundant marine mammal in its path. Since they spend most of their time at the surface of the water, they were unable to avoid the oil. When the oil began to penetrate their fur, destroying its insulation ability, they may have groomed obsessively, increasing their ingestion of oil. Almost a thousand sea otter carcasses were picked up in the weeks following the spill, but the number that died may have been three or four times as high. Although many otters were found dead, others were taken to rehabilitation facilities. Of the 357 captured alive, 123 died during treatment. Some of their stomachs had lesions, many were hemorrhaging badly, and their livers and kidneys were damaged. Before the spill, biologists who studied sea otters reported that most carcasses they found were either from very young otters, or very old ones. In the two years after the spill, many of the dead animals were in their prime, between the ages of two and eight. This is disturbing, because it indicates that the breeding population may be dying from exposure to the oil.

In the months following the spill there was a 35 percent decline in the number of sea otters in Prince William Sound. In succeeding years there appeared to be no recovery, largely because they continued to be exposed to the oil. Unweathered oil still remains under and within mussel beds, one of their staple food items. Unlike some other animals, which change their eating habits when faced with contamination, the sea otters have not. They continue to eat the contaminated foods in the same contaminated places. In 1996 their populations had still not recovered in some areas such as Knight Island, and ongoing studies are trying to determine why.

Figure 11.2. Harbor seal populations were affected by the oil spill in Prince William Sound and have not recovered even eight years after the spill.

The extreme vulnerability of sea otters, and their apparent failure to recover in Prince William Sound, suggests that they may be a good indicator of the effects of oil pollution. If other spills happen where sea otters live, special attention should be directed at monitoring their populations, both for their own sake as well as for that of the recovery of the system.

Harbor seals in Prince William Sound also could not escape the oil (Fig. 11.2). They lived in the waters, hauled out on the rocks, and gave birth to pups on oil-covered rocks. In the early summer after the spill, anywhere from 50 to 100 percent of the seals were oiled, most severely. Despite their heavy oiling, few dead harbor seals were collected after the *Exxon Valdez* spill, largely because they do not float as sea otters do, but instead sink like stones. Those that were most heavily oiled died immediately. Seals, like other mammals, have enzyme systems that allow them to detoxify and excrete oil hydrocarbons from their bodies, making those that survived the initial oiling less affected. However, the levels of oil in mammary tissue and milk were higher than in any other tissues, which may account for the large number of young that died. Not only were young found dead following the spill, but a number of dead fetuses were collected.

A second disturbing effect observed with harbor seals was a change in behavior. Normally wary, oiled harbor seals were sick, lethargic, and unusually tame. They allowed close approach, and remained on rocks rather than slipping into the water as boats approached. People could walk to within a few yards of them and they would merely look up. When such seals died, biologists dissected them and found that some had debilitating lesions in the thalamus region of the brain, the part that serves as the center to control swimming, diving, feeding, and escape behavior. Such effects are relatively long-lasting and will impair these seals for many years. Even today, in 1996, harbor seal populations are not recovering in Prince William Sound, although this may not be due entirely to oiling, since the declines are over a much wider area and had begun before the oil spill. The native Alaskans—who hunt seal as an important part of their culture—are very disturbed by continued problems with harbor seals because they do not want to hunt injured seals and because it means their homeland has not recovered from the oil.

The most dramatic marine mammals of Prince William Sound are the killer whales, which travel in large groups called pods. There are many pods in the sound; some are more resident, and some more transient. Many people view whales differently from many other mammals: Whales have an emotional appeal that is irresistible. We think of them as individuals that have weathered time. To some extent, this has influenced how scientists study them. Using individual differences in color patterns and fin injuries, biologists can identify the whales as individuals.

One of the main resident pods contained thirty-six members in the days before the *Exxon Valdez* spill, and it had remained stable at thirty-six for several years. This pod of whales was sighted swimming through the oil slick soon after the spill, when the oil was especially toxic. Shortly thereafter seven individuals were missing, and the following year six additional whales were missing. This is unusually high mortality, since before 1989 the average annual mortality was only 2 percent—two whales in the main pod died about every two years. The 1989 rate was ten times higher than expected, and the 1990 rate was just as high. Dead killer whales sink, so we have no corpses to examine. Some of the males in the pod still have collapsed dorsal fins, which may be related to poor nutrition. Since 1992, seven whales in the pod have died: Two were calves orphaned during the spill, one was a male whose fin had collapsed during the spill, one was a reproductive female who lost most of her relatives during the spill. These deaths seem related to the oil spill and indicate the long-range effects of a spill. In 1995 and 1996 there were additional losses from this heretofore stable pod—and this does not bode well for full recovery.

There is a real chance that the main affected pod will not recover, but there is hope, as some calves are being born. Little can be done to help their recovery, except to reduce whatever human disturbance there is.

Overall, there was no evidence that marine mammals avoided oil from the *Exxon Valdez* spill; some seals even went to oiled beaches to pup, and most species were observed swimming through oil. During this time, the consequences of inhaling petroleum vapors led to pulmonary emphysema and neurological lesions in some species.

Effects on Sea Turtles

When oil spills happen where there are sea turtles, some die and become stranded on beaches. After the Ixtoc 1 oil spill off Mexico, a number of dead, oiled sea turtles washed up on beaches in Mexico and Texas. Most of these were Kemp's ridley, the most highly endangered sea turtle in the world because the whole population breeds on one beach in Mexico, just south of Brownsville, Texas. When examined, these dead sea turtles had elevated levels of oil in their tissues. Other stranded sea turtles had oil in their digestive tracts; sometimes they even had relatively large tar balls that they obviously swallowed when they were eating other things.

Although not considered sea turtles, diamond-backed terrapins live entirely in coastal waters and the sea from Maine to Texas. Following the Arthur Kill pipeline leak in the winter of 1990, eleven terrapins emerged from their underground hibernation sites, and they were heavily oiled. Another two found dead were also oiled. The live terrapins were removed to Staten Island Zoo for rehabilitation, and when I saw them a few weeks later, they were still leaking oil, even though their water was changed every few hours. They showed a number of behavioral abnormalities that included impaired walking and swimming, inability to orient correctly, a tendency to fall off inclines, and slower movement than unoiled terrapins. Ultimately, most of them died. Like most of the marine mammals and sea turtles exposed to oil, when dissected they had a number of sores and inflammations in their digestive tracts and livers.

Overall, marine mammals and sea turtles are vulnerable to oil spills through oiling of their fur and skin, inhalation of toxic fumes, and eating of oil-contaminated foods. Over time, they develop lesions in their liver, kidney and digestive tract, and may ultimately die. Some marine mammals may be able to sense oil spills, but there is little evidence that they avoid them. Many remain in their home ranges, even though those areas are oiled.

Chapter Twelve
Effects on Humans

● ● ●

When slicks of oil pour from injured tankers, forming a thick black mousse over the water, our hearts go out to the oil-covered birds and marine mammals that sink lower and lower in the water, unable to escape or remove the oil. For the most part, oil spills pose no direct threat to humans, but spills do affect humans in a number of diverse ways, from accidents suffered by those on damaged tankers or those involved in cleanup, to illness caused by toxic fumes or eating contaminated fish or shellfish. However, no one dies immediately from eating oiled fish. The economic and psychological losses for humans are far greater than any known health threat. Oil can cause disruptions and losses for commercial and recreational fisheries, seaweed harvesting, subsistence harvesting, tourism, hiking and camping, bathing, boating, and a variety of other uses. More difficult to measure, but no less real, is the devastating emotional effect that oil spills have on fishing communities, subsistence harvesters, and others, who feel a sense of loss when their wilderness is spoiled by black oil that drifts with the winds and currents and smothers the beaches.

In this chapter I explore the ways people are affected by oil spills. These include human health considerations as well as direct and indirect monetary losses, and aesthetic losses.

Occupational Exposure

Oil spills harm humans either through illness and injury during the spill or cleanup or through the consumption of tainted or contaminated fish or shellfish. Drinking supplies can be fouled as well. I believe that we can also be harmed by the emotional stresses of oil spills, although this is seldom considered. This latter hazard will be discussed separately.

When an oil well explodes, a pipeline bursts, or a supertanker runs aground or collides with another, the crew can be injured. Many super-tanker accidents at sea have resulted in injury or death to crew members, either because of accidents on board or because help did not come soon enough to rescue the crew before the tanker sank. When the tanker *San-sinena* exploded in Los Angeles nine crew members were killed, and fifty were injured. In December 1976 the *Grand Zenith*, registered in Panama and carrying 8.2 million gallons of oil, vanished in a winter storm, along with a crew of thirty-eight. A massive air–sea search turned up only two life jackets with the name of the ship—the crew all perished. Only a month later, a small tanker, the *Chester A. Poling*, broke apart in storm weather, and one crew member was lost. In 1979, the tanker *Atlantic Express*, fully laden with oil, collided with the *Aegean Captain* northeast of Tobago, spilling nearly 49 million gallons of oil. Both ships burst into flames; twenty-six seamen died, and many others were injured.

The International Maritime Organization examined the number of casualties worldwide from 1974 to 1988. Over the fifteen-year period 1,209 lives were lost, an average of 81 a year. Of these, 67 percent were a result of fires and explosions. The number of deaths due to fires has decreased since then, mostly due to a new requirement that vessels have inert gas systems, reducing the likelihood of explosions. Workers exposed to burning oil can fall ill because of sulphur and other contaminants in the smoke. The 650 oil wells the Iraqis set afire on their retreat after the Gulf War released as much as 29.2 tons of smoke per day per well, an impressive exposure for personnel trying to cap the wells and stop the fires. Although air quality measurements in populated areas of Kuwait were within the standards of most Western nations, workers at the wells were clearly exposed to blinding smoke and burning oil. The black smoke near some wells contained high levels of polyaromatic hydrocarbons (PAHs) and nickel.

There are remarkably few studies of the health responses of local people exposed in the months following a spill. However, following the grounding of the tanker *Braer* in Shetland in 1993, local exposed people were questioned about their general health in telephone interviews nearly six months after the spill. In general, these people reported significantly more symptoms, and a greater proportion felt that their health had deteriorated compared with unexposed people. Several psychiatric symptons were also detected.

Ingestion

In addition to possible injury or death from oil spill accidents, eating contaminated fish or shellfish poses a hazard to humans. Most fish and shellfish contaminated with oil either smell or look bad, but do not pose a real hazard to humans because people do not voluntarily eat bad-smelling or -tasting fish. However, the PAHs contained in most crude and refined oils are carcinogenic to mammals. Mollusks, such as mussels and clams, are efficient accumulators of PAHs, thought they rapidly lose them when placed in clean water. Consumption of contaminated shellfish could result in food poisoning.

The greatest commercial impact of oil spills probably comes from the public's fear of tainting, defined as the change in color or taste, that may be caused by petroleum hydrocarbons taken up by tissues. The degree of tainting depends on the kind of oil and the species of fish. Fatty fish, such as salmon or herring, are tainted more readily than other fish. In some countries, shrimp and mollusks are boiled in bulk before sale, and under these conditions one or two tainted shellfish can spoil the whole batch. Perceptions that fish may be tainted or spoiled can have as devastating an effect as the tainting itself. Fish sales in Paris markets fell by half during the *Torrey Canyon* event, regardless of the quality or the origin of the fish. Word that fish from the Brittany shores smelled bad spread rapidly through France, and people avoided fish markets. Similar perceptions accompanied the *Exxon Valdez* oil spill twenty years later, mostly for the native Alaskans who harvest on a subsistence basis. Perceptions of a hazard can have as significant an effect on fishing as the reality of oil contamination.

Oil spills affect people in many other ways, and these will be discussed later. Mostly they involve loss of revenues, either directly from the immediate death of resources such as seaweed, fish, and shellfish or indirectly from decreases in resource populations, tourism, recreation, subsistence, or religious activities.

Loss of Commercial Fisheries

Oil spills have seriously impacted fisheries and shellfisheries ever since the first oil slick slipped across the oceans. For many years these losses were ignored, undocumented, unmeasured, and uncompensated. With increases in the size of oil tankers, the potential for large spills that can have massive effects on commercial fisheries increased. Over time, fishermen and the general public have become more militant in their desire to be paid for these losses. This feeling has been translated into laws that codify damage assessment and compensation for lost natural resources.

Fishing is the key industry affected by oil spills, followed closely by tourism. After the grounding of the barge *Florida* in Massachusetts in 1969, large numbers of soft-shelled and hard-shelled clams, scallops, lobsters, and finfish drifted onto the beaches. They lay dying, dead, or decaying, and with each new tide more washed ashore. One estimate put the loss of soft-shelled clams and scallops at $250,000, just from the dead bodies found along the shore. This did not include losses from other commercial products such as lobsters, fish, and hard-shelled clams, or the fish that died in the seas, undetected. The main Falmouth shellfishing areas were closed for several years following the spill. Ten years after the spill fishing and shellfishing were still restricted.

Because of the severe impact of the spill on the local economy, the state of Massachusetts filed suit against the owners of the barge and settled out of court. The town of Falmouth received $100,000 and the state of Massachusetts received $200,000 in payment of damages. This was clearly insufficient to cover even the direct losses from fish and shellfish found dead along the shore, but this was in the early 1970s, and damages were not usually assessed. Oil spills were considered a necessary cost of the benefits of having oil. Losses due to damaged natural resources were not clearly mandated by law as they are today, and the procedures for determining appropriate compensation for losses of natural resources were not developed fully.

In August 1974, winter in the Southern Hemisphere, the supertanker *Metula* ran aground in the Strait of Magellan and spilled 14 million gallons of oil into the cold waters between Patagonia and Tierra del Fuego. Much of the oil was deposited along seventy-five miles of shoreline. This area was used by local fishermen for centuries, as evidenced by the middens left by the Indians, which contain mussel shells and whale bones. Following the spill, local fishing grounds were contaminated; the meat in the mussels along the rocky shores turned brown and smelled of oil; they could no longer be harvested. The fishermen moved elsewhere, traveling long distances over perilous seas to reach sites free from oil. Although the local fisheries were completely disrupted for years, the extent of the damage was never documented, and the fishermen were not compensated in any way for their losses. They took their losses, and continued to struggle against the forces of the seas.

The grounding and breakup of the *Amoco Cadiz* in 1978 caused significant decreases in the fisheries, shellfisheries, and seaweed harvest along the northern coast of Brittany. This region produced about 40 percent of the total fish sold in France. Finfish, crustaceans, cultured oysters, other mollusks, and marine algae flowed from the shores of Brittany to all of France. Many local people depend on the harvesting of seaweed; over six hundred harvesters gather the algae. After the spill, fishing vessels lay in port, their bows blackened by oil, leading to public pressure to do something about oil spills.

Barely a year later, the second-largest accidental release of oil occurred when the *Ixtoc 1* oil well blew out and caught fire. For months the oil flowed into the Gulf of Mexico, drifting north to the coast of Texas and Florida, where tar balls landed on beaches. Oysters are an important resource along the shores of the Gulf. The whole coastal area, much of it oiled by the spill, is a rich fishing ground for shrimp; the shrimp boats from Carmen alone caught shrimp worth over $50 million in 1978. To the northeast of the blowout are the Campeche Banks, one of Mexico's richest grounds for shellfish, as well as for snappers and groupers. The combined United States and Mexico shrimp fishery in the Gulf of Mexico was worth about $230 million annually. Fishing resumed the following spring, but catches were below normal for several years.

The *Exxon Valdez* spill, as the largest oil spill in U.S. history, seriously affected fisheries in the months following the spill because of the problem the oil caused the fishing gear. The fish, for the most part, were under the water. As long as they remained there, most were safe. However, pulling pots, long lines, nets, and other gear up through the water exposed the catch to oiling. Only a few oiled fish could taint the whole catch. And finally, the fish could be tainted or contaminated during the transfer to larger boats or to the processing plant, or during processing itself. State management officials decided it was best to simply close fisheries rather than to administer closures on a stream-by-stream or fish-by-fish case. This resulted in a season's loss of income for most commercial fisherman.

The closures started with the herring fisheries, where fisherman work with gill and purse seine nets to collect the eggs or roe. The roe, however, are released near the surface on seaweed. The spill coincided with the herring spawning season, and it was impossible to seine for roe without facing oil contamination of the roe. When this fishery was closed, options were limited for fisherman who relied on the lucrative Asian market for herring roe to bankroll their later fishing for salmon, halibut, or others. Other closures followed, including shrimp, king and Dungeness crab, and virtually all salmon. This left only bottom-dwelling fish such as rockfish, and they were seriously overfished in 1989. With fisheries shut down, hatcheries lost their income, canneries closed, and local residents lost their jobs.

Losses for the fishing industry were carefully monitored following the grounding of the *Exxon Valdez*. Pink salmon, an important commercial and recreation fish in the area, were severely affected by the oil. Mortality of eggs was 67 percent higher in the spawning streams where there was oil, and this decrease persisted for several years. Juveniles grew more slowly, and 45 percent fewer survived to adulthood than salmon who grew in un-oiled streams. With fewer eggs, and fewer juveniles making it to adulthood, there were fewer fish to catch. Fishing was severely limited in 1989 because of the presence of oil, but in 1990 through 1992 the catch of pink salmon was 6 to 28 percent lower than usual in the sound's southwest district, the area hardest hit by the spill. Pacific herring in Prince William Sound showed effects for at least three years following the spill, and the fishery was entirely closed from 1994 through spring 1996. Although it is difficult to come up with a figure for the economic losses, estimates of losses incurred in the 1989 and 1990 seasons by commercial fishermen reached $135 million.

There were many direct fishing losses for at least four years following the *Exxon Valdez* oil spill, and pacific herring, sockeye salmon, and pink salmon have not fully recovered even in 1996. Thus, there continues to be ongoing injury to commercial fishing. Fisherman lost income because of the low yields and restricted fishing areas; and guides and hotels lost money because recreational fisherman did not come to the sound for many years. Fisherman and guides simply lost their jobs, and with them, their lifestyle.

The ramifications of a collapsed fishing industry for Prince William Sound, Cook Inlet, and the Gulf of Alaska are enormous, and the effects are cascading. Much of the local economy depends on fishing, either directly or indirectly. Although fisherman could make claims to Exxon for lost fishing opportunities, this was not easy except in the case of captains, who, using tax returns, could show a continuous record of fishing. This was impossible for many who were newly in the business or had interrupted their fishing for a year or two, or for those who worked different fishing districts in different years. Furthermore, Exxon would not entertain claims unless a vessel was geared up and ready to go when the fishery was closed. Thus, some captains had to spend money to hire crews and supply ships even though it was a near certainty that the fishery would be closed a day or two before the scheduled opening. Confusion reigned for everyone involved.

The press played up the money that vessel owners could make by leasing their boats to Exxon for the cleanup effort. However, this was greatly exaggerated. Roughly three hundred Kodiak-based vessels work the area's fisheries, and the majority did not find work on spill cleanup. Jobs were not as plentiful as the press made it seem, nor as equitably distributed as one might hope.

One interesting case involves the sockeye salmon population that spawns in the Kenai River system of Cook Inlet. When the oil from the *Exxon Valdez* spread out of Prince William Sound, no one expected it to end up in Upper Cook Inlet. However, prevailing water currents swept the oil up into the inlet. Tar balls and thick mousse forced commercial fisheries to halt operations. As a result, three times as many sockeye salmon made it to the Kenai River to spawn as usual. Remarkably, the oil halted the fishery but did not affect the number of sockeye migrating to freshwater streams. When populations of adult fish were too high the masses of young fish they produced reduced the populations of their prey to such low levels that juvenile sockeye in the following season were no longer able to eat enough to achieve growth or body fat necessary for the long winter. Many young sockeye died during their first winter because they had insufficient food reserves from summer feeding. The starvation of the young sockeye had tremendous effects on the local fishery. The Cook Inlet sockeye fishery accounts for $30 million to $120 million in annual income for the several cities and towns on the Kenai Peninsula. Tourism from sport fishing also brings in additional money. Subsistence and personal-use fishing are also important for the local people.

Losses to the fishing industry as a result of an oil spill, however, cannot always be predicted by the size of the spill, and its co-occurrence with spawning behavior of fish. For example, one of the largest oil spills in history happened when the tanker *Castillo de Bellver* broke apart, burned, and sank off the coast of South Africa in 1983. Although nearly eighty million gallons of oil spilled into the sea, strong winds and the Benguela ocean current blew the slick northwest, away from the coast and the spawning grounds. Detailed studies of fish were not conducted, but there was no obvious or apparent effect on the local fishing industry, which is substantial. Half of South Africa's rock lobster and half of the oceanic fish landings come from this area.

Today there is general agreement among fishery authorities that oil spills are damaging to finfisheries by excluding fishermen from fishing grounds for the period when the oil is on the water, by fouling fishing gear, by reducing fish stocks in succeeding years, and by creating concern over tainted fish, which can have a serious effect on the market. Since high levels of hydrocarbons can be deleterious to human health, the public's fear is sometimes justified. Direct fish kills are also critical, as hundreds or thousands of adult fish can be killed if the oil spill happens at the right time.

Recreation and Subsistence Harvesting

Whether people travel long distances to reach the wilds of Prince William Sound or merely walk down the street to a busy waterway, the pleasures derived from fishing are important. A large number of people sit along the shore, paddle small boats, or sail larger boats to fish or crab. Many are intent on catching fish or crabs that they can eat, but others are there for the pure thrill of catching something, of enjoying nature, or of merely being in a bit of wilderness. These pleasures can be immense, whether the wilderness is pristine like the shores of Alaska or the coast of Patagonia, or is merely a small bit of salt marsh tucked along the Arthur Kill near the urban sprawl of New York City.

When oil covers shorelines, it not only kills or injures the fish and crabs but it destroys the beauty of the experience. In some cases, it is even unsafe to eat the fish or to walk along the oiled beaches because of volatiles from the oil. Many shoreline activities cease for months or for years.

When the pipeline leaked into the Arthur Kill and spilled thousands of gallons of oil, many people who live in adjacent New York and New Jersey said, "If a spill has to happen, better here, in an area already spoiled by man." This response, however, did not come from the people who live along the Kill, or from those who spend hours crabbing and fishing there. It did not come from the small children who spend many a day wandering the shores in search of fiddler crabs and terrapins, or the older children who paddle about in small rowboats. It came from marina owners who rented slips to wealthier people who used the Kill only as a thoroughfare to the cleaner waters of the Raritan Bay. And it came from consultants hired by Exxon to determine whether people "suffered" any losses from the oil spill. However, had the Exxon officials or the consultants actually walked the shores of the Kill on any warm spring day before the spill they would have seen groups of people tending fishing poles, while others dipped strings baited with chicken bones into the water, waiting for blue crabs to cling. Carefully they haul them up, place the crab in a bucket, and begin anew.

Over 40 percent of those fishing or crabbing along the Arthur Kill are blue-collar workers who use their catch as a source of food, and another 40 percent are retired people whose catch is important both as food and recreation. To many of these people, the fish and crabs are important as a source of protein—sometimes their only protein. These are urban subsistence fishermen; perhaps "supplementation fishermen" may be a better term. But it is also very important socially, as parents come with young children, grandparents come with grandchildren, and young couples find it a nice place to relax after work. These activities are gender-free, and boys and girls of all ages fish beside one another and vie for the biggest catch.

Perhaps the best-studied subsistence harvesters are the native Alaskans who were affected by the *Exxon Valdez* spill. The advancing oil slick covered shorelines belonging to the Chugach people, shorelines used for subsistence hunting, fishing, and gathering for at least seven thousand years.

There are fifteen Alutiiq and other Aleut communities in the sound and the Gulf of Alaska, and they harvest many kinds of fish, shellfish, marine mammals, birds, and eggs. These resources are preserved for later use, when the cold winter weather sets in.

The Alutiiq were dismayed by the advancing oil. On the one hand they saw the oil-covered otters and birds drowning, and on the other they were told that they could tell by smell whether their traditional foods were safe to eat. Literally hundreds and thousands of birds and mammals were dying, covered with oil. The disruption of the lives of the people in subsistence-based villages was one of the most severe and long-lasting effects of the entire oil spill.

It was hard for the views of subsistence peoples to be heard: They were less organized than the fishing community, had fewer communication channels, and had no clear lobbying apparatus in place. When Vice President Dan Quayle came to visit he met with mayors from affected communities. One woman representative from Eyak talked for five minutes about the meaning of subsistence to her people. The vice president listened, but his only reply was, "All the fishermen will be paid." This missed the point completely. Money was an important issue, but it was not the issue that these people were most worried about. The real fear, especially among the older village leaders, was that the very foundation of their communities would collapse. When subsistence harvesting is disrupted for several years, the life of the community can change, and it is hard to return to the old ways.

Subsistence harvests virtually ceased after the spill, declining by as much as 14 to 77 percent in the various communities. The variation was partly due to whether many animals from upland habitats free from the oil spill were harvested. In the mid-1980s, the residents of Chenega Bay on the sound averaged a subsistence harvest of 342 pounds per person per year; after the spill it declined to 148 pounds. In English Bay on the Kenai Peninsula, harvesting declined from 289 pounds to 141 pounds per person per year. Not only did the residents decrease their consumption but they harvested fewer different species, from twenty-three to twelve. This reflects their fear of contamination of shellfish, fish, birds, and marine mammals. Although mussels from Prince William Sound are quite small, they are one of the few foods that are readily available when the snows are deep. The intertidal zone, where mussels grow, was exposed to oil with every low tide.

Both federal and state governmental agents collected samples of the subsistence foods and tested them for contaminants. They then informed the Alutiiq that PAHs were sufficiently low in the edible tissue, and that there was nothing to worry about. They organized a series of community meetings to tell them that their concerns were unwarranted. This was less than reassuring when birds and seals were still dying, when populations were

Figure 12.1. Author with mussel beds and barnacles in Prince William Sound. Several beds of mussels still contain high levels of PAHs, indicative of oil pollution.

depleted, and when they could see oil covering some mussel beds. When they saw that recreational fisherman were no longer fishing in the sound, their fears were further confirmed. Altogether, government agents tested 309 samples of fish and 1,080 samples of shellfish from 146 sites over the three years following the spill. None of the fish had levels of PAH sufficient to pose a health hazard, and the vast majority of shellfish were deemed safe to eat. This was not satisfying. If the vast majority are safe, then some are not, and how is anyone supposed to know which ones are which?

The *Exxon Valdez* Oil Spill Trustee Council, mandated by the legal settlement to undertake the damage assessment and the restoration of Prince William Sound organisms, has set up its own sampling regime for subsistence resources. But unlike the previous sampling, it is employing Alutiiq to help collect the shellfish, fish, birds, and mammals to be tested, and is testing the tissues the Alutiiq normally eat. This has the advantage of making sure the right species are examined, the right tissues are examined, and the resources are collected in the places traditionally used for subsistence harvesting.

Even so, the anxiety persists, and many Alutiiq are unsure what foods they can harvest. The mussel beds in many coves are still contaminated, and the mussels are small to begin with (Fig. 12.1). Subsistence hunting and fishing is no longer as pleasant, and the people are no longer at peace with their lifestyle. To them, the sound is still polluted because there are nooks and crannies with oil, and there are beaches where the mussels are too contaminated with oil to be eaten.

Tourism

Tourism is the major industry for many coastal areas around the world, surpassing even fishing. Lovely scenery, picturesque fishing villages, and clean beaches are the major drawing cards for many coastal regions. Oil mars these images, and people leave the shores and flock to the mountains. The effect can be both real and perceived. The image is real when, of course, oil or tar balls are present on otherwise pristine beaches. However, many people are kept away by the mere thought that the beach may be oiled, or their fear that oil may be on the shore, a fear fueled by the press. After the Ixtoc 1 disaster, there were continuous and alarmist reports in the papers about damage to the beaches of Texas and Mexico. Both regions suffered great losses in tourism revenues because people avoided these places.

The devastating effect that oil can have on beaches used for bathing cannot be underestimated, particularly for shore communities, for which tourism is the main industry. As early as the *Torrey Canyon*, officials dealing with the spill were pressured to prevent the oil from fouling the Cornish beaches in England. They waited too long, however, and the oil reached the shores. Only then did they dump two million gallons of detergents on the beaches to clean them. This "cure" proved worse than the disease; the detergents were very toxic to a wide variety of intertidal animals such as limpets, clams, and mussels. Hordes of touring British avoided the shores that were fouled with sticky oil, globs of detergent, and dead creatures. The surf foamed with large bubbles blackened by the emulsified oil.

Bathing beaches have been closed officially because of oil spills since the 1970s. In July 1971, several beaches along the Jersey shore were closed because of an oil spill from a Navy ship at Bayonne, and subsequently, Coney Island in nearby New York was also closed. In August 1978, the New York City commissioner of health closed beaches from Breezy Point to Far Rockaway when no. 6 fuel oil leaked from a sunken barge off Breezy Point. The four-mile slick moved toward the beaches in the middle of the hot summer, and the public was not pleased.

Tourism suffers for many other reasons as well: Birdwatchers do not want to see oiled birds struggling in the surf, photographers do not want to take pictures of soiled shores, and people who enjoy seeing active fishing villages do not want to see idle fleets sitting in docks or lined up along oil-stained beaches. The restaurants and hotels suffer directly, and then the whole community suffers, as local residents have less money to buy luxuries, and some cannot even buy necessities. The economy of the community can collapse.

Psychological Effects

Only in recent years have we started to realize the huge psychological toll that results from human-made disasters. Catastrophes that are acts of God such as earthquakes, tidal waves, and hurricanes are bad enough, but they are not of our doing. No one is at fault; one can find peace with an earthquake. The devastation that follows the loss of one's job or lifestyle because of an oil spill is far worse.

Nearly everyone connected with the *Exxon Valdez* oil spill recognized from the very start that the social and psychological effects for a wide range of people were tremendous, from the fishermen and guides who lost their jobs, to the people who were suddenly thrust into working eighteen hours a day to ferry cleanup crews to the sound, to the subsistence communities that were forced from their homes. Everyone suffered stress when the cleanup operations ceased, many lost their jobs, and most lost income either directly or indirectly. Alaska's dependence on oil for 85 percent of its income presents its own stresses when oil spills threaten that calm. The anxiety and stress of the cleanup activities was enormous, but so too was the letdown that occurred after everyone left, and the sound was empty.

The stress to the residents of small fishing villages on Prince William Sound was severe, not only because of the loss of their subsistence fishing, but because their culture was disrupted. J. S. Picou and others found that these villages showed a continuing pattern of stress and disruption some eighteen months after the spill, and some of these effects are still present. Chronic stress and disruption was evident thirty-two and forty-eight months later, well after cleanup crews left the area. Partly, the stress-related effects come about because the oil spill was never truly over or final, and the technological disaster continues to influence their culture. Natural disasters do not cause such chronic effects; indeed, the residents of some Alaskan fishing communities said that the 1964 earthquake in the same region was less traumatic than the oil spill, even though many people were killed in the earthquake. Technological disasters apparently leave in their wake a greater sense of uncertainty about future cultural and economic losses.

A tremendous amount of time, money, and thought has gone into restoring the environmental damage caused by the *Exxon Valdez* oil spill. Picou and other sociologists suggest that true restoration must also include the reestablishment of a social balance between the biological and physical environment, and the human community using those resources. This may be difficult, but should involve measures to resolve community conflict and uncertainty, reduce psychological stress, and restore the quality of life for the affected communities.

Chapter Thirteen
Hazards, Risk, and
Perceptions

● ● ●

Oil clearly poses a problem for plants, animals, and the ecosystems they are part of, as well as humans. How we choose to examine that risk, perceive the dangers, and act on them is up to us. In recent years, governmental agencies and academics have developed a process known as risk assessment to evaluate the risks that chemicals and other disturbances pose. When applied to humans, it is called human health risk assessment; when applied to other organisms, it is called ecological risk assessment. In this chapter I briefly describe how scientists and governmental agents view risk assessment, examine the relationship between risk and perception, and consider how these views affect our future actions with oil spills.

Risk Assessment

Risk assessment is a relatively new field of science, brought about by our need to figure out a standard way to compare hazards and to decide which ones we must do something about. Risk assessment examines all aspects of a given action, situation, food, or chemical to decide whether it poses a problem and to determine the magnitude of the problem. The process makes sense only when there are choices to make, as, for example, when governmental agencies must decide whether to allow or forbid the use of a particular chemical. Humans are excellent risk assessors, even though we seldom realize we are doing so.

For most of human history, the hazards we faced had to do with what foods to eat, how to obtain those foods, what mates to seek, how to obtain those mates, how to defend food and mates from others, and how to avoid being killed and eaten in the process. For example, in the search for meat, early humans had to balance whether to go hunt wild game for themselves or to wait to eat the leavings from other carnivores such as lions. The risks of hunting on their own were obvious: One could get killed by other predators either while hunting or carrying the food back to camp, one could waste valuable energy pursuing a prey item that was too fast to catch or too big to kill even if it could be caught. Cutting up and eating the meat on the open grasslands of Africa would expose the hunter to danger from a wide variety of animals. The risks to feasting on the meat or bones left by other carnivores were similar, but may have been less since the local carnivores would have already had their fill of the carcass. The other animals that move in to pick at the bones—vultures and hyenas—presented far less of a threat. Making a decision about which foraging method to use was a risk assessment for these early humans. Indeed, anthropologists now believe that early humans in Africa waited, and moved in to carry the bones back to camp, where they cut them open to expose the nutritious bone marrow.

Today we make similar decisions every day. We decide what the costs and benefits are of crossing the street at the crosswalk rather than in the middle of the block; we decide whether we should eat a cheeseburger or a fruit salad; or we decide which of two alternative routes to take to work. In the first case, we consider the relative risks of being hit if we cross in one of two places; in the second, we may be balancing the risks from cholesterol against our pleasure; and in the third, we may be balancing time and distance against hassle or toll costs, or even the possibility of an accident blocking the road.

Risk assessment is just a formalized way to compare the hazards associated with decisions. The formalization was necessary because different people were conducting assessments in different ways, and it was not possible to compare the risks. For example, one governmental agency was using one methodology to determine the risk of cancer from a given chemical, while another agency was using a different methodology. They came up with different risk estimates. It was particularly difficult because the government was trying to assess the risks to human health of a wide variety of chemicals. It was impossible for an ordinary citizen or even the government to decide which risk was the greater.

In 1983, the National Academy of Sciences organized a committee to consider various aspects of risk. It published a book called *Risk Assessment in the Federal Government: Managing the Process*, which laid out a formal approach for risk assessment. Although controversial, most people agree with the basic steps that were defined, including hazard identification, dose-response analysis, exposure assessment, and risk characterization. In the hazard identification phase, the nature and kinds of adverse effects are enumerated. For example, lead causes learning difficulties in infants and children, as well as other problems ranging from anemia to sensory damage. In the dose-response phase, the relationship between the amount of the hazard and the effect is examined. For example, at certain blood lead levels, IQ is affected to a certain degree, and at higher lead levels, it is affected to a greater degree. In the exposure assessment phase, the routes of exposure are examined, as well as the time course of exposure. For example, children may obtain lead through their mother's placenta, through the liquids or foods they consume, from breathing leaded dust, or from eating paint chips. In this case, one important route of exposure for young children was from eating lead paint that flaked from walls or dirt contaminated with lead from automobile emissions. Risk characterization is the process of examining the importance of the risk to individuals and society. For example, by lowering IQ, lead may affect future job prospects and the earning power of individuals, and exact a high cost for society if more people end up jobless or with other societal needs as a result of lead exposure early in life. This led directly to the banning of leaded paint and the removal of lead from gasoline in the United States. The risk assessment that was conducted with lead did result in regulatory action in many countries, and blood lead levels have decreased markedly. Today we realize that even very low levels of lead can lead to developmental problems for children.

The risk assessment conducted for lead examined the hazard it posed for humans. However, the removal of lead from gasoline had a direct effect on other organisms: At the same time that lead levels decreased in humans, they also decreased in birds and in mammals that lived near highways.

In ecological risk assessment, the initial hazard identification phase has been expanded to include a problem formulation stage, in which the nature of the problem is discussed by managers and scientists in detail. Defining the problem is more complicated in ecological risk assessment because there are so many more organisms to consider, with so many diverse life history stages, living in so many different habitats. Many species of plants and animals have complex life history strategies: They may live in water for part of their life cycle, and in air the other part; some live as a caterpillar for many weeks or months, and then become transform into a flying insect. Similarly, there are many different lifespans, from bacteria that may live for a period of minutes, to sea turtles that may live three hundred years, and redwoods and other trees that may live for fifteen hundred years.

Another difference between human health risk assessment and ecological risk assessment is the role of individuals. In human health, we are interested in the well-being and quality of life of every individual. Human health risk assessment takes into account the seventy-year life-span of each individual. In ecological risk assessment, we are interested in healthy populations rather than each individual. Except in the case of an endangered or threatened species, the individual is of no immediate concern. What is of importance is the maintenance of a healthy population that is stable, or, in the case of threatened or endangered species, is growing.

This means that in ecological risk assessment we concentrate on whether population numbers and stability have been disrupted by a chemical such as oil, and whether reproductive success is "normal" or similar to prespill levels or control populations. For example, an ecological risk assessment for oil requires examining the adverse effects of oil on different populations of birds, mammals, reptiles, amphibians, fish, and invertebrates living in a variety of habitats. Since it is clearly impossible to examine all species in the world, indicator species must be selected. These are then used as surrogates for the ecological world in general.

Indicator species are those that show effects, that are responsive when exposed to low levels of toxic chemicals, that can serve as a warning of impending danger, that are high enough on the food chain to show effects early, that are common enough to monitor, that can be monitored with a reasonable amount of time and money, and that people are interested in. It is difficult to obtain monies to monitor fiddler crabs or insects, but many people support monitoring bird populations. Thus, some species of birds serve as indicators. They are also used because they may be at the top of food chains, and thus show effects sooner than organisms lower on the chain. For chemicals that are persistent and remain within the body, each organism at a higher step on the food chain accumulates more of the chemical, until the top predators have the greatest concentrations in their tissues. Levels of the contaminant stored in their tissues will be detectable sooner than with other organisms.

Another aspect of ecological risk assessment is the importance of measuring community and ecosystem effects. Communities and ecosystems have several characteristic features that if disrupted will prevent the system from functioning normally. Measures of ecosystem function include number of species, nutrient cycling, energy relationships, and predator–prey relationships. These functions are difficult and time-consuming to measure, but are critical for determining the risks associated with a particular chemical, such as oil.

A Risk Assessment for Oil

A risk assessment for oil begins by examining the types of effects caused by oil on a wide variety of organisms (Table 13.1). This is the hazard identifica-

Table 13.1. Some Oil Spill Effects That Would Be Examined in a Risk Assessment

Target	Effects	Type of exposure
Humans	Death Nausea Poisoning	Accidents involving crew on tankers or cleanup Toxic fumes (clean-up) Contaminated food
Other mammals		
Marine mammals	Death Lowered breeding success Brain lesions Tameness Sluggishness	Oiling of fur/skin; internally from swallowing Contaminated food
Muskrat	Death Nausea	Oiling of fur, internally from swallowing
Deer	Nausea	contaminated water
Birds	Death Nausea Internal lesions Poisoning Lowered breeding success	Oiling of plumage, unable to thermoregulate Contaminated food Oiling of eggs or chicks
Sea turtles, terrapins	Death/nausea Premature emergence	Oiling of shell/skin, unable to breathe through skin Contaminated food
Fish	Death Nausea Internal lesions Poisoning Lowered breeding success Genetic abnormalities Effects in second generation	Oiling of scales, unable to swim upstream Contaminated food Oiling of eggs or fry
Invertebrates	Death Impaired behavior Premature emergence from hibernation	Oiling Contaminated food Continued low-level exposure to chronic oil

tion phase. Although these effects were described in more detail in Chapters 5 through 11, generalizations are more useful in this section. The main effects of oil on a wide variety of organisms include death, nausea, abnormal behavior, external lesions and internal sores, elevated blood levels of hydrocarbons, abnormal reproductive success, deformities in embryos or offspring, second-generation effects, and decreased population levels. Although these vary by species and by degree of exposure, the effects on ecological systems are impressive.

The effects discussed in previous chapters, and shown in Table 13.1, are individual and population effects. Very few people have examined community and ecosystem effects because of the difficulty of doing so, and the costs involved. Yet many effects have been described or inferred by the failure of some populations to recover. For example, following the Arthur Kill oil spill, there was an increase in the number of small, young forage fish and a decrease in the number of large, older forage fish preferred by fish-eating birds. The increase in the number of small fish was a direct result of the killing of the larger fish that normally prey on the smaller fish. Without the larger forage fish predators, a higher percentage of the small fish survived in the years following the spill. With fewer large forage fish, the night herons and snowy egrets had difficulty finding enough food to bring back to their nestlings, and their reproductive success was lower than usual for a number of years. This is an example of a community-level effect (Fig. 13.1).

An example of an ecosystem-level effect occurred following the *Amoco Cadiz*. *Laminaria* and other algae increased in abundance and size because of the release of nitrogen and phosphorous when a large number of oiled animals decayed after dying. The change in nitrogen and phosphorus levels affected the ecosystem for many months.

Regardess of the size of the spill, adverse effects on plants and animals follow every major spill. The challenging aspect has been to figure out the relationship between amount of oil and level of effects. Gathering this kind of information is difficult because there are so many different types of oils, they persist for different amounts of time, and wind and weather conditions affect where the oil goes and how quickly it disperses in the ocean. Nonetheless, it is clear that larger oil spills cause greater problems.

Furthermore, the demonstration of dose-response relationships, particularly for human carcinogens, usually occurs in the laboratory, where the exposure to a chemical can be carefully controlled and where the organisms are all living under the same conditions. There can be no laboratory study of the effect of oil on a whole ecosystem, making risk assessment difficult.

For the purposes of risk assessment, there is a dose-response relationship between oil and adverse effects in laboratory studies. A variety of experiments have been conducted with oil in the laboratory, by oiling eggs to

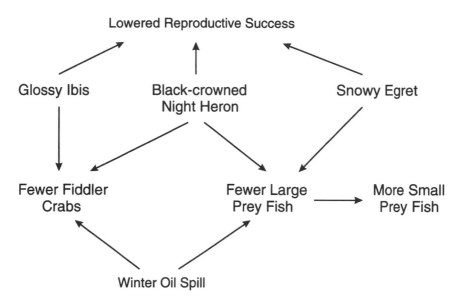

Figure 13.1. Community-level effects of oil: Shown are effects on fish, glossy ibis, night-heron, and snowy egret.

determine hatching rate; by feeding food laced with oil to birds or small mammals to determine lesion rates, growth rates, and death rates; and by exposing invertebrates to oil in their water to determine death rates and growth rates. In general, with increasing amounts of oil, a higher percentage of bird eggs fail to hatch, more experimental animals show lesions, nausea, or other abnormalities, and more die.

There are also clear examples of dose-response relationships in oiling field studies. Usually these are conducted by measuring the rate of oiling at different distances from the oil spill and comparing these with effects on plants or animals at these same distances. For example, after the Arthur Kill oil spill, the invertebrates living in creeks closest to the spill suffered higher mortality than those living in creeks several miles from the spill (Fig.13.2). There are numerous examples of fisheries being disrupted for months following an oil spill. When the *Amoco Cadiz* grounded, the fishing along the French coast was depressed for months, and fish and shellfish supplies in France were cut by over 25 percent. The tourist industry suffered even more because no one came to the oiled beaches.

There is also a dose-response relationship between depletion of fish stocks because of oil and the effects on people. Native Americans and others who rely on subsistence fishing, or who count hunting and fishing as an important aspect of their culture, are seriously affected by oil spills.

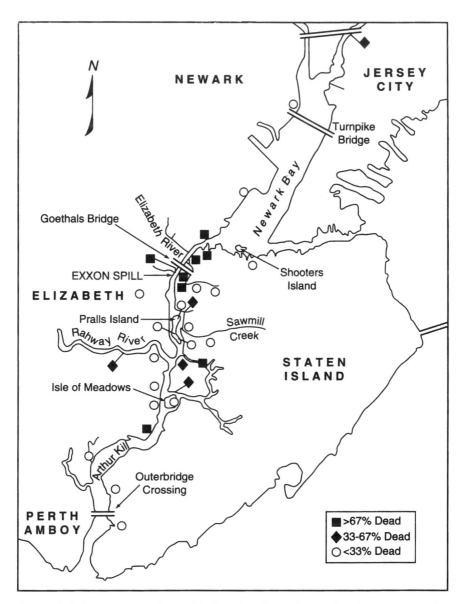

Figure 13.2. Dose-response relationship for oiling of mussels as a function of distance from spill. Percent mortality correlated with amount of oil on mudflats. (Source: Adapted from J. Burger, ed., 1994, Before and after an oil spill: The Arthur Kill *[Rutgers University Press, New Brunswick, N.J.])*

The native Alaskans in Prince William Sound found their fish and marine mammal stocks decreased after the *Exxon Valdez* oil spill, and some have not recovered even seven years later. Harbor seals, an important part of their hunt, still suffer low population numbers, and the people fear that those remaining are not safe to eat. The native Alaskans from some villages recount that the pain and stress from this oil spill is greater than from the 1964 earthquake, which killed 25 percent of their people.

Exposure assessment requires determining how organisms encounter oil, and how much they take into their bodies. Exposure to oil is normally determined by taking samples of soil from different places and measuring the levels of oil in the samples, by collecting organisms and measuring oil in different tissues, and by visual estimates of oiling of vegetation at different distances from the spill. The knowledge of how to measure exposure to oil has developed markedly over the years, and through fingerprinting it is possible to determine whether the oil in a given sample of a soil, plant, or animal came from a particular spill.

Risk characterization, or the final stage in classical risk assessment, is putting together all of this information to determine the magnitude or importance of the risk from oil. We know enough today, and have for some time, to say that oil can be devastating to organisms and ecosystems within the short term. When plants and animals are oiled, many die and others are so stressed that they die within a few months. Tens of thousands of birds may die following a large oil spill, and hundreds of marine mammals may perish. Oiling can have devastating effects on shellfisheries, fisheries, industries that rely on tourism along coasts, and on native American cultures.

The long-term effects of oil spills are more contentious, as some systems have recovered within a few years or decades of a major spill. Nevertheless, some systems have not completely recovered, and oil still remains. Moreover, it is clear that if a system requires twenty years to recover, it could not sustain another large spill within this period or recovery would be drastically delayed. The greater danger, then, may not lie in a single spill, but in the potential for repeated spills, which would render it impossible for populations and ecosystems to ever recover completely.

The cost and risks from oil spills have been sufficient to prompt Congress to pass the Oil Pollution Act of 1990 and to have continuing commissions examine the safety of supertankers and associated facilities. As more oil is shipped to more destinations around the globe, we must improve technology to decrease the risks that oil imposes on humans, as well as other organisms.

Risk Assessment and Perception

Whereas risk assessment is the process of examining the level of risk posed by a particular stress, risk perception is how the public views that risk. The two are not the same. For example, many smokers view the risk from smoking as relatively small compared with other risks they go way out of their way to avoid, such as exposure to some chemicals or cholesterol. When expert risk assessors and the general public are asked to rank risks, the results differ markedly (see Table 13.2). In general risk assessors and the public rank motor vehicles, smoking, and handguns as posing some of the highest risks, but other hazards such as nuclear power and police work are ranked higher by the public than by experts.

People also rank hazards differently depending upon whether they have control over them, whether they feel they could have control, and whether they choose the risk. Most people will rank the risk lower when they choose the hazard. For example, people choose to go skiing and to smoke, but they have no control over exposure to most chemicals. In many cases, people rank the dangers from exposure to chemicals as posing a higher risk than these other activities. Yet the actual risk of danger from skiing and smoking is greater than from exposure to most chemicals.

There are also differences as a result of one's involvement with the hazard. Following the *Exxon Valdez* accident in Prince William Sound, the native Alaskans suffered losses of their subsistence harvest. But they also suffered because their homeland was fouled. They perceived the risks from the oil spill as devastating, while other local Alaskans I talked to rated the risk relatively low, claiming that Prince William Sound looks just like it always did.

There are many other examples of the difference between risk and risk perception. For years, Congress delayed acting on oil spill legislation, preferring to let oil contamination fall entirely under the Clean Water Act. This resulted in relatively small fines, and no collection of damages for destroyed natural resources. However, after the 1989–90 season, when there were seven major oil accidents that spilled over twelve million gallons in several ports in the United States, oil spill legislation became a high priority for Congress, and the Oil Pollution Act of 1990 was passed. The actual hazards and dose-reponse relationships of oil contamination were the same; what differed was public perception of the oil spill problem. Before the *Exxon Valdez* over twenty oil spill incidents in the world that were larger had occurred, yet Congress had ignored the call. Some of these accidents were caused by American-owned ships, for example the *Amoco Cadiz*, which spilled nearly sixty-nine million gallons of oil.

Table 13.2. Perception of Risks by the General Public and Risk Assessors

	Public	Experts
Motor vehicles	2	1
Smoking	4	2
Alcoholic beverages	6	3
Handguns	3	4
Surgery	10	5
Motorcycles	5	6
X-rays	22	7
Pesticides	9	8
Electric power (nonnuclear)	18	9
Swimming	19	10
Contraceptives	20	11
General (private) aviation	7	12
Large construction	12	13
Food preservatives	25	14
Bicycles	16	15
Commercial aviation	17	16
Police work	8	17
Fire fighting	11	18
Railroads	24	19
Nuclear power	1	20
Food coloring	26	21
Home appliances	29	22
Hunting	13	23
Prescription antibiotics	28	24
Vaccinations	30	25
Spray cans	14	26
High school and college football	23	27
Power mowers	27	28
Mountain climbing	15	29
Skiing	21	30

Source: From League of Women Voters Survey in Oregon.

Different members of society view the risks from oil spills differently. People who are dependent upon the estuaries or oceans for their livelihood, such as fishermen and those in the tourist industry, are likely to rate the risks from oil spills higher than people living in the interior of the country, where oil spills are unlikely and who are unaffected by one that occurs along the coast.

Another risk perception issue with oil is the difference in perception as a result of the organisms effected. In general, the risk to humans from oil spills is relatively small, except for the potential risk to ship crews. Although the crew sometimes lose their lives when oil supertankers collide or beach on shoals, the incidence is relatively rare. Other risks to cleanup crews come from exposure to volatile fumes from the oil and thermal stress while cleaning up beaches in cold climates. The only other direct danger to humans lies in eating contaminated fish and shellfish, and this risk is lowered because of food testing.

The main victims of oil contamination are plants and animals living in coastal and oceanic environments. As described in Chapters 8 through 11, the risks to these organisms can be significant, and many populations take years to recover, while others never do. Plants can be severely affected if they are high on the marsh, where there is little tidal inundation to remove the oil. The oil seeps down in the peat and remains for decades, where it can adversely affect both plants and animals. The marsh vegetation is the base for salt marsh ecosystems, and without it there is no food or shelter for the myriad of invertebrates and small fish that live there. Salt marshes are often the nurseries for many species of shellfish and fish.

The animals most at risk are either top predators, which can bioaccumulate hydrocarbons, and invertebrates and other organisms that are relatively sedentary and cannot escape the oil that is buried in the peat and rocks and remains for many years. Here again, perceptions vary somewhat from reality. In general, humans perceive the risks to top predators because we notice when whales or seals are declining; we are less likely to perceive the risk to barnacles or fiddler crabs, yet they are sometimes more affected. The exception is native peoples, who may rely on barnacles or mussels for food; they are acutely aware of lowered populations or decreased size.

It is important for us to understand the difference between risks and our perceptions of these risks. The danger of assuming that our perceptions are correct is to fail to protect some species from the hazards of oil pollution. If the hazards to species that are relatively low in the food chain are ignored, the whole food chain may collapse, as many of these species form the basis of the food web. Without them, species that we do cherish may also perish.

Chapter Fourteen
Alternatives and the Future

● ● ●

The types and size of oil spills in the future will depend upon changing political and economic conditions, changes in reliance on fossil fuels throughout much of the world, and changes in the amount of tanker traffic. However, these changes will be matched by developments in tanker technology, port operations, and legal constraints that may reduce the number and size of spills.

In this chapter I discuss the alternatives to petroleum as an energy source, methods of preventing oil spills, and the future of oil use and oil spill prevention. Although this book has concentrated on oil spills, the problem of oil in the oceans is much broader. Nonetheless, we possess the methods to decrease the oil that enters the oceans from large spills, which would lower overall marine pollution.

Alternative Energy Sources

The global consumption of energy will increase in the future, particularly for developing countries. Energy experts believe that worldwide needs will increase by at least 25 to 30 percent over the next twenty years (Fig. 14.1). The question is not whether we will continue to require energy to fuel our world but rather what type of energy will be used. The energy sources currently in use will be those of the future; there are no new alternatives on the horizon. The main energy sources are wood, oil, natural gas, coal, nuclear power, wind, hydroelelectric, and solar. The world has more coal reserves than either natural gas or petroleum, and if availability of oil decreases—either because of overexploitation or because of wars and other political

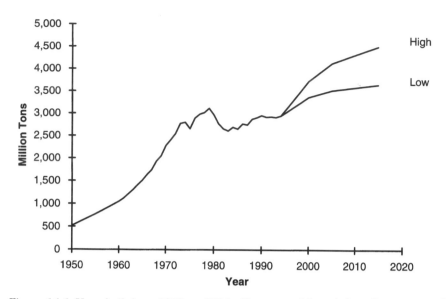

Figure 14.1 Use of oil from 1920 to 2010. (Sources: *Adapted from Department of Energy, 1994,* International energy annual report [*U.S. Department of Energy, Washington, D.C.*]; *Cutter Information Corp., 1995,* International oil spill statistics: 1994 [*Cutter Information Corp. Arlington, Mass.*])

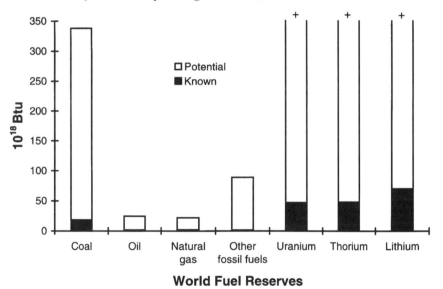

World Fuel Reserves

Figure 14.2. World fuel reserves, both potential and known. The potential reserves of uranium, thorium ("Btu" stands for "British thermal unit" a measure of the potential heat content of a fuel) and lithium are very large, but undetermined. (Sources: *Adapted from Department of Energy, 1994,* International energy annual report [*U.S. Department of Energy, Washington, D.C.*]; *Cutter Information Corp., 1995,* International oil spill statistics: 1994 [*Cutter Information Corp., Arlington, Mass.*])

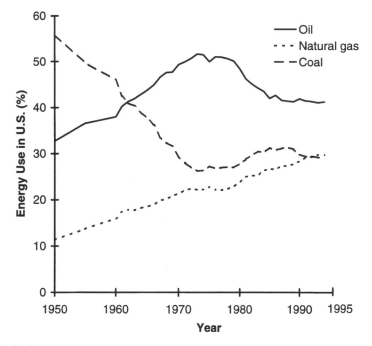

Figure 14.3. General use of fuel in the United States over the last forty-five years. (Sources: *Adapted from Department of Energy, 1994,* International energy annual report [*U.S. Department of Energy, Washington, D.C.*]; *Cutter Information Corp., 1995,* International oil spill statistics: 1994 [*Cutter Information Corp., Arlington, Mass.*])

problems—coal may increase in importance (Fig. 14.2). Even so, the use of coal has declined over the years in favor of both natural gas and oil.

Oil and natural gas account for about 60 percent of energy use worldwide. Energy use has changed over the past fifty years in the United States: Even as late as the 1950s coal was the prime source of energy, whereas oil is today (Fig. 14.3 and 14.4). The changes since the late 1800s have been even more dramatic.

The energy source of choice is a matter of availability, suitability, price, and public perception. Choices occur both at the individual and community level. Any country may have only certain energy sources available, and people must choose from these. Most forms of energy are available in developed countries, but this is far less true in developing ones. Personal choices often are limited within any one economy or nation. People living in the forests of New Guinea or Tibet may have only firewood or dried cattle dung as a viable option because they have no money to pay for other fuel types. Although firewood can be in short supply, it may be the only available energy source. Also, making use of natural gas or oil requires a large investment in both methods of delivery and storage, as well as the presence of

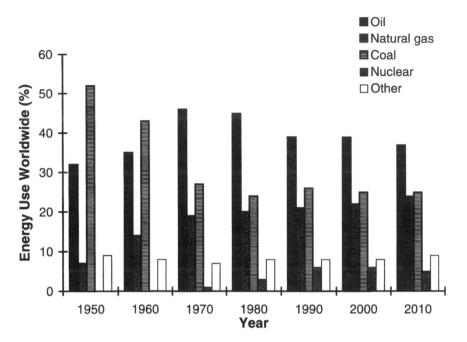

Figure 14.4. Comparative use of fuel in the world over the last forty-five years. (Sources: *Adapted from Department of Energy, 1994,* International energy annual report [*U.S. Department of Energy, Washington, D.C.*]; *Cutter Information Corp., 1995,* International oil spill statistics: 1994 [*Cutter Information Corp., Arlington, Mass.*].)

stoves and heaters in homes. People who live near natural gas reserves may find it to be the most economical and available energy source, while people living near coal mines may rely heavily on coal.

Even when different fuels are available, people may make choices based on price or convenience. When oil prices soared in the mid-1970s and mid-1980s, many people switched from oil to natural gas, which required costly new heaters and hookups. But the rapid increase in oil costs panicked people and stimulated a shift in behavior—subsequently, oil prices dropped. Price plays a role in gas consumption as well; when prices are high, people use less fuel for car travel.

Finally, public perception plays a key role in some energy consumption decisions, particularly in developed countries. For a number of years in the 1970s and early 1980s, some people in rural areas of the United States returned to using wood-burning stoves—perceived as ecologically friendly. However, we soon learned that they contributed more to the carbon monoxide and polyaromatic hydrocarbon problem than did burning oil. Some towns even passed ordinances banning wood-burning stoves.

Nuclear energy provides another example of the importance of public perception. Its use is far more common in Europe than it is in the U.S., largely because people here perceive that nuclear power is a threat to their life and health, fears that were increased by the Three Mile Island and Chernobyl accidents. Indeed, recent information from the region around Chernobyl shows an increase in childhood leukemia in children living near the site.

Americans have an inordinate fear of accidents from nuclear power plants. This is remarkable in some ways, since there are about forty Department of Energy facilities scattered about the United States that have enjoyed local support. Although only a few of these facilities have reactors and produced nuclear weapons during the cold war, many others stored or processed nuclear materials. Some of these facilities destroyed cultural and natural resources, particularly for native peoples. The DOE transported both weapons and radionuclides around the country, apparently without accidents. They used the rail and road systems without public knowledge, and with little response from a public used to hearing "national defense" as an excuse to avoid answering questions. Only recently have we realized the extent of nuclear contamination at these DOE lands. Nonetheless, many other nations—mostly in Europe—rely more heavily on nuclear power than does the United States. Nuclear power has proved to be inexpensive, compared with oil, but the management of high-level nuclear waste is a serious problem. It is not likely that Americans will return to nuclear energy in the next twenty-five years, nor is it likely that Europe will abandon it, although there have been protests in some countries.

Prevention

Oil will remain the primary source of energy for the world for the foreseeable future. Increased dependence on oil is likely to involve moving more oil around the world, with an increased potential for oil spill accidents. This can be countered only by methods to reduce the possibility of accidents in the first place, and methods to reduce the amount spilled and to clean up the oil once it has spilled.

For many years we thought of the oceans as an endless expanse of water that could produce an unlimited number of fish and other foods. We felt we could spill a few chemicals into the ocean with little effect: The oceans are so vast that oil and other chemicals discarded from our everyday lives will disappear when they drain from rivers and estuaries.

Increasingly, we are forced to face the problem of overexploitation and pollution of the oceans. Fishery after fishery is collapsing or being closed to

Table 14.1. Methods of Decreasing and Preventing Oil Spills

Legal constraints regarding
  • Tanker construction and materials
  • Tanker maintenance and inspections
  • Fines and penalties for spills
Tanker safety
  • Double hulls
  • Better materials and construction
  • Adequate space for maintenance and inspections
  • Increased tanker maintenance
  • Design for potential of groundings/accidents
Tanker traffic patterns
Ports and transfer facilities
  • Better construction and design
Pipelines and oil wells
  • Better design
  • Increased maintenance
Training of crew and personnel

protect the few remaining populations. Although we once believed that depleted fish stocks would recover in a few years if left alone, this has not happened in many places. The anchovy fishing fleet off the Peruvian coast is idle, the king crab traps lie unused in Alaska, and the California sardine canneries are closed, replaced by fancy boutiques and restaurants. This is all due to overfishing, but the fish populations have still not recovered. The fishing vessels move from one fishery to another as different fish populations collapse.

Although overfishing is the primary cause of fish declines, we cannot rule out the importance of chemical contamination—from oil as well as from hundreds of other toxins we release into the oceans. Although marine organisms are exposed to oil from natural seeps, we clearly are responsible for nearly 90 percent of the oil in the seas. Chronic oil pollution is an enormous problem and is compounded by a variety of small and large spills. We can affect oil pollution in the oceans by decreasing the number and size of oil spills. There are a number of ways to reduce oil spills, ranging from better tanker and barge design and different patterns of tanker traffic to more efficient cleanup methods (Table 14.1). Improved procedures to collect oil once it is spilled are particularly important, as this reduces pollution and recovers valuable oil.

Supertanker traffic around the United States already is very heavy. Of the 1.7 billion tons of crude oil transported annually around the world by sea, nearly a third passes through U.S. waters. This country's busiest ports are

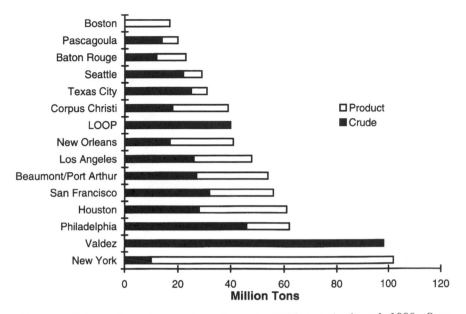

Figure 14.5. Tons of petroleum products that entered U.S. ports in the early 1990s. Some ports handle mostly crude (e.g., Valdez) while others handle mostly refined products (e.g., New York, Boston). (LOOP is the Louisiana Offshore Oil Port) (Source: Adapted from National Research Council, 1991, Tanker spills: prevention by design [National Academy Press, Washington, D.C.])

New York and Valdez, followed by Philadelphia (Delaware Bay), Houston, San Francisco, and Port Arthur, Texas (Fig.14.5). Mostly refined products come into New York, whereas mostly crude oil is moved into Valdez and the Louisiana Offshore Oil Port. Many of the other harbors import nearly equal amounts of crude oil and products. This traffic will increase because domestic production of oil is decreasing annually. The United States will rely increasingly on foreign oil. The National Academy of Science recently estimated that the United States' increasing reliance on foreign oil will raise the number of tanker port calls by 50 percent by the year 2000.

Of U.S. imports of crude oil, 30 percent comes from the Middle East, 25 percent comes from the Caribbean, and 20 percent comes from West Africa. On the West Coast, crude oil mostly comes from Alaska and Panama. Crude oil enters the Gulf states from the Caribbean; and crude and refined oil products enter the East Coast ports from the Persian Gulf, Africa, and the Caribbean. Although these are the major ports, oil must be transferred to smaller facilities all along the coasts. There will be an increase in the number of transfers from large supertankers to small ships and barges. With every "lightering" operation there is the potential for oil spills.

Not only is the direct traffic around the United States increasing, but

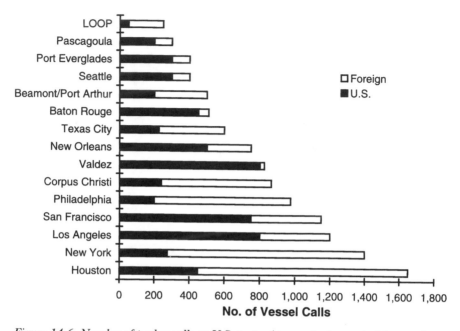

Figure 14.6. Number of tanker calls at U.S. ports: At some ports, most of the vessels are foreign-owned. It is clear by comparing Figures 14.5 and 14.6 that ports such as Houston have a large number of calls but handle less oil, suggesting that supertanker size is smaller. (Source: *Adapted from National Research Council, 1991,* Tanker spills: prevention by design [*National Academy Press, Washington, D.C.*])

there is an increase in the number of offshore ports where large supertankers transfer oil to smaller ships. These offshore ports are often in the open ocean, where they are exposed to severe storms, increasing the possibility for accidents. The relatively new development of offshore ports requires special technology for the safety of vessels and crew, and for the safe transfer of oil products in inclement weather. There are also offshore pipelines that lighten vessels and pump the oil into a refinery or holding facility on shore.

Tanker safety, construction, and training of the crew are critical for the reduction of oil spills. About fifteen hundred different supertankers call at the fifteen busiest ports in the United States, and the vast majority of these tankers fly foreign flags (Fig. 14.6). The problem is not quite as bad as the graph would suggest, however, because nearly half of the tanker calls involve ships under U.S. ownership. The ships that fly U.S. flags enter our ports more often each year than do individual foreign ships. The ownership of supertankers is important because construction standards are implemented by legislation in each country. Standards differ markedly.

Ships operating between U.S. ports are required by law to be constructed in the United States. However, there are no such restrictions on ships engaged in international trade with U.S. ports. This means that large supertankers are built at yards offering the lowest costs—and these are all outside the United States.

The Coast Guard can inspect foreign-flag tankers that enter U.S. ports to ensure that they comply with international standards, but not U.S. standards. U.S. law requires that a foreign vessel's casualty and pollution history be evaluated before it enters U.S. waters. Even so, a supertanker's condition is influenced by its age, size, country of registry, and owner maintenance policies.

Overall tanker construction has suffered over the years, largely due to the production of efficient, streamlined supertankers that have few of the traditional allowances for errors, deterioration, or unknown safety factors. Design standards need to be strengthened once again to include corrosion protection and high-tensile steel, and to allow for the possibility of collisions and groundings. Tankers are not designed with collisions and groundings specifically in mind, but only with transport. Imagine the lunacy of designing a car with no ability to withstand an accident. When we design cars, we do so with the intention of being able to survive collisions with other cars, trees, and rocks. Car manufacturers even advertise their cars by showing how little damage the car and passengers suffer following an accident. We should design supertankers similarly.

One aspect of tanker construction that could drastically reduce oil spills is double bottoms (only the bottom is doubled) and double hulls (the whole hull has a double skin). When double-hulled ships are used, there are almost no major oil spills; for more than five hundred ship-years (equals one ship running five hundred years, five hundred ships running one year each, or a combination thereof) there were seventy-seven groundings of tankers with double hulls, and none resulted in pollution. For all single-hulled accidents, about 9 percent result in pollution. This in itself is remarkable, that most supertanker accidents, whether of ships with single or double hulls, do not release oil into surrounding waters.

Knowing that oil spills could be drastically reduced by the use of double bottoms or hulls, however, does not ensure their use. It will take many years before all the world's supertankers—or even the U.S. fleet—have double hulls. Nearly 80 percent of the supertankers used worldwide have only a single hull at present. In the U.S. fleet, only one in six tankers has a double hull. The Oil Pollution Act of 1990 requires that all new tankers—those contracted for after June 30, 1990, or delivered after January 1, 1994—operating in U.S. waters be fitted with double hulls. Existing single-hulled boats are allowed to operate in U.S. waters only until January 1, 2010. Ships with double bottoms or double sides can operate until the year 2015. It will be 2015 before all tankers entering U.S. waters have double hulls! A recent National Academy of Science committee concluded that double hulls are the single-most important aspect of tanker design to reduce oil spills. Nothing else works as well. Yet the International Maritime Organization, the United Nations agency responsible for maritime safety and environmental protection of the seas, has not enacted rules about the use of double hulls.

The International Convention for the Prevention of Pollution from Ships, adopted in 1973 and amended in 1978, is the basic law limiting pollution from ships. It has provisions for structural and operational vessel safety on the high seas. All of the world's major shipping nations are members and are encouraged to adopt the international agreements. This convention does not require double hulls, although they do encourage several ballast tanks designed to reduce oil spillage.

Someday double hulls will be a reality for all supertankers—at least those entering U.S. territorial waters. Today, however, industries are starting to recognize the importance of using double hulls. In a recent copy of *Smithsonian*, I notice that DuPont has a full-page ad featuring a dolphin, a young seal, and a whale; the message reads: "Its energy unit, Conoco, will pioneer the use of double-hulled oil tankers to help safeguard the environment." It goes on to say that such tankers will cost 15 percent more than conventional oil tankers and will carry about 10 percent less oil, but that their use could eliminate or significantly reduce the damage from oil spills. It is a most effective ad, and perhaps suggests that public opinion might at last hold sway. I certainly will use Conoco whenever I can.

Size is another factor in oil spill accidents: Intermediate-sized tankers have the worst safety record. Intermediate-sized vessels have about the same rate of groundings and collisions as larger tankers, but worldwide they have 33 percent more fires and explosions. This suggests that either there is something about the design of these tankers or about their operations that make fires more likely. Part of the problem is that intermediate-sized tankers have less space between compartments, making safety inspections and maintenance more difficult. Fires and explosions have been largely eliminated from the United States fleet through increased safety training, improved maintenance, and better tanker design. Age is another factor that affects safety; older ships have more accidents, particularly fires and explosions. They do not have more collisions.

The oil that enters the oceans from accidents comes largely from fire and explosions, collisions, groundings, and structural problems (Fig. 14.7). We have nearly eliminated the amount of oil spilled because of tanker construction, although such accidents continue to happen. Oil spilled from collisions and groundings can be almost completely eliminated by double hulls, so even this type of accident should slowly decrease as we switch to double-hulled supertankers. Accidents from supertankers, however, ac-

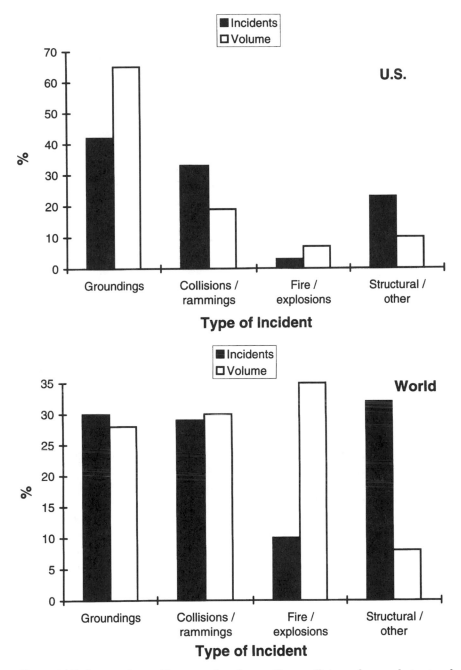

Figure 14.7. Supertanker accidents consist of groundings, collisions, fires, and structural problems. Although fires account for few of the incidents, they account for nearly 35 percent of the oil that spills into the oceans. (Source: *Adapted from National Research Council, 1991,* Tanker spills: prevention by design [*National Academy Press, Washinton, D.C.*])

count for something less than 20 percent of the oil that enters the oceans. Even if we reduce all oil spills from large tankers, we must work on decreasing the amount of oil that enters our oceans from other sources, such as runoff, river discharges, and small-scale transfer and use operations.

Legal constraints clearly can reduce the number of spills. The Oil Pollution Act of 1990's requirement concerning double hulls will drastically reduce large accidents in U.S. waters. In the year following the spill in the Arthur Kill, there were far fewer small spills, largely due to public attention and the reality of cleanup costs and large fines levied on Exxon for damages to natural resources.

The Future

Use of energy has increased worldwide over the past forty-five years (Fig. 14.8), a pattern that is expected to continue over the next fifty years. However, the transport of oil around the world will surely change with shifting political and economic climates and with the development of new oil reserves, particularly in offshore regions of the Middle East and Far East, and in arctic regions. As countries suffer internal strife, political upheaval, and bad economic times, they may become destabilized, requiring even more oil from external sources.

The U.S. consumption of oil is likely to increase slightly, and petroleum, natural gas, and coal will continue to provide most of its energy (Fig. 14.9). World oil prices, given current energy needs and production, are expected to remain relatively constant. Energy predictions do not call for the cost of oil reaching the highs of the mid-1970s and mid-1980s (Fig. 14.10). Since the American public is so concerned about the safety of nuclear power, this source is unlikely to become a major source of energy over the next few decades. Development of gas and oil reserves on the North Slope of Alaska, including the Arctic National Wildlife Refuge, will ensure that the United States will continue to produce the bulk of its requirements. Most Alaskans are in favor of oil development; they feel there is a lot of wilderness in Alaska, there are few people in Alaska, and they can absorb more development. Many Americans elsewhere question the wisdom of this exploitation; and it may be desirable to determine whether the harm to the wildlife refuge and wildlife can be offset by benefits from reduced oil spills.

The big change in energy development over the next fifty years will be continued oil exploration and drilling in arctic environments. This is the next frontier, particularly in Russia and Asia. Although most world production and proven oil resources are in temperate regions, there are enormous untapped oil reserves in arctic regions, and with development of new tech-

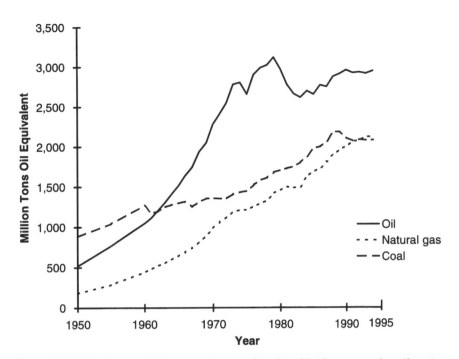

Figure 14.8. Relative use of oil, natural gas, and coal worldwide, converted to oil equivalent.

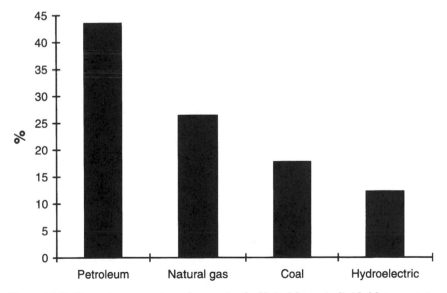

Figure 14.9. Current consumption of energy in the United States is divided between petroleum and natural gas, with less use of coal and hydroelectric.

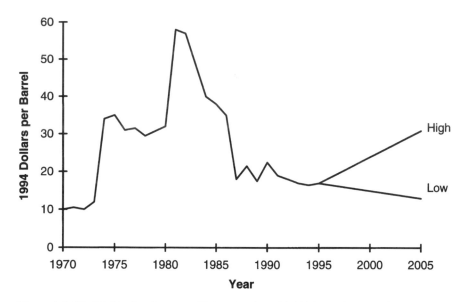

Figure 14.10. World oil prices were highest in the mid-1970s to the mid-1980s, but are expected to remain relatively low for the next decade. (Source: *Adapted from Department of Energy, 1994,* International energy annual report [*U.S. Department of Energy, Washington, D.C.*])

niques and equipment, these reserves will surely be explored (Figs. 14.11 and 14.12). Arctic environments provide unique challenges, both because it is difficult for machinery and men to work in such harsh and cold environments and because oil partially solidifies at low temperatures, and thus does not flow as easily.

Arctic ecosystems are also more fragile than temperate ones, and a large oil spill on a delicate tundra could foul it so that decades and centuries would pass before it would recover. At present, development of arctic reserves is occurring on land rather than offshore. This is positive for the oceans, but on land there is no possibility for dilution. In the oceans, oil diffuses away from the accident, and although slicks several miles long can drift from supertankers, over time, the oil is diluted by the vast quantities of water in the seas.

Oil that spills on the land normally seeps in, but in the arctic even this is prevented because of the permafrost layer that serves as a barrier. The oil remains on the surface, where it can kill everything in its reach. There are few microorganisms in the arctic that can biodegrade oil, and those that are there have little time to act, for most of the year is too cold. Natural biodegradation will proceed very slowly on a landscape that itself is covered with plants that grow very slowly. Giant lakes of spilled oil could mar the

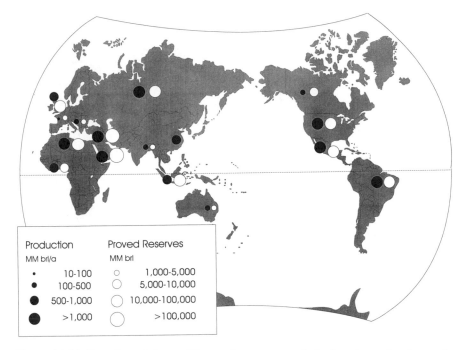

Figure 14.11. Location of the world's petroleum reserves, both those in production and proven reserves. (Source: *Adapted from E. N. Tiratsoo, 1984,* Oilfields of the world [*Scientific Press, Beaconsfield, England*])

arctic landscape if we are not careful. Presumably the oil in such lakes could be recovered, but collecting oil that is solidified and spread out in a thin sheet over miles of tundra would be a very difficult task. Also, when this happens in places facing tough economic times, as happened recently in Russia with the rupture in the Usinsk pipeline, there is little money for cleanup except what can be mobilized from foreign aid.

Species diversity is relatively low in the tundra, lower than almost anywhere else in the world. This means that the natural recovery rate is slow because nearly every organism must recover before the system can function properly. Recovery must be from the vegetation up, since it is here that the energy cycle begins. With many oil spills, the short tundra vegetation would be completely covered with oil, with high mortality and little chance for recovery for decades or centuries.

Repeated oil spills in any habitat can seriously damage it for decades, but this threat is more severe in the arctic. Habitats that are already stressed from other things—habitat destruction, other chemicals, human disturbance—may be less productive with repeated spills and may never be able to recover.

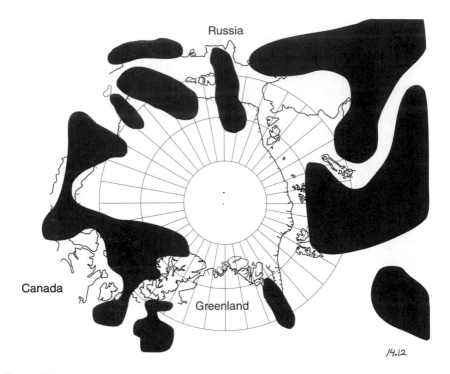

Figure 14.12. Location of suspected petroleum reserves in arctic regions. Few of these, except Alaska and Russia, have been explored extensively. (Source: *Adapted from F. R. Englehardt, 1985,* Petroleum effects in the arctic environment [*Elsevier Applied Science, New York*])

Petroleum and natural gas make up about 60 percent of the energy consumption of the world, and this will continue well into the next century. Most of the developed countries produce some oil, but not enough to satisfy their growing needs, so oil must be transported around the world from oil fields. The major oil wells and reserves are in the Middle East, and from there oil travels in supertankers to Europe, North America, and Japan.

There are many opportunities for oil to be accidentally spilled during exploration and drilling operations, en route, and during transfer or use at its destination. Oil enters the environment from occasional big, spectacular accidents as well as from countless small spills that happen during normal activities. Chronic oil pollution is a major problem because it actually contributes more oil to the world's oceans than do the major oil spills. Chronic oil pollution affects most major rivers, bays, and estuaries in both developed and undeveloped nations, although the problem is far worse in major seaports.

Although oil spills have been recorded since the turn of the century, they were relatively small and infrequent because the ships carrying oil held only so much oil, and no more could be spilled. However, in the 1950s small ships became tankers, and then tankers became supertankers able to carry 100,000 tons of oil. This drastically altered the amount of oil that could be spilled in any one accident. And even that amount would be doubled if two supertankers collide and burn, releasing all their oil into the seas or estuaries.

Oil spills increased in size and frequency in the late 1950s and 1960s, when environmental concerns prompted the drawing up of a number of world treaties to reduce the threats from oil pollution. This temporarily decreased oil pollution, but the pollution began to increase again with the building of larger supertankers, creating the possibility of gigantic spills. Over the last twenty years, the amount of oil spilled into the oceans has remained relatively constant.

The largest oil spill in history occurred during the Gulf War, when the Iraqis intentionally set over 650 Kuwaiti oil wells on fire and opened the pipes on oil terminals in the Gulf, allowing the oil to flow freely toward the desalination plants of southern Kuwait and Saudi Arabia. The threat of using oil as a military weapon is very real—it has been for hundreds of years—and one we must be prepared to fight.

With increasing reliance on oil, and increased transportation of oil around the world, the possibility of oil spills increases. This can be countered only with increased supertanker safety, better cleanup procedures, and stricter laws governing maintenance of vessels and inclusion of safety devices. One method to drastically reduce the amount of oil spilled is to require that all supertankers have double hulls. Double hulls may not decrease the number of collisions and groundings—pilot error and bad weather will continue—but they will reduce the amount of oil that flows into the oceans from these accidents.

Although the international regulations for supertankers do not require double hulls, U.S. regulations require that all new ships built after 1990 have double hulls, that all old ships that enter U.S. ports have double hulls or double bottoms by 2010, and that all ships be double-hulled by 2015. Since about one-third of the oil transported on the seas passes through U.S. waters, this will have a dramatic effect on oil pollution worldwide.

Other measures, such as safety maintenance and inspections, better tanker construction (noncorrosive materials, stronger steel), adequate space between compartments and hulls for safety inspections, and better radio and tracking equipment will also reduce the potential for tanker accidents. Similar considerations for nearshore oil transport and transfer will decrease oil pollution in bays and estuaries.

The importance of severe legal penalties and fines cannot be underestimated. If the total cost from an oil spill—cleanup costs, damages for natural resources, and criminal and civil fines—are less than the costs of implementing the safety measures, proper training for captain and crew, and building safe supertankers, then oil companies will simply absorb these as operating costs. The Oil Pollution Act of 1990 created a climate for higher fines and penalties in the United States, but many of its provisions have yet to be accepted internationally.

Finally, our biggest problem remains the chronic oil pollution along the coasts of the world. This oil comes from runoff, discharges from rivers and streams, and the hundreds of small leaks that occur with the everyday transport, transfer, and use of oil. These small spills of only tens of gallons or hundreds of gallons add up to millions of gallons because of the constant and continuous use of petroleum products worldwide.

Spectacular oil spills receive enormous media attention—as well they should—but we must now turn our attention to controlling chronic oil pollution or we will see life in the oceans deteriorate even more rapidly. Planktonic organisms floating in the seas will decrease in numbers, shellfish and other invertebrates will then decrease because their food supply has diminished, and small fish will decline as a result. The whole oceanic ecosystem in many parts of the world could collapse around us. This has happened in isolated places, largely due to overfishing and environmental contaminants. We now have the potential to produce large-scale death in the oceans.

We have the technological means and the legal means to drastically decrease the amount of oil that enters our oceans. Future technologies should, and must, be developed to decrease this possibility even further. It is up to us to force the companies that produce, transport, and transfer oil to eliminate the discharge of oil; we must force our local gas stations and others to prevent leaking of oil from underground tanks; and we must be vigilant to reduce our own individual releases when we change our car or lawnmower oil, handle heating oil, and maintain our oil-guzzling machines.

The plants and animals that live in the ocean have a remarkable ability to withstand oil pollution—indeed, some organisms have adapted to living off oil—but their adaptability is not limitless. They require time to recover from one environmental insult before being exposed to another. With each large oil spill, the ability to recover is diminished. At the very least, the time for populations to recover is extended. If oil spills occur too close together in time, the system cannot recover. If oil spills occur too close together spatially, recovery is delayed because there are no nearby organisms to move in and colonize the oil spill area. When spills happen close together in both time and space, the ecosystem can be devastated and recovery can take decades or centuries. Some may never recover.

Appendix:
Species Mentioned
in the Text

Plants
arrowhead, *Sagittaria*
black grass, *Juncus* spp.
cedar of Lebanon, *Cedrus libani*
cordgrass, *Spartina alterniflora*
dwarf willow, *Salix*
eelgrass, *Zostera* spp.
fucus (brown algae), *Fucus spiralis*
hemlock, *Tsuga canadensis*
kelp, *Laminaria digitata*
mangrove, *Rhizophora mangle*
plantagos, plantains, *Plantago* spp.
redwood, *Sequoia sempervirens*
salt hay, *Spartina patens*
saltwort, *Salicornia* spp.
seagrass, *Thalassia testudinum*
spruces, *Picea* spp.

Invertebrates
abalone (red abalone), *Haliotis rufescens*
American oyster, *Crassotrea virginica*
beach fleas, order Cladocera
blue crab, *Callinectes sapidus*
clam, *Mya arenaria*
copepods, orders Calanoida and Cyclopoida
crab, *Callinectes sapidus*
Dungeness crab, *Cancer magister*
edible crab, *Cancer pagurus*
fiddler crabs, *Uca* spp.

grass shrimp, *Palaeomonetes* spp.
hard-shelled clam, *Mercenaria mercenaria*
horseshoe crab, *Limulus polyphemus*
king crab, *Lopholithodus mandtii*
lobsters, *Homarus* spp.
mud snail, *Melampus bidentatus*
mussel, *Geukensia demissus*
oyster, *Crassostrea virginica*
periwinkle, *Litorina litorea*
razor clams, *Solen* spp., *Ensis* spp.
ribbed mussel, *Modiolus demissus* (or *Geukensia demissus)*
sand worm, *Nereis virens*
scallop (Mexico), *Aequipecten irradians*
shore crab, *Carcinus maenas*
shrimp, *Palaemonetes* spp.
soft-shelled clam, *Mya arenaria*
spot shrimp, *Leander serratus*
worm, *Capitella*

Fish
anchovy, *Anchoa* spp.
Atlantic croaker, *Micropogonias undulatus*
Atlantic silversides, *Menidia menidia*
bluefish, *Pomatomus saltatrix*
chum salmon, *Oncorhynchus keta*
cod, *Gadus morhua*
cutthroat trout, *Salmo clarki*
dab, *Limanda limanda*
Dolly Varden trout, *Salmalinus malma*
English sole, *Parophyrys vetulus*
gray mullets, *Mugil* spp.
groupers, *Epinephelus* spp.
killifish, *Fundulus heteroclitus, F. majalis*
mackerel, *Scomber scomber*
mullet (white mullet), *Mugil curema*
mummichog, *Fundulus heteroclitis*
Pacific herring, *Clupea harengus*
pink salmon, *Oncorhynchus gorbuscha*
plaice, *Pleuronectes platessa*
pollack, *Gadus pollachius*
rockfish, *Sebastes* spp.
salmon, *Salmo* spp., *Oncorhynchus* spp.
sand eels, *Ammodytes* spp.
sand sole, *Psettichthys melanostichus*
sharks, order Squaliformes
smelt (topsmelt), *Atherinops affinis*
snapper (red snapper), *Lutjanus campechanus*

sockeye salmon, *Oncorhynchus nerka*
sole, *Solea vulgaris*
swordfish, *Xiphias gladius*
tuna, family Scombridae, *Thunnus* spp.

Reptiles
California desert tortoise, *Gopherus* (= *Xerobates*) *agassizii*
diamondback terrapin, *Malaclemys terrapin*
green sea turtle, *Chelonia mydas*
Kemp's ridley sea turtle, *Lepidochelys kempii*

Birds
anhinga, *Anhinga anhinga*
auk, *Alca torda*
bald eagle, *Haliaeetus leucocephalus*
black-backed gull, *Larus marinus*
blackbird, *Agelaius phoeniceus*
black-crowned night heron, *Nycticorax nycticorax*
black-footed penguin, *Spheniscus demersus*
black guillemot, *Cepphus grylle*
black-necked grebe (eared grebe), *Podiceps nigricollis*
black oystercatcher, *Haematopus bachmani*
black skimmer, *Rynchops niger*
Cassin's auklet, *Ptychoramphus aleuticus*
common eider, *Somateria mollissima*
common murre, *Uria aalge*
common tern, *Sterna hirundo*
crows, *Corvus* spp.
dunlin, *Calidris alpina*
eider, *Somateria mollissima*
fork-tailed storm petrel, *Oceanodroma furcata*
Forster's tern, *Sterna forsterii*
fulmar, *Fulmarus glacialis*
gannet, *Sula bassanus*
glaucous gull, *Larus hyperboreus*
glaucous-winged gull, *Larus glaucescens*
glossy ibis, *Plegadis falcinellus*
goldeneye, *Bucephala clangula*
great cormorant, *Phalacrocorax carbo*
great-crested grebe, *Podiceps cristatus*
great black-backed gull, *Larus marinus*
great egret, *Egretta alba*
grebes, family Podicipiidae
guillemot, *Uria aalge*
gulls, *Larus* spp.
hairy woodpecker, *Picoides villosus*
harlequin duck, *Histrionicus histrionicus*

herring gull, *Larus argentatus*
horned grebe, *Podiceps auritus*
jackass penguin, *Spheniscus demersus*
Japanese quail, *Coturnix coturnix*
kittiwake, *Rissa tridactyla*
Kittlitz's murrelet, *Brachyramphus brevirostris*
laughing gull, *Larus atricilla*
Leach's storm petrel, *Oceanodroma leucorhoa*
least tern, *Sterna antillarum*
little auk (dovekie), *Alle alle*
long-tailed duck, *Clangula hyemalis*
loons, *Gavia* spp.
Louisiana heron, *Hydranassa tricolor*
magpie, *Pica nuttalli*
mallard, *Anas platyrhynchos*
Manx shearwater, *Puffinus puffinus*
marbled murrelet, *Brachyramphus marmoratus*
marsh hawk, *Circus cyaneus*
mergansers, *Mergus* spp.
murres, *Uria* spp.
oldsquaw, *Clangula hyemalis*
Olrog's gull, *Larus atlanticus*
petrels, family Hydrobatidae
pigeon, *Columba livia*
pigeon guillemot, *Cepphus columba*
piping plover, *Charadrius melodus*
puffin, *Fratercula arctica*
raven, *Corvus corax*
razorbill auk, *Alca torda*
red knot, *Calidris canutus*
rhinoceros auklet, *Cerorhinea monocerata*
sanderling, *Calidris alba*
sandwich tern, *Sterna sandvicensis*
scaups, *Aythya* spp.
scoters, *Melanitta* spp.
sea ducks (eiders, *Somateria* spp.; scoters, *Melanitta* spp.; oldsquaw, *Clangula hyemalis*)
semipalmated sandpiper, *Calidris pusilla*
snowy egret, *Egretta thula*
snowy owl, *Nyctea scandiaca*
Socotra cormorant, *Phalacrocorax nigrogularis*
sooty gull, *Larus hemprichii*
sooty tern, *Sterna fuscata*
sparrows, *Ammodramus* spp.
steamer duck, *Tachyeres leucocephalus*
streaked shearwater, *Calonectris leucomelas*
vultures, family Cathartidae
wedge-tailed shearwater, *Puffinus pacificus*

western grebe, *Aechmophorus occidentalis*
white-winged scoter, *Melanitta deglandi*
yellow-billed loon, *Gavia adamsii*

Mammals

arctic fox, *Alopex lagopus*
bison, *Bison bison*
black bear, *Ursus americanus*
caribou, *Rangifer tarandus*
deer, *Odocoileus* spp.
dire wolf, *Canus dirus*
dugong, *Dugong dugon*
European otter, *Lutra lutra*
fur seal, *Callorhinus ursinus*
giant ground sloth, *Megatherium*
glacier seal = harbor seal = *Phoca vitulina*
harbor seal, *Phoca vitulina*
humpback whale, *Megaptera novaeangliae*
hyena, *Crocuta crocuta*
killer whale, *Orcinus orca*
lemming, *Lemmus trimucronatus, Synaptomys borealis, Dicrostonyx groenlandicus*
manatee, *Trichechus manatus*
muskrat, *Ondatra zibethicus*
orca, *Orca orcinus*
polar bear, *Ursus maritimus*
raccoon, *Procyon lotor*
reindeer = caribou = *Rangifer tarandus*
ringed seal, *Phoca hispida*
river otter, *Lutra canadensis*
saber-toothed cat, *Smilodon*
sea lion (California = *Zalophus californianus*; Steller or northern = *Eumetopias jubatus*)
sea otter, *Enhydra lutris*
squirrel (California ground squirrel), *Citellus beecheyi*
walrus, *Odobenus rosmarus*
white-sided dolphin (Pacific), *Lagenorhynchus obliquidens*

Selected Readings

General

BAKER, J. M., R. B. CLARK, P. F. KINGSTON, AND R. H. JENKINS. 1990. Natural recovery of cold water marine environments after an oil spill. Thirteenth annual Arctic and Marine Oil Spill Program, Edinburgh, Scotland.

BOESCH, D. F., AND N. N. RABALAIS. 1984. *Long-term environmental effects of offshore oil and gas development.* Elsevier Applied Science, New York.

CAHILL, R. A. 1990. *Disasters at sea: Titanic to Exxon Valdez.* Nautical Books, San Antonio, Tex.

CAIRNS, J., JR., AND A. L. BUIKEMA, JR. 1984. *Restoration of habitats impacted by oil spills.* Butterworth Publishers, Boston.

CAIRNS, W. J., AND P. M. ROGERS. 1980. *Onshore impacts of offshore oil.* Applied Science Publishers, London.

COX, G. V., A. BARNETT, J. R. COULD, K. G. HAY, J. HIROTA, C. D. MCAULIFFE, AND A. D. MICHAEL. 1980. *Oil spill studies: Strategies and techniques.* Pathotox Publishers, Park Forest South, Ill.

CUTTER INFORMATION CORP. 1995. *International oil spill statistics: 1994.* Cutter Information Corp., Arlington, Mass.

DEPARTMENT OF ENERGY. 1980–94. *International energy annual reports.* U.S. Department of Energy, Washington, D.C.

DOERFFER, J. W. 1992. *Oil spill response in the marine environment.* Pergamon Press, New York.

ENGELHARDT, F. R. 1985. *Petroleum effects in the arctic environment.* Elsevier Applied Science, New York.

LANE, P. 1995. *The use of chemicals in oil spill response.* ASTM Publishers, Philadelphia, Pa.

NATIONAL RESEARCH COUNCIL. 1991. *Tanker spills: Prevention by design.* National Academy Press, Washington, D.C.

PAYNE, J. R., AND C. R. PHILLIPS. 1985. *Petroleum spills in the marine environment.* Lewis Publishers, Chelsea, Mich.

PRITCHARD, S. Z. 1987. *Oil pollution control.* Croom Helm, London, England.

SPAULDING, M. L., AND M. REED, EDS. 1990. *Oil spills: Management and legislative implications.* American Society of Civil Engineers, New York.

TIRATSOO, E. N. 1984. *Oilfields of the world.* Scientific Press, Beaconsfield, England.

Selected Readings for Chapter 1

BURGER, J., ED. 1994. *Before and after an oil spill: The Arthur Kill.* Rutgers University Press, New Brunswick, N.J.

EXXON VALDEZ OIL SPILL TRUSTEE COUNCIL. 1995. *1995 status report.* Exxon Valdex Oil Spill Trustee Council, Anchorage, Alaska.

MOLAK, V., W. DAVIS-HOOVER, S. KHAN, AND M. MEHLMAN, EDS. 1992. *A comprehensive approach to problems with oil spills in the marine environments: The Alaska story.* Princeton Scientific Publishing, Princeton, N.J.

Selected Readings for Chapter 2

CUTTER INFORMATION CORP. 1995. *International oil spill statistics: 1994.* Cutter Information Corp., Arlington, Mass.

DEPARTMENT OF ENERGY. 1988. *International energy annual report.* U.S. Department of Energy, Washington, D.C.

————. 1994. *International energy annual report.* U.S. Department of Energy, Washington, D.C.

NATIONAL RESEARCH COUNCIL. 1996. *An assessment of techniques for removing offshore structures.* National Academy Press, Washington, D.C.

PRINGLE, L. 1993. *Oil spills: Damage, recovery and prevention.* Morrow Junior Books, New York.

SCHACKNE, S., AND N. D. DRAKE. 1960. *Oil for the world.* Harper, New York.

TIRATSOO, E. N. 1984. *Oilfields of the world.* Scientific Press, Beaconsfield, England.

Selected Readings for Chapter 3

CAHILL, R. A. 1990. *Disasters at sea:* Titanic *to* Exxon Valdez. Nautical Books, San Antonio, Tex.

CHASSE, C. 1978. The ecological impact on and near shores by the *Amoco Cadiz* oil spill. *Marine Pollution Bulletin* 9:298–301.

CUTTER INFORMATION CORPORATION. 1995. *International oil spill statistics:* 1994. Cutter Information Corp., Arlington, Mass.

GUNDLACH, E. R., P. D. BOEHM, M. MARCHAND, R. M. ATLAS, D. M. WARD, AND D. A. WOLFE. 1983. Fate of the *Amoco Cadiz* oil. *Science* 221:122–129.

JACOFF, F. S., ED. 1979. *A small oil spill at West Falmouth.* Environmental Protection Agency, EPA 600/9-79-007, Washington, D.C.

JONES, P. H., J. Y. MONNAT, C. J. CADBURY, AND T. J. STOWE. 1978. Birds oiled during the *Amoco Cadiz* incident: An interim report. *Marine Pollution Bulletin* 9:307–310.

METZ, W. D. 1978. Mexico: The premier oil discovery in the Western Hemisphere. *Science* 202:1261–1265.

MOLDAN, A.G.S., L. F. JACKSON, S. McGILLON, AND J. V. DERWESTHUIZEN. 1985. Some aspects of the *Castillo de Bellver* oil spill. *Marine Pollution Bulletin* 16:97–102.

WALDICHUK, M. 1980. Retrospect of the Ixtoc 1 blowout. *Marine Pollution Bulletin* 11:184–186.

Selected Readings for Chapter 4

BORNE, W.R.P. 1995. Viewpoint: Persian/Arabian Gulf wars and the environment. *Pacific Seabirds* 22:3–6.

BURGER, J., ED. 1994. *Before and after an oil spill: The Arthur Kill.* Rutgers University Press, New Brunswick, N.J.

CAHILL, R. A. 1990. *Disasters at sea:* Titanic *to* Exxon Valdez. Nautical Books, San Antonio, Tex.

EXXON VALDEZ OIL SPILL TRUSTEE COUNCIL. 1995. *1995 status report.* Exxon Valdez Oil Spill Trustee Council, Anchorage, Alaska.

———. 1996. *Restoration plan: Draft update on injured resources and services.* Exxon Valdez Oilspill Trustee Council, Anchorage, Alaska.

FALL, J. A. 1993. Subsistence uses of fish and wildlife. *Alaska's Wildlife* 25:4–6.

FRAKER, M. 1993. In the wake of the spill: Injury, assessment and restoration. *Alaska's Wildlife* 25:3.

GORBICS, C. 1993. The fate of sea otters following the spill. *Alaska's Wildlife* 25:16–17.

HUSAIN, T. 1995. *Kuwaiti oil fires: Regional environmental perspectives.* Pergamon, Tarrytown, New York.

KADO, R., H. TOKUDA, H. SATOH, S. HANAWA, AND Y. MURATA. 1993. Influence of a big oil spill during the Gulf War on intertidal invertebrates. In *Proceedings of 1993 International Oil Spill Conference,* pp. 859–860. American Petroleum Institute, Washington, D.C.

KHORDAGUI, H., AND D. AL-AJMI. 1993. Environmental impact of the Gulf War: An integrated preliminary assessment. *Environmental Management* 17:557–562.

LOUGHLIN, T. R., ED. 1994. *Marine mammals and the* Exxon Valdez. Academic Press, New York.

MOLAK, V., W. DAVIS-HOOVER, S. KHAN, AND M. MEHLMAN, ED. 1992. *A comprehensive approach to problems with oil spills in marine environments: The Alaska story.* Princeton Scientific Publishing, Princeton, N.J.

PARRISH, J. K, AND P. D. BOERSMA. 1995. Muddy waters. *American Scientist* 83:112–115.

PIATT, J. 1993. The oil spill and seabirds: Three years later. *Alaska's Wildlife* 25:11–13.

ROGERS, M. 1978. Black day for Brittany. *National Geographic* 154:124–135.

WALSH, J. 1968. Pollution: The wake of the *Torrey Canyon. Science* 160:167–169.

Selected Readings for Chapter 5

ALLEN, A. A., R. S. SCHLUETER, AND P. G. MIKOLAJ. 1970. Natural oil seepage at Coal Point, Santa Barbara, California. *Science* 179:974–977.

CLARK, K. E., L. J. NILES, AND J. BURGER. 1993. Abundance and distribution of migrant shorebirds in Delaware Bay. *Condor* 95:694–705.

KVENVOLDEN, K. A. 1983. Reassessment of the rates at which oil from natural sources enters the marine environment. *Marine Environmental Research* 10:223–243.

WILSON, R. S., P. H. MONAGHAN, A. OSANIK, L. C. PRICE, AND M. A. ROGERS. 1974. Natural marine oil seepage. *Science* 184:857–865.

Selected Readings for Chapter 6

HAUGE, P. M., AND R. K. TUCKER. 1994. Governmental cooperation. In *Before and after an oil spill: The Arthur Kill* (J. Burger, ed.), pp. 23–43. Rutgers University Press, New Brunswick, N.J.

JOHNSON, G. J. 1994. Legal considerations. In *Before and after an oil spill: The Arthur Kill* (J. Burger, ed.), pp. 44–63. Rutgers University Press, New Brunswick, N.J.

NATIONAL OCEANIC AND ATMOSPHERIC ADMINISTRATION. 1995. *Reversing the tide: Restoring the nation's coastal and marine natural resources*. NOAA, Washington D.C.

PIPER, E. 1993. *The* Exxon Valdez *oil spill: Final report, state of Alaska response*. Alaska Department of Environmental Conservation, Anchorage, Alaska.

Selected Readings for Chapter 7

ALBERS, P. H. 1979. Oil dispersants and wildlife. In *Proceedings of the 1979 Pollution Response Workshop*, pp. 67–71. U. S. Fish and Wildlife Service, Washington, D.C.

ATLAS, R. M., AND R. BARTHA. 1992. Hydrocarbon biodegradation and oil spill remediation. *Advances in Microbial Ecology* 12:287–338.

BURGER, J. 1994. Bioremediation and the Arthur Kill. In *Before and after an oil spill: The Arthur Kill*. (J. Burger, ed.), pp. 99–114. Rutgers University Press, New Brunswick, N.J.

FRINK, L. 1994. Rehabilitation of contaminated wildlife. In *Before and after an oil spill: The Arthur Kill* (J. Burger, ed.), pp. 83–98. Rutgers University Press, New Brunswick, N.J.

KELSO, D. D., AND M. KENDZIOREK. 1991. Alaska's response to the *Exxon Valdez* oil spill. *Environmental Science and Technology* 25:16–22.

LANE, P. 1995. *The use of chemicals in oil spill response*. ASTM Publishers, Philadelphia, Pa.

LINDSTEDT-SIVA, J., P. H. ALBERS, K. W. FUCIK, AND N. G. MAYNARD. 1984. Ecological considerations for the use of dispersants in oil spill response. In *Oil spill chemical dispersants: Research, experience, and recommendations* (T. E. Allen, ed.), pp. 363–377. American Society for Testing and Materials, Philadelphia, Pa.

NATIONAL RESEARCH COUNCIL. 1989. *Using oil spill dispersants on the sea*. National Academy Press, Washington, D.C.

PIPER, E. 1993. *The* Exxon Valdez *oil spill: Final report, state of Alaska response*. Alaska Department of Environmental Conservation, Anchorage, Alaska.

SINGER, M. M., D. L. SMALHEER, AND R. S. TJERDEMA. 1991. Effects of spiked exposure to an oil dispersant on the early life stages of four marine species. *Environmental Toxicology and Chemistry* 10:1367–1374.

SPAULDING, M. L., AND M. REED, EDS. 1990. *Oil spills: Management and legislative implications*. American Society of Civil Engineers, New York.

Selected Readings for Chapter 8

BAKER, J. M. 1971. Seasonal effects of oil pollution on salt marsh vegetation. *Oikos* 22:106–110.

———. 1979. Responses of salt marsh vegetation to oil spills and refinery effluents. In *Ecological processes in coastal environments* (R. L. Jeffries and D. J. Davy, eds.), pp. 529–570. Blackwell Scientific Publications, Oxford, England.

———. 1993. Long-term fate and effects of untreated thick oil deposits on salt marshes. In *Proceedings of 1993 International Oil Spill Conference*, pp. 1–22. American Petroleum Institute, Washington, D.C.

BURGER, J. 1994. Effects of oil on vegetation. In *Before and after an oil spill: The Arthur Kill* (J. Burger, ed.) pp. 130–141. Rutgers University Press, New Brunswick, N.J.

GARRITY, S. D., S. G. LEVINGS, AND K. A. BURNS. 1994. The Galeta oil spill: I. Long-term effects on the physical structure of the mangrove fringe. *Estuarine, Coastal and Shelf Science* 38:327–348.

HERSHNER, C., AND J. LAKE. 1980. Effects of chronic oil pollution on a salt-marsh grass community. *Marine Biology* 56:163–173.

JACKSON, J.B.C., J. D. CUBIT, D. B. KELLER, V. BATISTA, K. BURNS, H. M. CAFFEY, R. L. CALDWELL, S. D. GARRITY, C. D. GETTER, C. GONZALEZ, H. M. GUZMAN, K. W. KAUFMANN, A. H. KNAP, S. C. LEVINGS, M. J. MARSHALL, R. STEGER, R. C. THOMPSON, AND E. WEIL. 1989. Ecological effects of a major oil spill on Panamanian coastal marine communities. *Science* 243:37–44.

LECK, M. A., AND R. L. SIMPSON. 1992. Effect of oil on recruitment from the seed bank of two tidal freshwater wetlands. *Wetlands Ecology and Management* 1:223–231.

Selected Readings for Chapter 9

Alaska Department of Fish and Game. 1993. Biological effects of the *Exxon Valdez* oil spill. *Alaska's Wildlife* 25:1–46.

BAKER, J. M., R. B. CLARK, P. F. KINGSTON, AND R. H. JENKINS. 1990. Natural recovery of cold water marine environments after an oil spill. Thirteenth Annual Arctic and Marine Oil Spill Program, Edinburgh, Scotland.

BOLZE, D., AND M. LEE. 1989. Offshore oil and gas development: The ecological effects beyond the offshore platform. In *Proceedings of the Sixth Symposium on Coastal and Ocean Management.* NOAA, Charleston, S.C.

BRZORAD, J. N., AND J. BURGER, 1994. Fish and shrimp populations in the Arthur Kill. In *Before and after an oil spill: The Arthur Kill* (J. Burger, ed.), pp. 178–200. Rutgers University Press, New Brunswick, N.J.

BURGER, J., J. N. BRZORAD, AND M. GOCHFELD. 1994. Fiddler crabs (*Uca* spp.) as bioindicators for oil spills. In *Before and after an oil spill: The Arthur Kill* (J. Burger, ed.), pp. 160–177. Rutgers University Press, New Brunswick, N.J.

CONAN, G. 1982. The long-term effects of the *Amoco Cadiz* oil spill. *Transactions of the Royal Society of London* B:297:323–333.

COOPER, K. R., AND A. CRISTINI. 1994. The effects of oil spills on bivalve mollusks and blue crabs. In *Before and after an oil spill: The Arthur Kill* (J. Burger, ed.), pp.142–159. Rutgers University Press, New Brunswick, N.J.

ELMGREN, R., S. HANSSON, U. LARSSON, B. SUNDELIN, AND P. D. BOEHM. 1983. The *Tsesis* oil spill: Acute and long-term impact on the benthos. *Marine Biology* 73:51–65.

FUCIK, K. W., T. J. BRIGHT, AND K. S. GOODMAN. 1984. Measurements of damage, recovery and rehabilitation of coral reefs exposed to oil. In *Restoration of habitats impacted by oil spills* (J. Cairns, Jr., and A. L. Buikema, Jr., eds.), pp. 115–133. Butterworth Publications, Boston.

GARRITY, S. D., AND S. C. LEVINGS. 1993. Effects of an oil spill on some organisms living on mangrove (*Rhizophora mangle*) roots in low wave-energy habitats in Central Panama. *Marine Environmental Research* 35:251–273.

GRASSLE, J. F., AND J. P. GRASSLE. 1974. Opportunistic life histories and genetic systems in marine benthic polychaetes. *Journal of Marine Research* 32:253–284.

JACKSON, J.B.C., J. D. CUBIT, D. B. KELLER, V. BATISTA, K. BURNS, H. M. CAFFEY, R. L. CALDWELL, S. D. GARRITY, C. D. GETTER, C. GONZALEZ, H. M. GUZMAN, K. W. KAUF-

MANN, A. H. KNAP, S. C. LEVINGS, M. J. MARSHALL, R. STEGER, R. C. THOMPSON, AND E. WEIL. 1989. Ecological effects of a major oil spill on Panamanian coastal marine communities. *Science* 243:37–44.

MAHONEY, B.M.S., AND G. S. NOYES. 1982. Effects of petroleum on feeding and mortality of the American oyster. *Archives of Environmental Contamination and Toxicology* 11:527–531.

SANDERS, H. L., J. F. GRASSLE, G. R. HAMPSON, L. S. MORSE, S. PRICE-GARNER, AND C. C. JONES. 1980. Anatomy of an oil spill: Long-term effects from the grounding of the barge *Florida* off West Falmouth, Massachusetts. *Journal of Marine Research* 38:265–380.

SHAW, D. G., L. E. CLEMENT, D. J. MCINTOSH, AND M. S. STEKOLL. 1981. *Some effects of petroleum on nearshore Alaskan marine organisms.* U.S. Environmental Protection Agency, EPA-600.S3–81–018, Washington D.C.

Selected Readings for Chapter 10

ALASKA DEPARTMENT OF FISH AND GAME. 1993. *Alaska's wildlife: The* Exxon Valdez *oil spill.* Alaska Department of Fish and Game, Anchorage, Alaska.

ALDRICH, J. W. 1970. *Review of the problem of birds contaminated by oil and their rehabilitation.* U.S. Department of the Interior, resource publication 87, Washington, D.C.

BOERSMA, P. A., E. M. DAVIES, AND W. V. REID. 1988. Weathered crude oil effects on chicks of fork-tailed storm petrels (*Oceanodroma furcata*). *Archives of Environmental Contamination and Toxicology* 17:527–531.

BOURNE, W.R.P. 1969. Chronological list of ornithological oil-pollution incidents. *Seabird Bulletin* 7:3–8.

BUTLER, R. G., A. HARFENIST, F. A. LEIGHTON, AND D. B. PEAKALL. 1988. Impact of sublethal oil and emulsion exposure on the reproductive success of Leach's storm-petrels: Short- and long-term effects. *Journal of Applied Ecology* 25:125–143.

EASTIN, W. C., AND D. J. HOFFMAN. 1979. Biological effects of petroleum on aquatic birds. In *Proceedings of the Conference on Assessment of Ecological Impacts of Oil Spills* (C. C. Bates, ed.), pp. 561–582. American Institute of Biological Sciences, Arlington, Va.

EVANS, P.G.H., AND D. N. NETTLESHIP. 1985. Conservation of the Atlantic Alcidae. In *The Atlantic Alcidae* (D. N. Nettleship and T. R. Birdhead, eds.), pp. 427–488. Academic Press, New York.

EXXON VALDEZ OIL SPILL TRUSTEE COUNCIL. 1995. *1995 status report. Exxon Valdez* Oil Spill Trustee Council, Anchorage, Alaska.

FORD, R. G., M. L. BONNELL, D. H. VARBUJEAN, G. W. PAGE, N. R. CARTER, B. E. SHARP, D. HEINEMANN, AND J. L. CASEY. 1996. Total direct mortality of seabirds from the *Exxon Valdez* oil spill. *American Fish Society Symposium* 18:684–711.

FRY, D. M., J. SWENSON, L. A. ADDIEGO, C. R. ADDIEGO, C. R. GRAU, AND A. KANG. 1986. Reduced reproduction of wedge-tailed shearwaters exposed to weathered Santa Barbara crude oil. *Archives of Environmental Contamination and Toxicology* 15:453–463.

HOLMES, W. N., AND J. CRONSHAW. 1985. Biological effects of petroleum on marine birds. In *Effects of petroleum on arctic and subarctic marine environments and organisms* (D. C. Malins, ed.), pp. 359–398. Academic Press, New York.

HUNT, G. L., JR. 1985. Offshore oil development and seabirds: The present status of knowledge and long-term research needs. In *Long-term environmental effects of off-shore oil and gas development* (D. F. Boesch and N. N. Rabalais, eds.), pp. 539–586. Elsevier Applied Science, New York.

JOENSEN, A. H., AND E. B. HANSEN. 1977. Oil pollution and seabirds in Denmark: 1971–1976. *Danish Review of Game Biology* 10:3–31.

NISBET, I.C.T. 1980. Effects of toxic pollutants on productivity in colonial waterbirds. *Transactions of the Linnean Society of New York* 9:103–114.

PAGE, G. W., H. R. CARTER, AND R. G. FORD. 1990. Numbers of seabirds killed or debilitated in the 1986 *Apex Houston* oil spill in central California. *Studies in Avian Biology* 14:164–174.

PIATT, J. F., H. R. CARTER, AND D. N. NETTLESHIP. 1990. Effects of oil pollution on marine bird populations. In *The effects of oil on wildlife* (J. White, ed.), pp. 125–141. Sheridan Press, Hanover, Pa.

PIATT, J. F., C. J. LENSINK, W. BUTLER, M. KENDZIOREK, AND D. NYSEWANDER. 1990. Immediate impacts of the *Exxon Valdez* oil spill on marine birds. *Auk* 107:387–397.

STOWE, T. J., AND L. A. UNDERWOOD. 1984. Oil spillages affecting seabirds in the United Kingdom, 1966–1983. *Marine Pollution Bulletin* 15:147–152.

Selected Readings for Chapter 11

ALASKA DEPARTMENT OF FISH AND GAME. 1993. *Alaska's wildlife: The* Exxon Valdez *oil spill.* Alaska Department of Fish and Game, Anchorage, Alaska.

EXXON VALDEZ OIL SPILL TRUSTEE COUNCIL. 1995. *1995 status report. Exxon Valdez* Oil Spill Trustee Council, Anchorage, Alaska.

GERACI, J. R., AND D. J. ST. AUBIN. 1990. *Sea mammals and oil: Confronting the risks.* Academic Press, San Diego, Calif.

HAEBLER, M. 1994. Biological effects: Marine mammals and sea turtles. In *Before and after an oil spill: The Arthur Kill* (J. Burger, ed.), pp. 238–252. Rutgers University Press, New Brunswick, N.J.

HUTCHINSON, J., AND M. SIMMONDS. 1991. *A review of the effects of pollution on marine turtles.* Greenpeace International, London.

MATKIN, C. O, AND D. SHEEL. 1996. Comprehensive killer whale investigation in Prince William Sound, Alaska. In *Abstracts of 1995 Restoration Project Results*, p. 5. *Exxon Valdez* Oil Spill Trustee Council, Anchorage, Alaska.

Selected Readings for Chapter 12

BLUMER, M., G. SOUZA, AND J. SASS. 1970. Hydrocarbon pollution of edible shellfish by an oil spill. *Marine Biology* 5:195–202.

CAHILL, R. A. 1990. *Disasters at sea: Titanic to* Exxon Valdez. Nautical Books, San Antonio, Tex.

CAMPBELL, D., D. COX, J. CRUM, K. FOSTER, AND A. RILEY. 1994. Later effects of grounding of tanker *Braer* on health in Shetland. *British Journal of Medicine* 309:773–774.

CHASSE, C. 1978. The ecological impact on and near shores by the *Amoco Cadiz* oil spill. *Marine Pollution Bulletin* 9:298–301.

EXXON VALDEZ OIL SPILL TRUSTEE COUNCIL. 1995. *1995 status report. Exxon Valdez* Oil Spill Trustee Council, Anchorage, Alaska.

FALL, J. A. 1993. Subsistence uses of fish and wildlife. *Alaska's Wildlife* 25:4–6.

HUSAIN, T. 1995. *Kuwaiti oil fires: Regional environmental perspectives.* Pergamon, Tarrytown, N.Y.

JACOFF, F. S., ED. 1979. *A small oil spill at West Falmouth.* Environmental Protection Agency, EPA 600/9-79-007, Washington, D.C.

KHORDAGUI, H., AND D. AL-AJMI. 1993. Environmental impact of the Gulf War: An integrated preliminary assessment. *Environmental Management* 17:557–562.

MOLDAN, A.G.S., L. F. JACKSON, S. McGILLON, AND J. V. DERWESTHUIZEN. 1985. Some aspects of the *Castillo de Vellver* oil spill. *Marine Pollution Bulletin* 16:97–102.

PICOU, J. S., AND D. A. GILL. 1996. The *Exxon Valdez* oil spill and chronic psychological stress. In *Proceedings of the Exxon Valdez Oil Spill Symposium* (F. Rice, R. Spies, D. Wolfe, and B. Wright, eds.), pp. 1–15. American Fisheries Society, Bethesda, Md.

PICOU, J. S., D. A. GILL, C. L. DYER, AND E. W. CURRY. 1992. Disruption and stress in an Alaskan fishing community: Initial and continuing impacts of the *Exxon Valdez* oil spill. *Individual Crisis Quarterly* 6:235–257.

PIPER, E. 1993. *The Exxon Valdez oil spill: Final report, State of Alaska response.* Alaska Department of Environmental Conservation, Anchorage, Alaska.

Purrett, L. A. 1975. The second-biggest oil spill. *NOAA Magazine* (October):21–24.

WALDICHUK, M. 1980. Retrospect of the Ixtoc 1 blowout. *Marine Pollution Bulletin* 11:184–186.

WALSH, J. 1968. Pollution: The wake of the *Torrey Canyon. Science* 160:167–169.

Selected Readings for Chapter 13

BURGER, J., AND M. GOCHFELD. 1994. Ecological risk, risk perception, and harm: Lessons from the Arthur Kill. In *Before and after an oil spill: the Arthur Kill* (J. Burger, ed.), pp. 265–282. Rutgers University Press, New Brunswick, N.J.

———. 1996. Ecological and human health risk assessment: A comparison. In *Interconnections between human and ecosystem health* (R. T. DiGiulio and E. Monosson, eds.), pp. 127–148. Chapman and Hall, London.

NATIONAL RESEARCH COUNCIL. 1983. *Risk assessment in the federal government: Managing the process.* National Academy Press, Washington D.C.

———. 1993. *Issues in Risk Assessment.* National Academy Press, Washington D.C.

Selected Readings for Chapter 14

CUTTER INFORMATION CORP. 1995. *International oil spill statistics: 1994.* Cutter Information Corp., Arlington, Mass.

DEPARTMENT OF ENERGY. 1980–94. *International energy annual reports.* U.S. Department of Energy, Washington, D.C.

NATIONAL RESEARCH COUNCIL. 1991. *Tanker spills: Prevention by design.* National Academy Press, Washington D.C.

SPAULDING, M. L., AND M. REED, EDS. 1990. *Oil spills: Management and legislative implications.* American Society of Civil Engineers, New York.

Subject Index

Species Index

About the Author

Joanna Burger is Professor of Biological Sciences at Rutgers University, where she teaches animal behavior, ecology, and ecological risk. As a child she began watching salamanders, snakes, butterflies, and birds on her parent's farm in Niskayuna, New York. She has written over 350 scientific papers as well as essays for the general reader in *Natural History, Explorer's Journal,* and *New Jersey Outdoors.* Her eight books include *Before and After an Oil Spill: The Arthur Kill* and *A Naturalist Along the Jersey Shore* (both Rutgers University Press). She lives in Somerset, New Jersey, with her family on her own nature preserve.